PAT SPRINGLE

CONQUERING CODEPENDENCY

A Christ-Centered 12-Step Process

Learning Activities by Dale W. McCleskey

LifeWay Press
Nashville, Tennessee

ACKNOWLEDGMENTS

Rapha's 12-Step Program for Overcoming Codependency was originally co-published by Word, Inc. and Rapha Resources, Inc. and is available in its original version in Christian bookstores. We want to thank Rapha for making this book available to the LifeWay Press for its use.

Rapha is a manager of inpatient psychiatric care and substance-abuse treatment from a distinctively Christian perspective in hospitals located nationwide. For information about Rapha you may contact Rapha at 1-800-383-HOPE or write to Rapha, 12700 Featherwood, Houston, Texas 77034.

Conquering Codependency: A Christ-Centered 12-Step Process
Copyright © 1993 by Rapha Publishing
Reprinted 1997, 1999, 2001, 2002
All rights reserved
No part of this book may be reproduced or transmitted in any form or by any means, electronic or mechanical, including photocopying and recording, or by any information storage or retrieval system, except as may be expressly permitted in writing by the publisher. Requests for permission should be addressed in writing to LifeWay Press; One LifeWay Plaza; Nashville, TN 37234-0175.

ISBN 978-1515029380
Subject Heading: CODEPENDENCY // COMPULSIVE BEHAVIOR

Sources for definitions in *Conquering Codependency: A Christ-Centered 12-Step Process*: *Webster's Ninth New Collegiate Dictionary*. By permission. From Merriam-Webster's Collegiate Dictionary, Tenth Edition ©1993 by Merriam Webster Inc., publisher of the Merriam-Webster® dictionaries; *Webster's New Twentieth Century Dictionary*, Second Edition, Unabridged © 1983; W.E. Vine, *Vine's Expository Dictionary of Old and New Testament Words* (Fleming H. Revell Company, 1981).

Unless otherwise indicated, biblical quotations are from the *New American Standard Bible*. © The Lockman Foundation, 1960, 1962, 1963, 1968, 1971, 1972, 1973, 1975, 1977. Used by permission. Other versions used: From the Holy Bible, *New International Version*, copyright © 1973, 1978, 1984 by International Bible Society (NIV); the *King James Version* (KJV); Verses marked TLB are taken from *The Living Bible*. Copyright © Tyndale House Publishers, Wheaton, Illinois, 1971. Used by permission.

To order additional copies of this resource: WRITE LifeWay Church Resources Customer Service; One LifeWay Plaza; Nashville, TN 37234-0113; FAX order to (615) 251-5933; PHONE (800) 458-2772; EMAIL to *customerservice@lifeway.com*; ORDER ONLINE at *www.lifeway.com*; or VISIT the LifeWay Christian Store serving you.

Printed in the United States of America

Leadership and Adult Publishing
LifeWay Church Resources
One LifeWay Plaza
Nashville, Tennessee 37234-0175

Table of Contents

About the Authors 4

Introduction 5

Foundations for Recovery 9

STEP 1
    The Process Begins 25

STEP 2
    Changing the Cycle 43

STEP 3
    Turning It Over 64

STEP 4
    Honesty at Work 79

STEP 5
    Out of the Darkness 112

STEP 6
    Willing to Be Willing 123

STEP 7
    Ready for Change 137

STEP 8
    Choosing to Forgive 161

STEP 9
    Making Amends 179

STEP 10
    People of the Extremes 188

STEP 11
    A Growing Relationship 200

STEP 12
    Practicing and Sharing 215

The Twelve Steps of Alcoholics Anonymous 223

The Christ-Centered 12 Steps for Codependency 224

Course map .... Inside back cover

The Journey Begins

INTRODUCTION

> **ALWAYS GIVING—OR ALWAYS GIVING IN?**
>
> Darla lived to do things for others. People in her neighborhood and at her church thought she was the most giving person they ever had known. When someone on their block had a death in the family, Darla was the first person on the scene with a casserole. When someone's car wouldn't start, Darla offered the use of hers. When another couple in the neighborhood wanted to go out for dinner, Darla quickly offered to babysit with their children.
>
> Darla's desire to help extended far beyond these acts of generosity, however. When her teen-age daughter wrote checks that bounced, Rebecca covered for her time after time and did not require her daughter to feel the consequences of being irresponsible. Each time her younger child forgot his lunch—even one day when Darla was sick with the flu—she dutifully raced to school with the forgotten sack meal. When her husband decided to go fishing instead of attending a church committee meeting, she agreed to lie for him. She told the committee he was called out of town on business.
>
> Darla was compelled to rescue and "fix" others. She felt good about herself when she felt needed—even if she had to be untruthful or if she endangered her own health in the process. When Darla was a child, her parents constantly compared her to her older sister and told her she was no good. As an adult Darla decided she would prove her "goodness" by doing for others, even when she abused herself and compromised her principles in the process. Only trouble was—the exhilaration Darla felt after one of her successful rescues didn't last long. Soon she felt angry at herself for giving in—yet another time.

Why you may need this course

Does Darla remind you of yourself? Have you ever been so determined to please others that you end up rescuing them time and time again? You also may have some of these traits:
- difficulty seeing persons and situations realistically;
- belief that you are responsible for others' thoughts and actions;
- susceptibility to control by others and a tendency to control others;
- feeling unhealthy amounts of hurt and anger;
- feeling guilty about things over which you have no control;
- feeling that you live a life of loneliness without true intimacy.

Darla—and as many as 160 million Americans like her—suffer from the painful effects of codependency. Many times a person develops this condition because of circumstances that occurred during childhood. Other times codependency occurs because of our responses to circumstances that occur later in life. Many of us find ourselves in relationships with physically or psychologically abusive persons. We try to please, rescue, and serve others, but the more diligently we try, the less peace of mind, intimacy and joy we receive for our efforts.

What is codependency?

Conquering Codependency: A Christ-Centered 12-Step Process will help you to understand and begin to change the life-long habits of codependency. The term *codependency* originated in the 1970s to describe a spiritual, emotional, and psychological syndrome that first was identified among family members of chemical dependents. We since have discovered that a vast array of circumstances can cause the same problem. These circumstances can include any family difficulty which causes significant and unresolved hurt, anger, fear, or anxiety. *Conquering Codependency: A Christ-Centered 12-Step Process* will help you identify those patterns of thinking, feeling, and acting. It will enable you to understand better your emotions and actions. It will teach you to use the three-part process *identify*, *detach*, and *decide* to bring change into your life.

What is the 12-Step approach?

You will accomplish this as you work the Christ-centered 12 Steps. The 12 Steps show us a means for effective living. Many of us are familiar with a booklet called *The Four Spiritual Laws*. The booklet is an effective means by which we can share Jesus Christ with people. Through those concepts many of us have come to understand the facts so we could have a relationship with Christ. *The Four Spiritual Laws* booklet, by Bill Bright, presents extremely basic theology. It organizes the information in the Bible in a practical way, so we can apply it to our lives. The 12 Steps give us an organized plan to live life effectively. *The Four Spiritual Laws* is designed to help save our souls, while the 12 Steps are designed to save our lives.

Twelve-Step programs began with the establishment in the 1930s of the first program, Alcoholics Anonymous. Alcoholics Anonymous was adapted from a Christian revival organization known as the Oxford Group. The Twelve Steps were written in the laboratory of human experience as people sought God's solution for alcoholism, but they do not help only alcoholics. They are for everyone. They are God-centered. They are practical.

Those of us who have come to know Jesus through *The Four Spiritual Laws* have a special respect for the little booklet. Those of us who have experienced deliverance from life-crushing problems through the 12 Steps have a similar respect for the 12-Step program—or simply the *program*, as many people call it. We respect the program because the Steps have led us to know and love the Holy God who gave us the Steps. As a reference you'll find the Twelve Steps of Alcoholics Anonymous on page 223 and our adaptation of them—the Christ-Centered 12 Steps for Codependency—on page 224.

The purpose of this book is to help you begin and work the 12-Step process in your life. The writers have many years' experience with codependency and with the 12-Steps. You will find *Conquering Codependency: A Christ-Centered 12-Step Program* is true to the proven 12-Step recovery tradition. Without apology we identify Jesus Christ as our Higher Power. We desire to build bridges to the recovery community.

On the inside back cover you'll find a course map showing steps into and out of codependency. This drawing represents a further explanation of how the Christ-centered 12 Steps work. On the unit page of each Step, you'll find a cutaway drawing of some steps that will highlight for you one of the stages of the development of codependency and the Step that segment of material explains to help you change those learned behaviors. The steps into codependency are not are clearly defined as are the steps out. Some of us can identify particular steps like this; others of us seem not to be able to identify those as clearly.

Some new terms

If you are new to the 12-Step process, you will encounter in this book some terms that may not be familiar. They are expressions frequently used in 12-Step groups. Following is an overview of some of these terms.

- **Recovery**—The entire process of healing from the painful effects of dysfunctional behavior is called recovery. In a larger sense everything in Christian ministry is recovery. Think of it this way: God created us with a glorious purpose, which sin warped and twisted. Theologians call this the "fall" of humanity. We might call it the loss—loss of our innocence, purpose, dignity, and relationships to God and to others. Recovery is the process of restoring what sin took away. For some of us recovery is specialized. For example, for alcoholics recovery is restoration of sobriety. For codependents recovery includes restoring healthy boundaries and separateness.

- The **Program**—When we speak of "the program" we mean the entire process of restoration that comes through working the 12 Steps. The program includes attending meetings, participating in the sponsoring model of personal accountability and discipleship, and doing the written and verbal work to apply the Steps to our lives. The program essentially applies the teachings of the Christian faith to practical life situations.

- **Sponsor**—The 12-Step program uses the ancient biblical practice of apprenticeship for spiritual growth. Each person is encouraged to enlist a sponsor—someone who has progressed in the recovery process. The sponsor does not take care of, rescue, or fix the person he or she sponsors. The sponsor makes assignments and guides the newcomer to work the Steps. While working in this book, you will meet regularly with your sponsor to review your progress. Your *Conquering Codependency* group facilitator will explain more about how you select your sponsor. A companion product, *Conquering Codependency: A Christ-Centered 12-Step Process Facilitator's Guide* is available for free download at *www.lifeway.com/discipleplus/download.htm* (see p. 8).

- **Working the Steps** or **Step-work**—The goal of the program is to glorify God as we develop healthy, Christ-honoring behavior. Working the Steps is the entire process of learning and growing. The key parts of working the Steps include the relationship with a sponsor, attendance and sharing at meetings, and doing certain written work. *Conquering Codependency* is a workbook to help you work the Steps. *Conquering Codependency: A Christ-Centered 12-Step Process* is not merely designed for you to understand concepts. The purpose of this material is life change.

How this course fits in

Conquering Codependency is part of the LIFE® Support Group Series. The LIFE® Support Group Series is an educational system of discovery-group and support-group resources for providing Christian ministry and emotional support to individuals in the areas of social, emotional, and physical need. These resources deal with such life issues as chemical dependency, codependency, recovery from sexual abuse, eating disorders, divorce recovery, and how to grieve the losses of life. Participants in LIFE® Support Group Series courses will be led through recovery to discipleship and ministry by using these courses.

Conquering Codependency is an integrated course of study. To achieve the full benefit of the educational design, prepare your individual assignments and participate in the group sessions. It represents an opportunity to understand and change basic areas which have generated pain in your life.

Getting the most from this course

Study Tips. This book is written as a tutorial text. Study it as if Pat Springle is sitting at your side helping you learn. When he asks you a question or gives you an assignment, you will benefit most if you write your response. Yes—you read that correctly. We want you to write in your book! Many of us are caretakers who, while neglecting ourselves, take care of people who don't want or need our attention. We have a difficult time writing in books. We don't feel worthy. We just read the book, or we write on a separate sheet of paper. We plan to give the book to someone else—someone who doesn't want or appreciate it. One major step toward recovering from codependency is learning to write in your book! You can practice by doodling in the box that appears in the margin at left. Each assignment is indented and appears in **boldface type**. When you are to respond in writing, a pencil appears beside the assignment. For example, an assignment will look like this:

✎ **Read Psalm 139:13. Write what the verse tells about God's care for you.**

Of course, in an actual activity, a line would appear below each assignment or in the margin beside the assignment. You would write your response as indicated. Then, when you are asked to respond in a non-written fashion—for example, by thinking about or praying about a matter—a ⇨ appears beside the assignment. This type of assignment will look like this:

⇨ **Pause now to pray and thank God for accepting you unconditionally.**

In most cases your "personal tutor" will give you some feedback about your response. For example, you may see a suggestion about what you might have written. This process is designed to help you learn the material and apply the concepts more effectively. Do not deny yourself valuable learning by skipping the learning activities. Set a definite time and select a quiet place where you can study with little interruption. Keep a Bible handy for times in which the material asks you to look up Scripture. Memorizing Scripture is an important part of your work. Make notes of questions that arise while you study. You will discuss many of these with your sponsor or during your 12-Step meetings. Write these matters in the margins of this textbook.

Your 12-Step support group will add a needed dimension to your learning. If you have started studying *Conquering Codependency* and you are not involved in a group, try to enlist some friends or associates who will work through this material with you. Approach your church leaders about beginning such a group. *Conquering Codependency: A Christ-Centered 12-Step Process Facilitator's Guide* provides guidance in how to begin a Christ-centered 12-Step group as well as give suggestions for scheduling group meetings. It also provides guidance for sponsers as well as facilitators. It is available for free download at *www.lifeway.com/discipleplus/download.htm.*

A key decision

Conquering Codependency: A Christ-Centered 12-Step Process is written with the assumption that you already have received Jesus Christ as your Savior and Lord and that you have Him guiding you in the healing process. If you have not yet made the important decision to receive Christ, you will find in Step 3 guidance for how to do so. You will benefit far more from *Conquering Codependency: A Christ-Centered 12-Step Process* if you have Jesus working in your life and guiding you in the process.

Foundations for Recovery

FOUNDATIONS

HARMFUL MESSAGES

Will grew up in a family with an alcoholic father and a mentally ill mother. If Will came home to find his dad drunk and passed out on the floor, other family members told the boy, "He's really just asleep."

His family's message to Will was, "You aren't entitled to your feelings; you can't trust your own eyes; you certainly can't trust us, and whatever you do, don't talk to anyone about what is happening in this family."

Gloria came from a very different kind of family. Her father was a deacon in the church. Her parents really did care about her and love her, but Gloria's father came from a family in which no one ever showed him love. No one ever taught him the skills of giving love.

Gloria's father loved his daughter very much, but he didn't know how to show her how he felt.

Gloria grew up feeling shamed to the very core of her being because she believed her father cared nothing about her. She wondered, "What is wrong with me that my daddy doesn't love me?"

Read these lessons to learn more about what causes families to send these kind of messages and about how we respond to them.

Overview

Lesson 1: The Functional Family
   Goal: You will describe the operation of a healthy family.
Lesson 2: The Dysfunctional Family
   Goal: You will explain the creation and operation of the dysfunctional family.
Lesson 3: The Roles of the Dysfunctional Family
   Goal: You will identify the harmful roles which result from dysfunctional families.
Lesson 4: What Is Codependency?
   Goal: You will understand the key elements of the condition called codependency.
Lesson 5: How it Works: The Parts of the Program
   Goal: You will identify the four essential parts of an effective recovery program.

LESSON 1

The Functional Family

In our world we often speak of systems: school systems, engine systems, highway systems. We think of a system as a group of items that interact and that form a unit. But have you ever thought about *families* as systems? Families are systems in which each person's behavior affects all the other members.[1] Two types of family systems exist: the functional family and the dysfunctional family.

Key Concept:
Healthy families teach people to feel, trust, and talk.

The functional family helps its members grow and develop. This type of family certainly isn't perfect, but it does foster open, honest, loving communication. Both the parents and their children develop a strong sense of "self," or identity. They learn that they can trust, feel, and talk about many—if not all—the issues in their lives. The diagram below illustrates how a functional family operates.

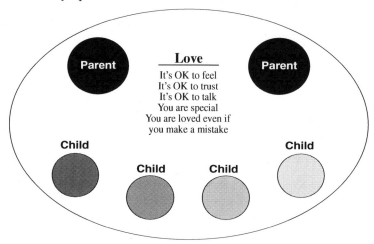

Families teach us how to live. The most important thing we learn from families is how to operate in relationships—how to give and receive love. Three **skills** are required for healthy, loving relationships to exist. These are the abilities to feel, to trust, and to talk. A functional family not only gives an individual permission to feel, trust, and talk, it also helps the individual develop skills he or she needs for living. Developing skills for living represents a major life task of the family.

skills–n. abilities, expertness. (Webster's) In studying about families, we use the word *skill* to refer to abilities that persons must develop to have successful relationships. Hitting a golf ball or frying an egg are skills. Saying "I love you," giving a hug, or asking forgiveness also are skills.

 The three drawings below are designed to help you remember these important skills. Under the appropriate cartoon write the skill shown.

You probably chose the first picture to illustrate the skill of trusting, the second picture to illustrate the skill of talking, and the third picture to illustrate the skill of feeling.

Parents help their children learn to trust by showing them that the parents are trustworthy. They teach their children to recognize and to deal with feelings. Parents do this by respecting their childrens' emotions and by showing how they as parents deal with feelings. This is called modeling. By being available and by valuing their children's ideas and opinions, parents show that it's OK to talk.

✎ **You have learned about three skills the family teaches. In the blanks beside the behaviors listed below write the name of one of the three skills you just learned which will help a child learn to feel, trust, and talk.**

1. By modeling consistency and dependability parents teach children to _____.
2. By respecting children as people with the right to their own emotions, hurts and joys, parents teach them to _____.
3. By taking time to listen to their children and valuing what they say, parents teach them to _____.

The correct responses were 1. trust, 2. feel, 3. talk. How well did your parents provide an environment that allowed you to feel, trust, and talk? Explain.

_____

_____

Important work

Cheryl, a wife and mother, does something incredibly wise. She learned this skill from her own functional family. When her children were young, Cheryl began a practice of having her "time" with them. Now, when her children come home from school, she sits and listens to the details of their day. Mother and child just "visit." She says finding time for these uninterrupted moments often is difficult to work into her (and their) busy days, but what she is doing is more important than is the work of kings and presidents. She is teaching basic life skills. These essential life skills are built on two basic truths: 1) I am special (that is, my worth is based on who I am) and 2) I will be loved even when I make a mistake (that is, my performance is not the basis for my worth).

✎ **Because learning these is so very important, will you please write below two basic truths the family teaches the children?**

1. That my worth *is* based upon who I am: I am _____
2. That my worth is *not* based upon my performance: I will be _____

God is the ultimate functional Father. He loves with a special kind of love called unconditional love. This love says "I love you because of who you are, and I will continue to love you no matter what." The answers to the exercise above were 1) I am *special* and 2) I will be *loved even when I make a mistake*.

Foundations

✏ In the diagram of the functional family, fill in the three skills and the two basic truths of self worth.

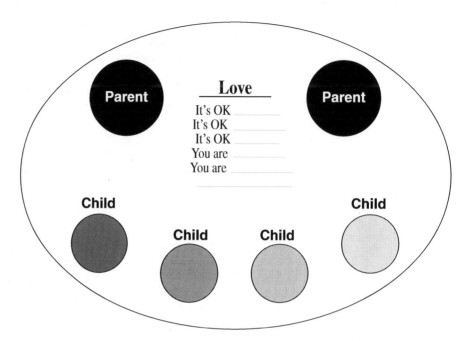

If you are uncertain about what to write on the chart, go back and check your answers with information you read in the lesson.

✏ At the close of this lesson on the functional family please take time to pray and thank God for the acts the following list describes. Check off each when you have thanked Him. Say, God, I thank You for:

- ❑ Loving me—I am special in your sight.
- ❑ Loving me no matter how great my mistakes.
- ❑ Desiring for me to trust You.
- ❑ Desiring to share my feelings.
- ❑ Taking time to talk with me and to listen to me.

Key Concept for Lesson 1
Healthy families teach people to feel, trust, and talk.

✏ Please pray and ask God how this concept can apply in your life. Now please review this lesson. What has God shown you that you can use in your recovery?

_____
_____
_____
_____

LESSON 2

The Dysfunctional Family

The functional family teaches its members basic skills: to feel, to trust, and to talk. These skills are built on the beliefs: I am special, and I am loved even when I make a mistake. The dysfunctional family simply lacks these skills. In a dysfunctional family system one or more of the following reasons keeps open, honest, loving communication from occurring:

Key Concept:
Dysfunctional families don't teach needed skills because they lack open, honest communication.

- Someone in the family is emotionally or physically abusive or absent, or a parent is an addict, so the parent spends on some other object the love family members need.

Describe three kinds of situations which can cause the family to be dysfunctional:

1. _____
2. _____
3. _____

- Someone in the family is physically or mentally ill. This requires family members' time and energy, so not enough time and energy is left for others.

- The family is organized around a set of sick rules such as: "Children are to be seen and not heard," or "We don't air our dirty laundry in public."

- The family is rigid. One member controls the other family members so that the others are like robots.

Foundations 13

Codependency first was observed to be a problem in alcoholic families. We now know that many events can cause a family to experience major dysfunction. Your answers may have included: *prolonged illness of a family member, emotional, sexual or physical abuse; the presence of a person with an addiction of any kind; a parent who was reared in a dysfunctional home;* or you may have given other answers. Something is dysfunctional if it keeps the family from teaching life skills.

Blind to the truth

The members of a dysfunctional family know something is wrong, but the rules against feeling, trusting, or talking make talking about the problem difficult. Denial results. Denial is an unwillingness or inability to be honest about our feelings. Denial becomes a life pattern so that family members don't "speak the truth in love" to themselves or each other. They eventually become people who are blind to the truth of their lives.

Loss of self

A nationally televised commercial about bad breath shows this type of pattern at work in our society. The people on the commercial have bad breath, but their family members won't tell them the truth. Only behind the person's back do the family members gesture that the person has a problem. In our society we don't learn to be honest with ourselves or with each other. The relatively harmless example of the commercial we just mentioned reflects on a much deeper problem in millions of wrecked lives and marriages. The diagram below shows how dysfunctional family systems hinder trusting, feeling, and talking. This results in each family member's growth and development being hindered. Because of this each person has a loss of identity, or "self."

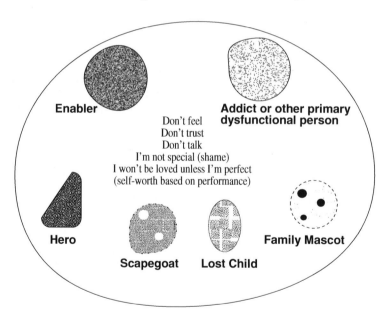

Go back to page 9 and reread the stories of Will and Gloria. Both Will and Gloria identify themselves as codependents. They received the same messages, although they learned them in different ways.

✎ **The messages in a dysfunctional family system are (check all that apply):**

❑ Don't talk.
❑ You are bad.
❑ Don't worry.

❑ People will love you only if you are perfect.
❑ Don't feel.
❑ Don't trust.

The reason a family is dysfunctional is because it doesn't work. It doesn't teach the skills people need for happy, effective living. One skill it does teach is worrying. All the answers apply except the third one on the list.

Who Is to Blame?

Now is a good time to deal with a basic misconception of recovery. The following cartoon depicts this misconception.

As we begin to recover from our destructive behavior we learn to work on our past. We begin to understand what dysfunctional messages run our lives. Some persons think this means we blame our parents for our condition. The truth is that we do **family of origin work** to understand what is happening in our lives so that we may become more, not less, responsible in the present.

Behavior that doesn't work is self-defeating behavior. These learned behaviors—like controlling instead of trusting, or **stuffing** instead of feeling—hurt us and our relationships. Instead of dealing with our feelings we stuff them inside and often pack something else on top. To get better we can spot these self-defeating patterns in our lives, and we can understand their origin. We don't go back in the past to blame. Instead we go back in the past to understand and unhook from these unhealthy patterns. Then healing begins.

Sometimes that unhooking and understanding involves experiencing some strong emotions. Many people feel that if they ever turn loose and begin to cry or to feel again, they will be unable to stop. We need the support of our group to deal with difficult issues. Remember, we do not go into the past to stay there, to blame, or simply to feel, but to understand and to detach.

family of origin work–n. a study of your personal history in order to identify the harmful patterns that are controlling your life.

stuffing–n. a descriptive term for denying our feelings. It's as though we take our feelings and stuff them in a drawer where they can't be seen or experienced.

Unhooking, understanding

✎ Mark the following statements as *T* (true) or *F* (false).

_____ 1. We don't need to study the past as we begin recovering from codependency.

_____ 2. We study our past in order to blame our parents or others for our problems.

_____ 3. We study our past in order to understand our own behaviors so that we may change them.

_____ 4. We study our past to feel the emotions and relive the past.

Foundations

Denying that the past is important continues to allow those events to control us. Blaming others does not free us and only keeps us stuck. Simply feeling the pain of past grief does not represent recovery from its control in our lives.

The only true answer in the above activity is number 3. The others are false. We study so that we may understand our habits of thinking, feeling, and acting and so that we may grow toward wholeness.

Andrew's story

Andrew grew up in a violent family. He recalls wanting to talk to his pastor or coach about what was going on in his home, but he was afraid. He was afraid of his father's anger. He was even more afraid of being disloyal to his family. Many years have passed, but Andrew still feels disloyal when he talks about his family.

Many choose to stay stuck in their sick behaviors because they, like Andrew, have a misplaced loyalty to family. Loyalty is an admirable attitude, but Andrew's loyalty is misguided. Please do not let a misguided loyalty keep you from recovery. The best thing people can do for their families is to find recovery for themselves.

> **Key Concept for Lesson 2**
> Dysfunctional families don't teach needed skills because these families lack open, honest communication.

 Please pray and ask God how understanding this concept can help you in recovery. Now please review this lesson. What has God shown you that you can use?

_____

_____

LESSON 3

Key Concept:
Dysfunctional families squeeze the members into rigid, inappropriate roles.

Roles of the Dysfunctional Family

Members in families naturally take on different roles. When an argument occurs, the family needs a peacemaker. When illness strikes, the family needs someone to provide care. When a family member excels, the family can have a healthy pride.

In a healthy family unit these roles are flexible. One day you may be the source of family pride. The next day your brother or sister may be the one getting the attention. The roles change as they need to do so and are appropriate to the situation. In dysfunctional homes the roles become fixed and rigid. Psychologist and author Sharon Wegscheider-Cruse has described these typical roles as that of the family hero, scapegoat, lost child, and mascot. Various members of the family share the role of enabler.

The dysfunctional family organizes itself around some problem. The problem shapes family living, while family members deny that the problem exists.

16   Foundations

Elephants and problems

Experts say this problem is like living with an elephant in the living room. Everyone in the house denies that the elephant exists. They do this even as they seek to avoid its swinging trunk and battering torso. People feel they must do something to take their minds off their problems. The rigid roles serve to do just that. Birth order (the order in which children are born into a family) does not always determine these roles but sometimes can be a factor. Below I have described these roles for you. As you read these, many of you will identify the fact that you have played more than one role. For example when the first child leaves home, the scapegoat sometimes becomes the family's hero.

Role #1: The Hero. The first-born child often assumes the role of the responsible one, or hero. Heroes often excel in sports and/or academics. Their achievement takes the focus off the family's problem. Heroes may make sure that younger siblings are cared for and arrive at school and home from school. In this caregiving role heroes become like surrogate parents—people who take on some of the same roles as parents. Claudia Black describes one such child "who had seven sheets of paper along the wall in her room outlining her duties every hour of the day, including one specific hour to relax and play."[2]

Old before their time

Heroes are little adults—old before their time—who never get to be children.

Role #2: The Scapegoat. This is the child who gets blamed for the family's problems. A 13-year-old boy was told that he was to blame because his father was an alcoholic. Finding the role of hero already filled, scapegoats seek attention by acting out, running away, or getting into trouble. All children crave attention. In a dysfunctional home, attention is in short supply. Addicted parents use all their energies to deal with the addiction. Codependent spouses are addicted to their addict, with all their energies spent on trying to control and cover up for him or her. Very little attention is left over for the children. The hero receives attention from teachers or coaches who are surrogate parents. The scapegoat gets attention by getting into trouble. The attention may be negative, but it's better than nothing.

Attention at any price

Role #3: The Lost Child. The lost child deals with the elephant in the living room by denying that it exists and by staying very quiet. The term *lost child* describes this situation well because these children are the ones no one notices. They never make waves. They never do anything to draw attention to themselves. They are masters at chamelionism—blending into the surroundings. What makes the lost child's situation even more tragic is that observers may think that the family's chaos does not affect these children, when in fact it affects them greatly. Lost children tend to be shy.

Never making waves

Role #4: The Mascot. This is the child who seeks to relieve the tension in a stress-filled family by telling jokes, making funny facial expressions, or doing humorous antics that relieve the tension some way. Mascots are the children who major on feelings. The trouble is that they major on fixing other people's feelings. They are masters at using comedy to relieve a tense situation. A mascot becomes an adult who is the life of the party but who is out of touch with his or her own feelings.

A laugh a minute

Role #5: The Enabler: The role of enabler traditionally is assigned to the addicted person's spouse. The wife of the alcoholic keeps the family secret. This enables the alcoholic to keep drinking. She phones in sick for him; she cleans up his messes. In the name of helping she sees to it that he never has the encounter with reality that might cause him to become responsible.

Keeping things the same

Foundations

Everybody's Role: Common elements exist for all the roles just mentioned. In these roles people try to escape pain, gain self-worth, and avoid reality. Everybody in the system strives to maintain some stability. The only order they know is the way things are. Each role serves to deny the existence of the elephant in the living room. Each allows the elephant to remain untroubled.

 The following sentences describe the roles of the dysfunctional family. Fill in each blank with the name of the family role that completes the sentence. I have completed for you the sentence about the role of the enabler because it is a role that all the other family members play.

1. The _enabler_ prevents people from experiencing the consequences of their behavior.

2. The _____ thinks that if he or she is perfect, the problems will go away.

3. The _____ rebels against the family problems and ultimately believes that he or she is the problem.

4. The _____ pulls into a shell, withdraws, and isolates himself or herself from meaningful relationships.

5. The _____ tries desperately to make everyone laugh in the midst of the tragedy of the family situation.³

Children in such systems rarely build healthy self-concepts. They are at great risk for multiple marriages, addiction, codependency, and stress-related physical problems. In the exercise above you showed growing understanding of the family by answering 2. hero, 3. scapegoat, 4. lost child, 5. mascot.

Understanding the roles of a dysfunctional family is a step toward understanding why we are what we are. The understanding will not make us better but can open the door to making some choices that can lead us to a better life. New solutions begin to appear when we learn to reframe the problems. Recovery is possible. Life can be a joy rather than a burden.

New solutions appear when we learn to reframe the problems.

At this point you may find yourself in an identification process. You may see yourself and your family members in the rigid roles of the dysfunctional family. Remind yourself this process is not about guilt and blame but is about release from the bondage of family patterns that held you captive in the past.

Check your feelings

Stop now for a feelings check. In the list of possible feelings below check all that apply for you right now. If you have feelings other than the ones listed for you, describe them in the blank after "other."

After learning these things I feel—

❏ hopeful, maybe change can occur in my life;
❏ exposed, has somebody been looking in our windows?;
❏ fearful, is something wrong with me?;
❏ excited, I think this just might work!;
❏ relieved, I'm not alone anymore;
❏ sad, I've missed so much.
❏ other _____

18   Foundations

> Do not be surprised if you find yourself feeling overwhelmed at times. All of us do as we process these matters. Recovery takes time, but it does work.

▷ Now take a moment to share your feelings with God in prayer. He loves you and wants to share your hurts, joys, insights, and fears.

> **Key Concept for Lesson 3**
> Dysfunctional families squeeze the members into rigid, inappropriate roles.

 Please ask God how this concept can apply to your life. Now please review this lesson. What has God shown you that you can use to find joy and healing?

_____

_____

LESSON 4

Key Concept:
The learned habits of a dysfunctional system become the roots of the condition called codependency.

What Is Codependency?

You have studied the functional and dysfunctional family. Codependency usually, but not always, results when a person is exposed to a dysfunctional family. A person from a functional family can become codependent because of life circumstances such as a job loss or other transition that initially might seem devastating to a person's self-concept.

The term *codependency* originated in the field of alcoholism treatment. Alcoholics have some common behaviors. Therapists treating families of these alcoholics observed that the family members also have a fairly consistent set of behaviors.

The alcoholic is dependent on alcohol. Family members are affected, too, so therapists began to call them *codependent*. At first people applied the term codependent only to families of alcoholics. Then people began using the term to refer to families of people who use other drugs besides alcohol. Today people use the word to describe anyone affected by a relationship with a person who is dependent, abusive, absent, or physically or mentally impaired.

Someone in a group once said, "There are those who are addicted and those who are afflicted." Codependents are people who have been afflicted by being in a relationship with a dysfunctional person or by being in a dysfunctional situation, such as having a parent absent because of death or divorce.

Rescue, fix, and help

Codependents have an imbalanced sense of responsibility to rescue, fix, and/or help people who usually don't want their help. People either consciously or unconsciously deprive the codependent of needed love and

Foundations 19

attention, so the codependent rescues as a way to gain that love he or she needs.

Many definitions of codependency exist. Melody Beattie defines a codependent as one who "has let another person's behavior affect him or her, and who is obsessed with controlling that person's behavior."[4]

compulsion–n. an obsessive, irresistible, driving urge

> We will define codependency this way:
> Codependency is a **compulsion** to control and rescue people by fixing their problems. It occurs when a person's needs for love and security are not met.

Matt's, Christine's stories

Matt grew up in a military family and had a drill sergeant for a father. His father planned every element of Matt's life. His father pushed the boy into sports to fulfill the father's failed dreams of being a professional ball player. Christine grew up in a home that was as unlike that of Matt's as anyone can imagine. Matt's all-powerful father controlled every element of Matt's life. Christine's home could be described as being totally out of control. Because her father was an alcoholic, she never knew whether her basic needs would be met. Later Christine's father found religion and became just as addicted to that as he had been to booze. Now Christine never knew if the bills would be paid, because he gave away the money that he once drank away.

Matt's and Christine's childhoods were vastly different, but both individuals learned that if any order in life was to exist, they would have to provide it.

Matt became a controller. He controlled his children, and they hated him. He controlled his wife, and she left him. He controlled his boss, and the boss fired him. Christine became a controller. She controlled her husband, and he ignored her. She controlled her children, and they defied her.

 Look at Matt's and Christine's stories. Do you see terms describing you or the family in which you were reared? Circle those terms or phrases.

 Carefully read the following paragraphs. Then fill in the blanks in the key statements that follow these paragraphs.

Codependency has three core perceptions and behaviors and three emotional results. The core symptoms are: a lack of objectivity, a warped sense of responsibility, and being controlled and controlling others.

Lack of objectivity is the inability to see things as they really are. Our views of ourelves and others makes it difficult to see reality in a clear, unbiased way. Past hurts keep warping our view of present events.

boundaries–n. an important recovery term, it means the invisible "fences" God gives us to protect us from allowing others to abuse us and to keep us from invading their space to abuse them. Good boundaries are like screen doors: they allow the fresh air in but keep the bugs out.

A warped sense of responsibility means we don't have good **boundaries** to tell us our duties and what others should do. As a result we tend either to feel guilty for and try to do everything, or we become super irresponsible and do nothing.

Being controlled and controlling others is another result of bad boundaries. Since we don't know where we stop and others begin, we alternate invading others' space and manipulating them with allowing them to invade our space and manipulate us.

✎ **The three core perceptions and behaviors of codependency are—**

1. a lack of _____;

2. a warped sense of _____;

3. being _____ and _____.

The three emotional results of codependency are: hurt and anger, guilt, and loneliness.

✎ **Think about the manipulative behaviors you have experienced. List several ways people have controlled you. You may think about people's efforts to control you at home, at work, or at school. You may think about verbal methods, physical methods, use of rewards, or threats of punishment.**

_____

_____

Master Control Artists

In a hopeless attempt to stop the pain from all the above, we become masters of the art of controlling. In fact, one of the best descriptions I know of codependency is that it is an addiction to controlling. Controlling is a lousy way to build loving relationships, so we let ourselves in for a huge amount of rejection. The rejection fuels the loneliness, and the cycle continues.

✎ **Review what you've read about the three emotional results of codependency. Then list them here.**

1. _____ and _____

2. _____

3. _____

These characteristics affect our every relationship and desire. Our goals in life are to avoid the pain of being unloved and to find ways to prove that we are lovable. This desperate quest is a compulsion to rescue others, a sense of having to get others' approval at all costs, and a need to control others' emotions, attitudes, and behaviors. The quest continues until the truth can penetrate and recovery can begin. The three emotional results are: hurt and anger, guilt, and loneliness. A pastor gave this testimony: "I had been in the ministry for 16 years and was striving to love and serve God, but something always was wrong. Nothing I did ever was good enough. I couldn't make myself pray as I felt I should. Guilt and shame stained every joy in my life. Then one day I heard about something called codependency. I saw a list that

Foundations 21

spelled out codependent traits. This list said, As codependents we—

- feel responsible for others' behavior;
- need to be needed;
- expect others to make us happy;
- can be demanding or indecisive;
- can be attentive and caring or selfish and cruel;
- see people and situations as wonderful or awful—one extreme to the other;
- seek affirmation and attention or sulk and hide;
- believe we are perceptive (and sometimes we are), but we often can't see reality in our own lives;
- see others either as being 'for us' or 'against us';
- use self-pity and/or anger to manipulate others;
- feel like we must rescue people from themselves;
- communicate contrasting messages, like 'I need you. I hate you';
- don't say what we mean and don't mean what we say;
- repent deeply but commit the same sins again and again.

"I saw that if what I had was a condition instead of just weakness and shame on my part, a solution might exist. My recovery began when I admitted my condition."

 In the above list underline the characteristics you see in your life.

These are symptoms of a hidden condition that for a long time has stolen our joy. The good news is that God has given us a cure for this condition!

The good news—a cure

> **Key Concept for Lesson 4**
> The learned habits of a dysfunctional system become the patterns of thinking, feeling, and acting for codependents.

 Please pray and ask God how knowing the roots of codependency can be important in your life. Now please review this lesson. What has God shown you for your recovery?

LESSON 5

How It Works

Discovery Is Not Recovery

Entering the office, they had a look I had learned to recognize—the look a husband and wife have when their marriage is on the rocks. I soon felt I had a clear picture of their problems. Clearly their codependent habits were destroying their marriage. I asked: "Are you familiar with the term 'codependency?'" Their response was a common one. They told me they had read *Codependent No More*, a book on codependency, several times.

Key Concept:
Recovery occurs by doing the necessary growth work with others' support.

22 Foundations

Rx For Healthy Lives:
A strong relationship with GOD.
A strong relationship with emotionally healthy people.

> **NOW HEAR THIS!**
>
> Codependency is a condition of learned and deeply ingrained behaviors. *Knowing* about the problem does a bit of good, but only *confronting* and *changing* the behaviors can bring healing.

A person can move toward recovery from destructive behavior on her own by studying and applying the principles in this material. I believe, however, that you can't really grow without being around some supportive people who will tell you the truth and will love you while you deal with it.

To live healthy lives we need a strong relationship with God and strong relationships with emotionally healthy people. We can't separate these two needs. We are deceived, sinful, needy people. We need Jesus Christ. He alone is the source of forgiveness, life, hope, love, and peace. We need emotionally healthy people because we can't live alone; we need each other. To communicate Himself to us, God provided two primary sources: the Bible and the Holy Spirit. The two main environments He provided are the family and the body of Christ. God intends for the family to model His nature for us while we are in the critical formative years. When that fails, other believers can help us overcome the things we lacked so we can know the reality of God.

We each need the encouragement, reproof, exhortation, comfort, teaching, love, and prayer that others can give. We also need a mature relationship with Christ and with each other. In the Scripture at left Paul described these relationships. People from dysfunctional families know less about healthy relationships and need healthy relationships more than do other people. Deception, abuse, neglect, and manipulation have scarred their lives.

What's Required for Recovery

Recovery requires four things for real growth and health: knowledge, relationships, spirituality, and time.
- **Knowledge.** As you understand yourself better, you can apply biblical truth to your deepest needs, hurts, and desires.
- **Relationships.** Growth occurs in an atmosphere of love and encouragement. Overcoming codependency alone is next to impossible. Let others support you as you go through this program of healing.
- **Spirituality.** As you examine God's truths and begin to experience His forgiveness and strength, you will grow in understanding of His character and His purposes in your life. You will gain a new attitude about accepting others and about sharing yourself with them.
- **Time.** Recovery is a process. Lasting change won't occur overnight. You will experience flashes of understanding, but the process of real growth is long, slow, and steady. Expecting too much too soon may cause you to become disillusioned and to pull out of the program completely. Be patient.

✎ **Will you prayerfully consider the truths that appear on the next page? We who have been in the process can assure you that the quality of your recovery depends on understanding these truths.**
  For recovery to work in my life I must grow in these areas:

---

until we all attain to the unity of the faith, and of the knowledge of the Son of God, to a mature man, to the measure of the stature which belongs to the fullness of Christ. As a result, we are no longer to be children, tossed here and there by waves, and carried about by every wind of doctrine, by the trickery of men, by craftiness in deceitful scheming; but speaking the truth in love, we are to grow up in all aspects into Him, who is the head, even Christ.
–Ephesians 4:13-15

Knowledge: I choose to learn by listening and reading with an open mind. ❑ Yes ❑ No

Relationships: I choose to do what's necessary—one baby step at a time—including participating in support groups and working with a sponsor or mentor. ❑ Yes ❑ No

Spirituality: I choose to build a relationship with God and to accept His care for me. ❑ Yes ❑ No

Time: I recognize that recovery is a process. I choose to allow the time necessary for this growth to take place in my life. ❑ Yes ❑ No

➪ **If you are afraid to work right now on these areas, please pray and ask God to strengthen you and to make you ready. All He requires is the "willingness to become willing."**

> But the vessel that he was making of clay was spoiled in the hand of the potter; so he remade it into another vessel, as it pleased the potter to make. The word of the LORD came to me saying, "Can I not, O house of Israel, deal with you as this potter does?" declares the LORD. "Behold, like the clay in the potter's hand, so are you in My hand, O house of Israel."
> –Jeremiah 18:4-6

In the passage at left about the potter and the clay, the job of making the desired object is the potter's and not the clay's. The potter finds, prepares, and shapes the clay. The clay's job is to remain in the potter's hand. God is the potter working with biblical principles to help you through the recovery process. For Him to complete His work, you must stay in His hand. God will make you pliable if you simply will stay in His hand.

Some people in recovery are willing to do the necessary work. They work through the difficult times and experience miracles of healing in their lives. Others quit because the going is too slow or the way is too difficult. As you practice the "Steps of progress," your behavior will begin to change. More importantly, your perception of yourself and of God and your relationships with others will improve. This will provide a strong foundation for a lasting recovery and for a healthy and productive life. The land where you go is well worth the journey.

Key Concept for Lesson 5
Recovery occurs by doing the necessary growth work with others' support.

✎ Please pray and ask God how this concept can apply in your life. Now please review this lesson. What has God shown you that you can use?

_____

_____

Notes

[1] Analyses adapted from Sharon Wegscheider-Cruse, *The Family Trap*, and John Bradshaw, *The Family*.

[2] Herbert L. Gravitz and Julie D. Bowden, *Recovery: A Guide for Adult Children of Alcoholics*, (New York: Simon & Schuster, Inc., 1985), 23.

[3] Adapted from Sharon Wegscheider-Cruse, *The Family Trap*, and John Bradshaw, *The Family*.

[4] Melodie Beattie, *Codependent No More* (New York: Hazeldon Foundation, 1987), 31.

STEP 1

The Process Begins

We admit that we are powerless over other people; our needs to be needed and our compulsions to rescue others have made our lives unmanageable.

Step 1 Into Codependency

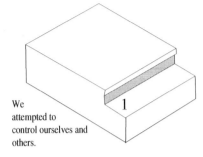

We attempted to control ourselves and others.

Step 1 Out of Codependency

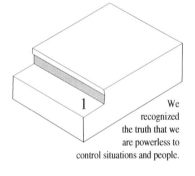

We recognized the truth that we are powerless to control situations and people.

Overview for Step 1

DETERMINED TO CONTROL

Pauline grew up in a family in which everything was out of control. She believed she could change the man she married even though he displayed negative character traits. He became an abusive alcoholic. Her children either became addicts or married compulsive people. Pauline no longer is married and is trying, but failing, to control her addict son and codependent daughter.

Pauline is hyper-organized. If you need someone to plan a convention for 500 people, give her the afternoon and she'll have it done, with time left over to make the centerpieces. Even when she relates the most painful details of past or present experiences, she always bubbles with enthusiasm.

Pauline is an extremely competent woman because her self-worth depends on her performance. She sees no connection between her family of origin and her present difficulties. Pauline also is completely out of touch with herself. She is a very miserable woman and possibly is headed for life breakdown. Read on following pages about what helps Pauline needs.

Blessed are the poor in spirit, for theirs is the kingdom of heaven.
—Matthew 5:3

Lesson 1: "Unmanageable, who me?"
  Goal: You will identify in your life the areas of unmanageability resulting from codependent behaviors.
Lesson 2: ". . . over other people"
  Goal: You will begin to identify the types of controlling behavior at work in your life.
Lesson 3: "that we are powerless"
  Goal: You will understand the basics of healthy boundaries.
Lesson 4: The Great Identity Crisis
  Goal: You will identify the process and results of choosing to be God vs. allowing God to have the job.
Lesson 5: Working Step 1
  Goal: You will explain what it actually means to work Step 1 in a regular way in your life.

LESSON 1

"Unmanageable? Who, Me?"

We admit that we are powerless over other people; our needs to be needed and our compulsions to rescue others have made our lives unmanageable.

> The wise woman builds her house, But the foolish tears it down with her own hands.
>
> –Proverbs 14:1

Key Concept:
Unmanageability means that old habits are running our lives.

Most of us have become highly controlling in several areas of our lives. Those areas are our safe havens. If those havens are in order, we feel secure, even if the rest of our lives are falling apart. If someone mentions that our lives are unmanageable, we proudly point to areas in which we feel we demonstrate control. We say that what the person says about us is ridiculous.

We focus our overresponsibility in those aspects of our lives, but we fail to see the chaos and the pain in other areas. We also fail to see how we view matters in a very surface way.

For example, a woman whose husband is an alcoholic and has lost his job regularly during the past 12 years is a perfectionist about her clothes and home. However, she never has talked to her husband about how insecure, hurt, or fearful she feels because he behaves irresponsibly.

A young man from a home in which his parents were divorced keeps an orderly schedule, but his relationships are shallow. He controls his time carefully. He also controls people by not letting anyone get too close to him emotionally.

A tragic trait

One of the most tragic traits of codependency is the loss of identity. We learn from our dysfunctional families that we must please others to gain others' approval. Therefore, we lean to one extreme or another. We may give up our identity by thinking what we believe others want us to think, feeling what we believe others want us to feel, and acting the way we believe others want us to act.

Or, we may be very defiant about defending our separate identity. Because we feel threatened, we may argue about the smallest point, or we may hold to a point of view even after we realize it is wrong or unreasonable. We childishly may demand our own way. Both of these extremes are common at some time in most of our lives.

Learning to see clearly is a long, slow process.

Step 1 is the first step into reality. It is not the end; it is only the beginning. (You've probably already taken the first step or two, or you wouldn't be reading this workbook now!) Learning to see clearly is a long, slow process.

We will see only a little at first, and most of us will be confused by what comes into view! If you reach a point in the workbook which you don't understand or where you can't identify yourself, that's OK. You may understand much more as you discuss with a group of people what you've learned; you may understand it months later, or it may be a sub-point that may not relate to you or your situation at all. Be patient.

✎ The following questions are taken from a helpful analysis of adult children of alcoholics, but they apply to all codependents. Answer the following.

❑ Yes ❑ No 1. Do I often feel isolated and afraid of people, especially authority figures?
❑ Yes ❑ No 2. Have I observed myself to be an approval-seeker? Do I lose my own identity in the process?
❑ Yes ❑ No 3. Do I feel overly frightened of angry people and of personal criticism?
❑ Yes ❑ No 4. Do I often feel I'm a victim in personal and career relationships?
❑ Yes ❑ No 5. Do I sometimes feel I have an overdeveloped sense of responsibility, which makes it easier to be more concerned with others than with myself?
❑ Yes ❑ No 6. Is it hard for me to look at my own faults and my own responsibility to myself?
❑ Yes ❑ No 7. Do I feel guilty when I stand up for myself instead of giving in to others?
❑ Yes ❑ No 8. Do I feel addicted to excitement?
❑ Yes ❑ No 9. Do I confuse love with pity, and do I tend to love people I can pity and rescue?
❑ Yes ❑ No 10. Is it difficult for me to feel or to express feelings, including feelings such as joy or happiness?
❑ Yes ❑ No 11. Do I judge myself harshly?
❑ Yes ❑ No 12. Do I have a low sense of self-esteem?
❑ Yes ❑ No 13. Do I often feel abandoned in the course of my relationships?
❑ Yes ❑ No 14. Do I tend to be a reactor instead of an actor?

The total number of: no answers: _____ yes answers: _____

I experienced shock when I first encountered this list. I wondered how anyone possibly could know me so well. All of the yes responses indicate that you have some element of codependency in your life. If you, like the author, answered yes to several or most, . . . "We have good news for you!"

At first you may think these traits represent charges against you. You may think that we are saying that something is wrong with you. As you work the first Step, you will find that something entirely different is true.

A pain-creating habit

These codependent traits are the marks of a wonderful, caring, strong person with a great deal of creativity. At a time of stress or unmet need you may have taken on one of these traits in order to deal with the situation. The problem is that the means of getting through that time in your life may have become a pain-creating habit which now spoils your joy.

 Read these descriptions of common defense mechanisms in codependents. Underline the phrases you see that apply to your life.

Defense Mechanism #1: The Perfectionist
Perfectionists somehow get the message: "You will be accepted if you perform perfectly." They are driven to try to earn self-worth by performance. The sad part is that nothing on this planet ever can be perfect, so they always are doomed to feel inadequate.

Step 1

Charles grew up in a home with critical parents. His parents felt they showed love to their children if they pointed out their children's mistakes. No matter what Charles did, his parents always felt he could have done it a little better. Charles now is a driven professional. He is successful in everything except what counts—relationships.

Defense Mechanism #2: The Martyr
Martyrs find that they can get praise or acceptance by holding up under pain. The greater the pain, the more praise they earn. The more others pity them, the more attention they receive. To feel worthwhile they develop a need to hurt.

Defense Mechanism #3: The People Pleaser
People pleasers discover the way to gain acceptance is never to make anyone angry. They become unable to say no and feel that others' needs, wants, or opinions are more important than are their own. Since they must please everybody, they take on more than any human could hope to accomplish. Then they become angry about the fact that they can't get everything done. Since they lack the skills to express anger appropriately, people pleasers either turn anger inside on themselves or on innocent victims. People pleasers endure life rather than enjoy life.

Defense Mechanism #4: The Caretaker
Caretakers learn to obtain praise by taking care of other people's responsibilities. They need to take care of people, so they either find or create emotional cripples. Then they complain bitterly about the burden they bear.

Do these sound familiar?

Defense Mechanism #5: The Stuffer
Stuffers learned that expressing certain emotions is inappropriate. They say to others: "Big kids don't cry." Since a link exists between feeling and expressing feelings, stuffers stop feeling in part or completely. As a child, Don had a "crying corner." When he cried, his parents told him to go his corner. No doubt his parents thought they were teaching him to be strong. What they really taught is that to cry is both wrong and humiliating. Before Don began recovery, if someone asked him how he felt, he would respond, "I don't know what you are talking about."

Defense Mechanism #6: The Martha Complex
These persons learn that work is the way to gain approval. Their self-worth depends on always being busy whether or not they actually have anything to do. This complex gets its name from the biblical character Martha, a friend of Jesus, who chose to busy herself with household activities rather than to stop and learn at Jesus' feet. Martha Complex sufferers feel guilty any time they aren't busy doing something. They don't "do" loving relationships, because relationships require time. People in the program often call this the "craziness of the busies."

Defense Mechanism #7: The Fixer
Fixers learn that the way to gain approval and a measure of control is to take care of other people's emotions. You don't have to deal with your own pains when you're busy patching someone else's. Fixers develop a need to fix hurting people, so something drives them to find dependent, sick relationships. Fixers mistake *need* for *love*. They tend to fall "in love" because they feel someone needs them.

In which of the defense mechanisms have you recognized yourself?

_____

_____

_____

 Likely you spotted yourself in one or more of the defense mechanisms you just read. In the margin box list the ones with which you identify.

What does this understanding say about who is controlling your life? Below check all that apply to how you feel after reading on the previous page the descriptions of defense mechanisms.

❏ Frightened. "I don't want to be powerless."
❏ Relieved. "I thought I was just weak and hopeless."
❏ Dazed. "What do I do now?"
❏ Hopeful. "You mean I can find a way out?"
❏ Angry. "This isn't fair!"
❏ Doubtful. "I don't believe it; none of this applies to me."
❏ Other _____

The good news is that we can find freedom in Christ!

 Reflect on the Scripture appearing in the margin. Does God intend for the defense mechanisms you read about to control you? ❏ Yes ❏ No

you shall know the truth, and the truth shall make you free. . . If therefore the Son shall make you free, you shall be free indeed.
                    –John 8:32,36

Key Concept for Lesson 1
Unmanageability means that old habits are running our lives.

 Please pray and ask God how this concept can apply in your life. Now please review this lesson. What has God shown you that you can use?

_____

_____

_____

LESSON 2

Key Concept:
Attempting to control myself and others results in greater pain and chaos.

"... over other people"

We admit that we are powerless over other people; our needs to be needed and our compulsions to rescue others have made our lives unmanageable.

> *But let each one examine his own work, and then he will have reason for boasting in regard to himself alone, and not in regard to another. For each one shall bear his own load.*
>   –Galatians 6:4-5

The Birth of an Addiction

Ross is an alcoholic. He tells this story about how his addiction was born: "I always felt out of place, like others knew something I didn't. One night I drank for the first time, and the feeling of emptiness and loneliness went away. From that time on I kept returning to the alcohol for relief."

Ann is a sex addict. Her story is amazingly similar to Ross'. When she first acted out sexually, she experienced a temporary relief from her low self-worth and loneliness. Millions of addicts have this same kind of story. We use SOMETHING to stop the real or imagined pain.

We use SOMETHING to stop the real or imagined pain.

Codependency is a form of addiction as well. Many consider it the underlying condition of all addiction. We find that we can relieve the pain by taking the focus off ourselves. By taking care of someone else, by putting up a front, or by retreating inside their walls, we can avoid our pain.

We are addicted to compulsive controlling. We sometimes don't look like controllers, but we are. All of us have learned that by using certain behaviors—defense mechanisms—we can control our lives and the lives of those around us. For a moment we learn to stop the pain. The trouble is, like all addictive behaviors, this results in more and greater pain.

For example:
- Lin learned that he could control by being angry.
- Joy learned that she could control by being helpless.
- Dan learned that if he never completed a job, then no one could criticize it.
- Nancy learned that she could control her feelings by consuming food.
- Fred learned that he could get attention by being sick.
- David learned that he could control by speeding excessively when he drove.
- Forrest learned that he could control by whining.
- Sharon learned that she could control by being compulsively neat.
- Al learned that he could control by leaving a mess.

By the way, Sharon married Al because he admired her "having it all together," while she was attracted to him as a "free spirit."

 Describe what you think occurred in their relationship because of these traits after Sharon and Al married.

_____

_____

All of the real-life cases above are examples of controlling behavior. Some behavior, such as passivity and irresponsibility, looks like the extreme opposite of control but is in fact another form of control. Passivity limits people's access to hurt you. Irresponsibility is a way to avoid failure or rejection. In the above exercise, you may have written that after Sharon and Al married, the traits that attracted them to each other were the very things that irritated each other the most.

What Is Controlling?

 In the following paragraphs, underline examples of controlling behavior, and circle examples of healthy behavior. Then answer the questions that follow the paragraphs.

All people have to deal with stress in healthy or destructive ways. The healthy way is to use some method that gets it out, experiences it, and gets rid of it. Some examples of healthy methods include talking to a friend, taking a walk, writing in a journal about what's going on in your life, and taking appropriate action. Unhealthy methods are those that either 1) keep the stress inside and numb the pain, or 2) dump it on somebody else. When we manipulate ourselves or others, that is controlling.

One way people control in an unhealthy manner involves becoming numb: exercising until you drop, acting out a compulsive ritual, or doing anything compulsively. Another example of an unhealthy control method includes controlling others: by rage, rescue, withdrawing, fixing, blaming, or smothering. All these are compulsive ways to lose ourselves in others.

✎ **The differences between healthy methods and controlling are:**

Losing ourselves in others

1. Healthy stress relievers _____

2. Unhealthy controlling methods either:

   a. _____ or

   b. _____ and always contain a common

   element of _____ behavior.

The line between healthy and controlling behavior is not easy to draw. A particular activity, like exercise, can be healthy for one person while it becomes destructive for others. The problem occurs when you begin to use for an excessive time some behavior to avoid dealing with your feelings. Healthy methods help us experience our feelings and get them out. Unhealthy methods either numb our feelings or dump them on someone else. The common element among all of these is compulsive behavior.

Codependency is cultivated in families that have great needs. Such families may be characterized by at least one person who is an alcoholic, drug dependent, physically, mentally or emotionally ill, or very needy in some other way. Those who come from such families don't learn needed stress management skills. Everyone's energies are focused on getting through the crises and on **rescuing** the family problem person.

rescuing–v. occurs when we take on a responsibility that properly belongs to someone else. When we rescue we hurt ourselves and we keep the ones we rescue from growing up.

✎ **Check whether or not the statements below apply to you.**

❑ Yes ❑ No 1. Did you feel you have to rescue certain persons in your family?
❑ Yes ❑ No 2. Do you feel that some persons in your present family or among your friends can't get by without your help?
❑ Yes ❑ No 3. Do you find yourself taking on the tasks that others should be doing?
❑ Yes ❑ No 4. Does the irresponsibility of others irritate you?
❑ Yes ❑ No 5. Do you do things for others and then find they are ungrateful or even irritated by your help?

If you answered yes to any of the questions above, that yes answer points to those "self-defeating learned behaviors" of codependency in your family. Relationships and self-esteem in families like these are based on **denial**, an unwillingness or inability to recognize the problems in one's life. This denial breeds still more denial.

denial–n. a developed blindness, an inability to see the truth in an area of our lives.

Step 1 31

Denial —
it isn't a river in Egypt.

✎ **Where do you see yourself in these descriptions? Underline those that seem to apply to you.**

- Others control me, but I think I control them.
- I smother and manipulate others but think I am providing a loving environment for them.
- I thrive on being needed, but rescuing only satisfies me for a short time. Then I feel compelled to rescue again.
- I take care of others but neglect my own needs.
- In the desire to please I give up my own identity (my thoughts, beliefs, feelings, and decisions) and develop an identity that pleases others.

✎ **Take time to answer the following questions.**

Who in your life are you trying to control but actually is controlling you? Describe the situation.

_____
_____

Who are you trying to love but actually are smothering with affection, directions, and attention? Explain.

_____
_____

In what relationships are you unable to be honest about how you really feel? What keeps you from being honest?

_____
_____

In what relationships does your need to be needed drive you to rescue and rescue again? What is the effect on you and on the other person?

_____
_____

What needs in your own life are you neglecting in order to caretake someone else's need? With what result?

_____
_____

How have you given up your identity to please someone else?

_____
_____

For am I now seeking the favor of men, or of God? Or am I striving to please men? If I were still trying to please men, I would not be a bond-servant of Christ.
—Galatians 1:10

✎ **Read Galatians 1:10 appearing in the margin. What does being a people pleaser do to your relationship to Christ?**

_____

_____

_____

As long as your life is governed by people-pleasing habits, you cannot experience the practical benefits of the lordship of Christ.

> **Key Concept for Lesson 2**
> Attempting to control myself and others results in greater pain and chaos.

✎ **Please pray and ask God how this concept can apply in your life. Now please review this lesson. What has God shown you that you can use?**

_____

_____

_____

LESSON 3

Key Concept:
Trying to control things over which I am powerless is emotionally unhealthy.

I am powerless over—
_____
_____
_____

"... that we are powerless"

We admit that we are powerless over other people; our needs to be needed, and compulsions to rescue others have made our lives unmanageable.

   for when I am weak, then I am strong. –2 Corinthians 12:10

   I can do all things through Him who strengthens me. –Philippians 4:13

Our hope of health and recovery hinges on admitting that we are powerless. Powerless does not mean that you are weak, incompetent, or any of the hundred other things you may fear. Admitting we are powerless means we recognize the limits to our power. Admitting this does not make us weak. It makes us emotionally healthy. Take a moment to list in the margin box some things over which we all are powerless.

Your list could include a large number of things, like *flying the space shuttle*. I hope you also included some things like *I am powerless over other people's opinions, feelings, and behaviors.*

Rich is a pastor of a growing church. He is a diligent worker—everybody admires him—but Rich has a problem. He grew up in a violent home. He is

Step 1 33

terrified of authority figures and angry people. Whenever even the slightest confrontation occurs, Rich finds himself reliving his childhood terror.

Today Rich must be in control. He cannot delegate responsibilities and cannot let others do their ministry in the church. He can't confront problems when they are small and repairable. He waits until they become big and impossible to ignore. Most of all he cannot put himself under anyone else's authority. Rich cannot obey Ephesians 5:21: "be subject to one another in the fear of Christ," because to Rich, being subject to others means that others completely dominate him.

✎ Have you recognized this same need to be in control in your life?
❑ Yes ❑ No. If so, in what areas do you feel you need to maintain control?

_____

_____

What happens to you because you feel you need to control?

_____

_____

Do you think this behavior hurts or helps your relationships?

_____

Filing-cabinet messages

Our minds operate in the same way a filing cabinet does. The drawers have all files containing our life experiences. Each of the files has a tag that will trigger the contents of the file. The tag can be almost anything: a smell, a facial expression, a situation, or a word. When we open one of the files in our minds, the drawer immediately opens, and the file spreads itself across our desk. Our bodies still are in the present, but we wrestle with long-ago events.

A boy's parents told him: "You're not getting up from this table until you drink your milk." His parents didn't know the milk they asked him to drink was spoiled. Now, 40 years later, this man gets sick at the thought of milk.

A girl grew up with a mother who was a "helicopter" parent—always hovering around. The parent meant her hovering actions to be acts of love, but the daughter saw them as acts of distrust and disapproval. Now as an adult with her own family this woman feels put down whenever her husband tries to help.

In turn the husband feels rejection and bewilderment. He is learning to maintain a distance from his wife. His distant behavior causes her still more rejection and pain. Neither spouse is aware of the filing-cabinet messages involved in the marriage.

We spend a lot of time wrestling with ghosts. Past pains keep spilling over into the present. Living with a codependent can be like a real roller-coaster ride. Family members and friends never know for sure if they are dealing with the here and now or with some folder from the filing cabinet.

✎ **Do you recognize any of these or other file folders active in your life?**
❏ Yes ❏ No

What sort of situations trigger your files?

_____

What feelings do these occasions bring up for you?

_____
_____
_____

for when I am weak, then I am strong.
—2 Corinthians 12:10

I can do all things through Him who strengthens me.
—Philippians 4:13

✎ **This lesson began with the Scriptures listed in the margin. What hope do these passages give you to encourage you to accept your appropriate powerlessness?**

_____
_____
_____

The Issue of Boundaries

Just as boundaries exist between countries or cities or subdivisions, boundaries exist between people. Boundaries represent the invisible places where "you stop and I start." Examples of important boundaries include my right to own my own feelings instead of letting other people tell me how to feel, to make my own choices instead of letting other people tell me what to do, and to make my own decisions about if and how much someone is trustworthy instead of blindly trusting him or her.

In recovery you will deal again and again with boundaries. Remember: a boundary is that God-given space around each of us. Healthy boundaries are like shields that protect us and others. They protect us from allowing others to violate our space. At the same time our healthy boundaries keep us contained and keep us from our violating others' space.

Healthy boundaries protect us from allowing others to violate our space.

When we don't admit our powerlessness, we violate others' boundaries. We try to control other people's lives. We think we know what is best for them.

✎ **Can you recognize ways that you have violated others' boundaries because you did not recognize powerlessness?** ❏ Yes ❏ No **If so, what are some of them?**

_____
_____

How long, O Lord, will I call for help, And Thou wilt not hear? I cry out to Thee, "Violence!" Yet Thou dost not save.
—Habakkuk 1:2

Habakkuk is a character in the Bible who had a boundary problem. When we first meet Habakkuk in the Scriptures (see the verse at left), he is telling God

Step 1 35

what to do. God is patient with Habakkuk as He is with us. Out of Habakkuk's impatience comes one of the great statements of all times. God says: "Behold, as for the proud one, His soul is not right within him; But the righteous will live by his faith" (Habakkuk 2:4).

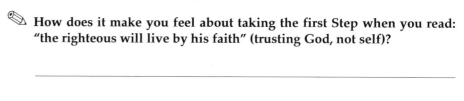 How does it make you feel about taking the first Step when you read: "the righteous will live by his faith" (trusting God, not self)?

Key Concept for Lesson 3
Trying to control things over which I am powerless is emotionally unhealthy.

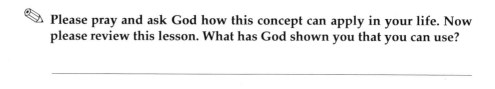 Please pray and ask God how this concept can apply in your life. Now please review this lesson. What has God shown you that you can use?

LESSON 4

The Great Identity Crisis

We admit that we are powerless over other people; our needs to be needed and our compulsions to rescue others have made our lives unmanageable.

And the serpent said to the woman, "You surely shall not die! For God knows that in the day you eat from it your eyes will be opened and you will be like God. . . ."

–Genesis 3:4-5

Key Concept:
Controlling behaviors are hopeless attempts to take God's place and do His job.

The problem with human beings is that we have dethroned God and have tried to take His place. Our first ancestors chose to try to be God instead of leaving the job to Him. Our destructive behavior is a direct result of that choice. Someone in my group said, "I have discovered that I only have two problems. The first is that I keep getting mixed up and thinking I am God. The second is that I don't do it very well."

The next to last thing many of us believe is that we are trying to be God, but the last thing we want to do is surrender control. Because we have experienced a situation in which we felt out of control, we grab now for whatever power we can get. We move God aside and take His place.

36   Step 1

In the Newcomer's Pack for the group was a poster that read: "For Serenity's Sake Resign as General Manager of the Universe"

A new world awaits you

This first Step to recovery is so difficult because it requires that we let go. No matter how painful the outcome is, we have depended upon ourselves. Now we learn we must do NOTHING, and it scares us to death.

We thrive on being needed. We gain our sense of value and significance by meeting others' needs. The greater the needs, the more that "rescuing" gives us importance and approval, or so we hope. We really are trying to be God to the people whose lives we attempt to run. We do this in the vain hope of working diligently enough to earn self-worth.

✎ **The root cause of our problem is our desire to** _____.

This is because we try to get our self-worth by _____

Everyone must have a basis for self-worth. God intends for that self-worth to originate from grace—a free gift. From the cradle we learn that we are loved and valuable to our parents because of who we are, not because of what we do. In time we learn the same lesson in our relationship to God. We are valuable to our Heavenly Father because He values us.

Our problems stem from our desire to be God. We try to gain self-worth by meeting others' needs. We never realize we are running their lives for them.

Step 1 frightens many of us because our defense mechanisms are all that stand between us and feeling like the hole in the middle of the doughnut. If you can begin to take this Step, a whole new world awaits based on your identity in Christ.

Our Identity in Christ

✎ **As you read the following passage, please underline the statements that point out our identity in Christ.**

> *just as He chose us in Him before the foundation of the world, that we should be holy and blameless before Him. In love He predestined us to adoption as sons through Jesus Christ to Himself, according to the kind intention of His will, to the praise of the glory of His grace, which He freely bestowed on us in the Beloved. In Him we have redemption through His blood, the forgiveness of our trespasses, according to the riches of His grace. . . . In Him, you also, after listening to the message of truth, the gospel of your salvation—having also believed, you were sealed in Him with the Holy Spirit of promise, who is given as a pledge of our inheritance, with a view to the redemption of God's own possession, to the praise of His glory.*
>
> –Ephesians 1:4-7,13-14

✎ **In this exercise are several phrases that God says about you. After each phrase, write how you feel when you read it.**

"He chose us" _____

"to adoption" _____

_____

"His grace, which He freely bestowed" _____

_____

"the forgiveness of our trespasses" _____

_____

"the riches of his grace" _____

_____

"you were sealed in Him with the Holy Spirit of Promise" _____

_____

"a pledge of your inheritance" _____

_____

"God's own possession _____

_____

> There is therefore now no condemnation for those who are in Christ Jesus.
> —Romans 8:1

✎ **Condemnation is defined as "censure, criticism, disapproval, damnation, punishment." Exactly how much condemnation does the verse at left say exists for those who are in Christ?**

❏ some ❏ none
❏ only when we sin ❏ a train load

> See how great a love the Father has bestowed upon us, that we should be called children of God; and such we are. For this reason the world does not know us, because it did not know Him. Beloved, now we are children of God, and it has not appeared as yet what we shall be. We know that, when He appears, we shall be like Him, because we shall see Him just as He is.
> —1 John 3:1-2

✎ **Please read 1 John 3:1-2, which appears in the margin. What do believers already have in Christ? What does this verse promise us?**

_____

_____

_____

John says believers have the privilege of being God's children. We look forward to seeing Him and being like Him.

Key Concept for Lesson 4
Controlling behaviors are hopeless attempts to take God's place and do His job.

---

38   Step 1

✏️ Pray and ask God how this awareness applies in your life. Now please review this lesson. What has God shown you that you can use?

___

LESSON 5

Working Step 1

We admit that we are powerless over other people. Our needs to be needed and our compulsions to rescue others have made our lives unmanageable.

> *For I know that nothing good dwells in me, that is, in my flesh; for the wishing is present in me, but the doing of the good is not.*
> –Romans 7:18

Key Concept:
Step 1 is a life-style, not an act. It is a doorway to a new life.

Many of us have approached Step 1 with great fear. We have lost so much in life that we cannot bear the thought of giving up our power. We benefit from looking at the true wording of the Step. In it we do not give up our power. We recognize reality: we never had this deceptive power in the first place.

 Read again Romans 7:18—the Scripture at the beginning of this lesson. The apostle Paul speaks of his personal admission of powerlessness. Which statement best describes what he does in the passage?

❑ 1. Surrenders to God a power he previously held.
❑ 2. Recognizes he has no power in an area of his life.
❑ 3. Puts himself down and says he is worthless.

By his statement the apostle was not degrading himself. His words are the very basis for overcoming defeat. He was not surrendering his personal power. Paul simply was recognizing that he had personal limitations. The answer is number 2.

In the Extremes

Either great or terrible

We tend to see life in the extremes. We have the habit of what experts call "black-and-white" thinking—we seldom view life in shades of gray. Life either is wonderful or awful. We think that people or situations are all good or all bad, that we must be all in or all out of relationships, and that we want all or nothing. Beware of thinking, "I must do Step 1 perfectly." You can't even <u>do</u> the first Step. It isn't a *do*, it is a Step. Step 1 isn't something you complete but is a door to a new life. Possibly "The Serenity Prayer, " written by Reinhold Niebuhr and commonly is used in 12-Step groups, says it best:

> *God,*
> *Grant me the serenity,*
> *to accept the things I cannot change,*
> *the courage to change the things I can,*
> *and the wisdom to know the difference.*
> *Amen.*[1]

Step 1

This is the step missing in millions of exhausted and miserable Christians' lives. They've heard all the things about duty and responsibility with no boundaries to help them sort it all out.

People try to do God's business for Him.

The result is that people frantically try to do God's business for Him, feel guilty, and eventually either drop out or become numb.

Step 1 is a step of reality. It is not even an action and certainly is not an accomplishment that you complete and then leave behind. Step 1 is—just as it says—an admission.

Cleve's story

Cleve once felt he must control other people's opinions of him. When he sensed that a customer disapproved of him, he felt depressed and guilty. Now he is learning to work on the first Step. When disapproval arises he asks," 'What am I powerless over here?' The opinions of others. 'Who am I responsible to please?' My Lord, family, etc." The first Step is not the final solution for Cleve. It is the doorway to a whole new life of peace, effectiveness, and obedience to Jesus.

Our thinking in the extremes leads us to spoil our lives in several other areas. Part of this extreme thinking leads us to be super responsible or to give up and be irresponsible, because we cannot live up to our own demands.

For each one shall bear his own load.
–Galatians 6:5

✏ **Read the verse at left. In what ways have you neglected to bear your own load? (That is, how have you failed to be responsible to make your own decisions, be yourself, and set limits in your responsibilities to others?)**

_____

_____

Paul also encouraged the believers in Corinth to give cheerfully: "Let each one do just as he has purposed in his heart; not grudgingly or under compulsion; for God loves a cheerful giver" (2 Corinthians 9:7). We may give cheerfully for a while, but we expect (or is it demand?) a positive response in return. When our "selfless giving" is not appreciated, we become resentful.

✏ **In what ways are you a cheerful giver?** _____

_____

Ways I've been resentful—
_____
_____
_____
_____
_____

In the margin box list examples of ways have you been resentful when people don't appreciate your "serving" and "helping" them.

We usually deny the hurt inside. We learn to put on pleasant fronts to hide our anger, pain, bitterness and depression. Or, we live from successful rescue to successful rescue. We seldom see a glimmer of the painful cause of our compulsive rescuing. Looking inside is painful but necessary if we are to experience genuine love, warmth, meaning, and intimacy.

Christ dealt strongly with the Pharisees, who looked stable and mature on the outside, but who had not dealt with the painful realities on the inside of their lives. On the next page read a Scripture describing this situation.

> Woe to you, scribes and Pharisees, hypocrites! For you clean the outside of the cup and of the dish, but inside they are full of robbery and self-indulgence. You blind Pharisee, first clean the inside of the cup and of the dish, so that the outside of it may become clean also. Woe to you, scribes and Pharisees, hypocrites! For you are like whitewashed tombs which on the outside appear beautiful, but inside they are full of dead men's bones and all uncleanness. Even so you too outwardly appear righteous to men, but inwardly you are full of hypocrisy and lawlessness.
> –Matthew 23:25-28

> For am I now seeking the favor of men, or of God? Or am I striving to please men? If I were still trying to please men, I would not be a bond-servant of Christ.
> –Galatians 1:10

To gain others' approval, I—

_____
_____
_____
_____

✎ **This is an exercise that will require great courage. As you read the Scripture appearing in the margin, please underline the phrases that you could apply to your "looking good at all costs" acts.**

As I read this passage, God convicted me of actions like "cleaning the outside of the cup" and "outwardly appearing righteous."

✎ **What are some ways that you appear strong and healthy on the outside? What do you do or say to appear that way?**

_____
_____

Why is it so difficult to be honest about the pain inside? _____

_____
_____

The Scripture at left shows what Paul wrote to the believers in Galatia about the compulsion to please people. To please people at all costs, we serve and fix and rescue and enable. That's why we allow ourselves to be so easily manipulated. And that's why we are so deeply hurt when someone doesn't appreciate us. Approval means everything to us. In the margin box at left write some things you do or say to win others' approval.

Step 1 is the doorway to a new life. This is not a doorway you will enter and then leave behind but one God will provide for you in every situation. Do you now choose to begin walking through that doorway? ❏ Yes ❏ No

---

Key Concept for Lesson 5
Step 1 is a life-style, not an act. It is a doorway to a new life.

✎ **Please pray and ask God how this concept can apply in your life. Now please review this lesson. What has God shown you that you can use?**

_____
_____

Step Review

✎ **Please review this Step. Pray and ask God to identify the Scriptures or principles that are particularly important for your life. Underline them. Then respond to the following:**

Restate Step 1 in your own words.

_____
_____

Step 1 41

What do you have to gain by practicing this Step in your life?

_____

_____

Reword your summary into a prayer of response to God. Thank Him for this Step, and affirm your commitment to Him.

_____

_____

Memorize this Step's memory verse:
Blessed are the poor in spirit, for theirs is the kingdom of heaven.
–Matthew 5:3

Notes
[1] Reinhold Niebuhr, "The Serenity Prayer," (St. Meinrad, IN: Abbey Press.)

STEP 2

Changing the Cycle

We increasingly believe that God can restore us to health and sanity through His Son Jesus Christ.

Step 2 Into Codependency

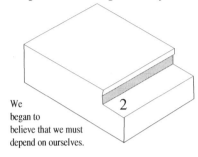

We began to believe that we must depend on ourselves.

Step 2 Out of Codependency

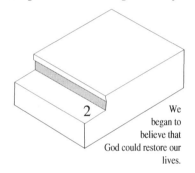

We began to believe that God could restore our lives.

CAUGHT UP IN BUSYNESS

Many people envied Jack because he seemed to be the most knowledgeable person in town about the latest movie or the most recent sporting event. Jack prided himself on how diligently he worked at "playing"—his constant flurry of activities gave the appearance that he thrived on a good time.

Although Jack would not admit it, he flitted from movie to symphony performance to professional baseball game because he hurt inside.

He and his wife and twin sons did not communicate well with each other, so he stayed busy to avoid intimacy with them. He also chose busy activities because the hubbub enabled him to avoid personal conversations with friends who might accompany him to these events.

Besides being a "good-time Charlie" Jack also was a model church participant. He taught a regular Bible study, chaired a demanding church committee, and visited church prospects weekly.

Despite his activity level Jack always seemed to feel his life was empty. Read on pages xx about what people like Jack need in their lives.

Jesus answered and said to them, 'This is the work of God, that you believe in Him whom He has sent.'

–John 6:29

Overview for Step 2

Lesson 1: Insanity Part One: The Core Symptoms
   Goal: You will describe how the three core symptoms of codependency result in self-defeating behavior.

Lesson 2: Insanity Part Two: Denial
   Goal: You will identify six defense mechanisms that blind us to the truth.

Lesson 3: The Origin of Our Concept of God
   Goal: You will describe one key influence in the development of your concept of God.

Lesson 4: Getting to Know Your Concept of God
   Goal: You will describe for yourself your concept(s) of God.

Lesson 5: Experiencing God from Psalm 139
   Goal: You will begin bringing your concepts of God in line with reality.

Lesson 6: Belief Systems
   Goal: You will describe the four false beliefs behind codependency and the four scriptural truths to overcome them.

LESSON 1

Insanity Part One: The Core Symptoms

We increasingly believe that God can restore us to health and sanity through His Son Jesus Christ.

> *For God did not send the Son into the world to judge the world, but that the world should be saved through Him.*
>
> –John 3:17

Key Concept:
Codependency is a disease with predictable symptoms and results.

In this Step you will distinguish between your concept of God and the God who lives and who loves you. Step 2 has three parts:

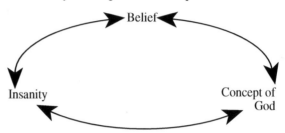

Part 1
We come to believe as we realize—
- the **insanity** (see definition at left) of our lives;
- the nature of the living God.

Part 2
We recognize our insanity as we see—
- our concept of God;
- the foolishness of our unbelief.

Part 3
We get to know the real God when we distinguish—
- our concept of God from
- the God who really is.

insanity–n. a recovery term that describes unreasonable or self-defeating thinking. This term is not used here in a clinical sense to refer to a mental disorder.

We find the process of believing with both our minds and our emotions extremely difficult because of the insanity of the condition. You recall the three core symptoms of codependency and the three emotional results as the diagram below shows.

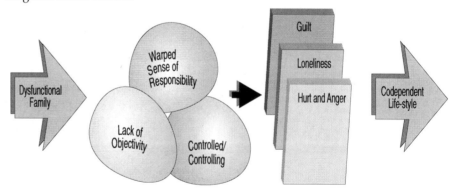

As painful as it is to think about, our three core symptoms cause us the three emotional results. We learned to experience this pain because of another person's actions or inaction, but now we are the actors. The ones who caused the original pain are gone, but we have taken their place. We are afflicting ourselves. Now, what could be more absurd than that? The solution is to have God actually operating in His place in our lives. We cannot have God in His rightful place in our lives because we have a mistaken concept of who He is. This makes it impossible for us to trust Him.

44   Step 2

A Lack of Objectivity

Objective means *impartial*, *unbiased*, or *unprejudiced*. An objective person sees things the way they really are. We, however, have a filing cabinet full of painful, distorted experiences that make objectivity difficult.

 Circle the numbers of the statements that reflect a lack of objectivity.

1. She did that just to hurt me.
2. I wonder what he meant by that remark.
3. I really like her a lot.
4. I'm having difficulty making friends.
5. Nobody likes me at that school.
6. I feel very awkward being in a new job.

People are self-motivated; they do what they do for their own reasons. We demonstrate a lack of objectivity when we think we are the reason others do what they do. When we make broad generalizations, we do the same thing. Numbers 1 and 5 show a lack of objectivity.

Our understanding of God

While dining with friends, I said, "We get our concept of God, especially how we feel about Him, from our parents." "Wow!" my friend Nancy said. "So that's why I'm always so angry at Him."

 Did Nancy demonstrate an objective view of God? ❑ Yes ❑ No

Why or why not? _____

When we were children, our parents literally were our God-figures. Long before we were old enough to have an intellectual (head-knowledge) understanding about God, we obtained ideas about God from our emotional understanding of Him.

What Nancy really was feeling was not anger at God; it was misplaced anger at her earthly father and mother. Her concept of God definitely was not objective. She dealt with two different concepts—one she knew in her intellect and one she felt in her emotions.

> **Who's in charge of Nancy's life?**
> _____
> _____
> _____

 Since my friend felt this way about God, would it be possible for her to trust Him and to allow Him to direct her life? ❑ Yes ❑ No

In the margin box answer this question: Who is likely to be in charge of Nancy's life in practical matters? If we cannot trust God because of an unhealthy image we have received from our distorted family experience, likely we either will attempt to run our lives ourselves and be miserable, or we will surrender to some person or system of belief and ask this person or system to run our lives for us.

 How could my friend's distorted view of God put her in the situation James describes in the passage in the margin? Have you ever felt you were in that situation—wanting to trust God but not able to do so?

_____
_____

> and every decision you then make will be uncertain, as you turn first this way, then that. If you don't ask with faith, don't expect the Lord to give you any solid answer.
> –James 1:7-8, TLB

Step 2

Torn apart at the seams

We often find ourselves in exactly the situation James describes. We have difficulty trusting God in our emotions. Because of the beliefs in our heads, however, we *know* we should trust Him. The result is literally a "double-minded" person who is torn apart at the seams.

 Below describe how lack of objectivity affects your life. Be prepared to share your insights with your sponsor or group this week.

___

___

Lack of objectivity feeds directly into the next characteristic of codependency.

A Warped Sense of Responsibility

Some words we use to define codependency are: *rescue, help, fix,* and *enable*. We see ourselves as saviors; we often feel responsible for everything and everybody. Usually we feel responsible for many things which are someone else's business. The result is that we have neither the time nor the energy to take care of our own business.

Usually we feel responsible for many things which are someone else's business.

Those of us who are overly responsible become consumed with taking care of others. In the role of caretaker we don't see the need to have our own identities, our own dreams, our own emotions, and our own schedules. We are driven to be and do and feel what other people want us to be and do and feel. We believe doing anything for ourselves is selfish. Our thinking goes something like this:

- If he is angry, it must be my fault.
- If she is sad, I must have done something to hurt her feelings.
- If she is afraid, I need to comfort and protect her.
- If he is happy, I must have helped him.

We want to be loved and accepted, and we want to avoid conflict, so we do whatever it takes to make people happy, especially the needy people in our families. We believe we can do no wrong and can rescue everyone in need. Our creed is,

- If someone has a need, I'll meet it.
- If a need doesn't exist, I'll find one, and then I'll meet it.
- If a small need exists, I'll make it a large one. Then I'll feel even better when I meet it.
- Even if nobody wants help, I'll help anyway.
- When I've helped, I'll finally feel good about myself.

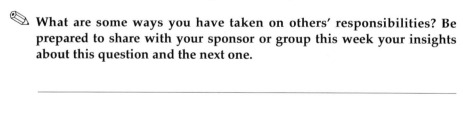 What are some ways you have taken on others' responsibilities? Be prepared to share with your sponsor or group this week your insights about this question and the next one.

___

___

How do you feel about the areas of responsibility you have taken on?

Many times we feel angry, bitter, or used because we take on other people's responsibilities. Some people feel guilty or righteous or needed.

Controlled and Controlling

Only emotionally sick people like to be controlled.

Since we cannot see objectively, and since we feel responsible for others' thoughts, feelings, and actions, we begin to try to control other people. Only emotionally-sick people like to be controlled, so the result is sick relationships or outright rejection.

Development of the people pleaser: Like everyone else, we need love and respect. Having been deprived of these precious commodities, we become determined to do whatever it takes to win the affirmation we crave. Our chief fear is that people will be unhappy with us. Those around us often learn to use praise or condemnation to manipulate us in the same way the operator manipulates a puppet on a string.

Development of the abusive codependent: Some of us lose hope of getting love by earning it, so we instead turn to demanding it. Our actions are the exact opposite of those of the people pleaser described above, but the same desperate needs motivate these actions.

✎ **What are the areas of your life over which you attempt to maintain control?**

In what ways do others attempt to control you?

How do you attempt to control them?

Congratulations on completing this lesson.

Key Concept for Lesson 1
Codependency is a disease with predictable symptoms and results.

Step 2

✏️ Please pray and ask God how this concept can apply in your life. Now please review this lesson. What has God shown you that you can use?

_____

_____

LESSON 2

Insanity Part Two: Denial

We increasingly believe that God can restore us to health and sanity through His Son Jesus Christ.

And they have healed the brokenness of My people superficially, Saying, "Peace, peace," But there is no peace.
—Jeremiah 6:14

Key Concept:
Since denial keeps us stuck, we need Jesus, each other and the program to help us face reality.

Denial creates a tremendous temptation to do in recovery as the false prophets did in the passage above. We are tempted to have wounds healed on the surface. Many people enter the recovery process, get some knowledge, and declare themselves healed. The result is like putting a dressing on a cancer.

✏️ Write your own definition of denial.

_____

_____

He who conceals his transgressions will not prosper, But he who confesses and forsakes them will find compassion.
—Proverbs 28:13

✏️ Explain in what way the Scripture at left warns us about what happens when we allow denial to work in our lives.

_____

_____

_____

I define denial as a "learned inability to see the truth." Look honestly at some of the obstacles that stand in your way of putting Step 2 into practice. Codependents' **defense mechanisms** prevent seeing the truth. Without seeing the truth, you won't get well.

defense mechanism–n. a habit of thought that keeps us from seeing painful reality. . . and getting well.

Among those habitual defense mechanisms are—

1. Selective Filtering of Information

Codependents learn to filter out unpleasant truth. A codependent's bulimic sister says for the umpteenth time, "It's over; I'm never going to binge and purge again." The codependent wants to believe this promise so badly that he feels great relief even though his sister has a poor record of keeping promises. Or, codependents may hear and see only what they dread. A codependent

Hearing bits and pieces

receives her performance review at work. Her boss tells her she has performed with excellence 20 actions and that she needs to improve only one area. Instead of rejoicing about her good work in most of the job, she will be crushed. The one area that needs some work consumes her mind.

2. Defending the Offender

Always an excuse

Instead of honestly feeling the hurt of betrayal and experiencing the anger of being abused or neglected, the codependent usually defends the offender. She makes excuses such as, "It's not really her fault," or, "She couldn't help it, and besides, it doesn't bother me when she curses me like that. I'm used to it by now." Or, she may say, "Yes, it hurts when he treats me that way, but I feel so sorry for him. He wants to stop drinking, but he just can't."

3. Redefining the Pain

psychosomatic–relating to bodily symptoms caused by mental or emotional disturbance (Webster's)

Being objective about their deep hurt and seething anger may be painful and/or guilt-inducing for codependents, but repressing these emotions often causes **psychosomatic** illnesses. Many people who experience the tremendous stress of pain, anger, and guilt develop severe tension headaches. Instead of admitting their stress, they say they are having migraine headaches. When I asked one man to describe the pain of his migraines, he did not describe a typical migraine—a headache characterized by a one-sided, light-sensitive, throbbing pain. His pain was from tension, but when he called it a migraine, this made the pain seem less threatening and more acceptable to him. By saying he had a tension headache, he would reveal to others that he was stressed—a situation he might not want to disclose. We often give to ailments a host of other labels that shift the source of the problem from repressed emotions to a purely physical cause. (We don't want to imply that we believe repressed emotions cause every sickness a codependent experiences. Buried emotions do, however, lower resistance to all kinds of physical problems.)

Shifting the source

✎ List the first three denial mechanisms.

1. Selective _____.

2. Defending the _____.

3. _____ the pain.

✎ Match the three mechanisms above to the following examples.

_____ a. He really couldn't help it. I shouldn't have. . . .
_____ b. No, the counselor said the . . . wasn't a problem.
_____ c. I can't go with you. My allergies are acting up again.

The exercise you just worked is designed to help you remember the first three means denial uses to hide painful reality and thus cause more pain. Thank you for correctly responding: a. 2, b. 1, and c. 3. Below are three more defense mechanisms that keep us from seeing the truth:

4. Diversions

Codependents use all kinds of activities to keep themselves so busy that they don't have time to reflect and feel. Working 70 to 80 hours a week,

A flurry of activity

participating in clubs, watching television, and many other diversions keep them preoccupied. Jack, the "good-time Charlie" introduced on the unit page, was a master at this defense mechanism. Like Jack, most codependents are unaware that the reason their lives seem empty is because they hurt. They may have a vague sense that something is wrong, but they have no idea what it is. They reject any hint that they may be dealing with repressed emotions.

5. Exchanged Emotions

Worry equals love

Because codependents haven't experienced much true love and intimacy or genuine support and encouragement, they often substitute one emotion for another. For instance one woman equated worry with love. She always *worried* about her son, but she very seldom expressed genuine affection for him. She substituted the intensity of her worry for the love he needed. Some people may use condemnation and praise to manipulate others rather than simply loving them. Some may substitute anger with a stoic calm that has the appearance of peacefulness but which in reality is denial.

6. Euphemisms

Altering words

To avoid being objective about their emotions, codependents often use words that don't reflect accurately how they really feel. The classic example of this occurs when people describe themselves as being *frustrated* instead of *angry*. People seem to think that it's OK to be frustrated with someone, but real anger is a different story. Real anger is too threatening to us, so we alter our words to make our emotions seem less severe. Though the word *frustrated* is a perfectly legitimate word to describe an emotion, we overuse it. In our office we have agreed that we will not use the word *frustrated*. Instead we agree to say that we are angry when that's truly how we feel. People found this to be difficult at first, but after a few days the honesty was very refreshing!

In our office we have agreed to say that we are angry when that's truly how we feel.

✎ **List the next three denial mechanisms.**

4. Staying too busy to face the truth _____.

5. Substituting something for real feelings _____ emotions.

6. Not saying what we really feel _____.

✎ **Match to the following examples the three mechanisms you just listed.**

_____ a. Let's gather the family up and see what's showing at the movies. I've been away from home for two weeks, and this would be a fun activity for us to do.

_____ b. I'm frustrated that you showed up late for work.

_____ c. I worry myself sick when you don't eat three meals a day.

The exercise you just worked is designed to help you remember the second three means denial uses to hide painful reality and thus cause more pain. Thank you for correctly responding: a. 4, b. 6, c. 5.

✎ **Pray and ask God to give you understanding about this very important information you've just processed; then go back and review the six denial mechanisms. In the descriptions of them circle words or phrases that you see apply to your life.**

Ephesians 4:15 describes the goal of healthy living: *but speaking the truth in love, we are to grow up in all aspects into Him, who is the head, even Christ.*

> **Key Concept for Lesson 2**
> Since denial keeps us stuck, we need Jesus, each other and the program to help us face reality.

 Please pray and ask God how the concept you just read can apply in your life. Now please review this lesson. What has God shown you that you can use?

LESSON 3

The Origin of Our Concept of God

We increasingly believe that God can restore us to health and sanity through His Son Jesus Christ.

But Thou, O LORD, art a shield about me, My glory, and the One who lifts my head.

–Psalm 3:3

Key Concept:
Our relationships with our parents shape our concept of God.

Your Parents and You

Our parents shape our views of God, our self-concepts, and our abilities to relate to others. If our parents were loving and supportive, we probably will feel that God is loving and strong. If our parents were harsh and demanding, we probably will feel God is impossible to please. What we see our parents model usually establishes the foundation of our emotional, relational, and spiritual health. The results can be wonderful or tragic.

To gain a better understanding of this shaping process, we will examine the characteristics of our parents and of our relationships with them. Ahead is an exercise to help you evaluate your relationship with your parents that you experienced while you were growing up. Perhaps your father was absent from your childhood home, but you may have had another significant, ongoing relationship with an adult man—perhaps a grandfather, uncle, or stepfather. If so, fill in the exercise according to how this individual related to you when you were younger. The same situation applies to those whose mothers were absent from your childhood home. If this was the case, base the exercise on your relationship with another significant adult woman—perhaps a grandmother, aunt, or stepmother.

Not fault or blame

Please be aware: The exercise you are about to complete is not about fault or blame but is about feelings. Feelings aren't right or wrong—feelings just *are*. Several children reared in the same home will answer this exercise very differently. The point is not what happened but how you reacted and felt when you were a child.

Step 2 51

My Concept of My Father

 Choose from each of the five groups of descriptive words that follow the one word that best describes how you felt about your father when you were a small child. On each line circle the words that applies.

1. gentle, harsh, loving, stern, disapproving, kind
2. distant, intimate, angry, caring, demanding, supportive
3. interested, discipliner, gracious, harsh, wise, impatient
4. unpredictable, sensitive, encouraging, passive, strong, wise
5. just, unreasonable, good, trustworthy, holy, joyful

What do those five words you circled tell you about your relationship with your father?

_____
_____

Years later John still tries to figure out why he has mixed feelings about God.

John has wonderful memories of his father. He felt that he was his father's "special son." But when John was eight years old, his father died. Years later John still tries to figure out why he has mixed feelings about God. He feels that God definitely loves him, but he also feels he cannot get close to God.

 Did any extraordinary life circumstances, such as death, divorce, or absence because of military service, affect your feelings about your father? ❏ Yes ❏ No If so, describe below.

_____
_____

If you were an objective observer of the relationship you described in answering the two previous questions, how would you feel about the father?

_____
_____

How would you feel about the child? _____
_____

My Concept of My Mother

 Choose from each of the five groups of descriptive words that follow the one word that best describes how you felt about your mother when you were a small child. On each line circle the word that applies.

1. gentle, harsh, loving, stern, disapproving, kind
2. distant, intimate, angry, caring, demanding, supportive
3. interested, discipliner, gracious, harsh, wise, impatient
4. unpredictable, sensitive, encouraging, passive, strong, wise
5. just, unreasonable, good, trustworthy, holy, joyful

What do those five words you circled tell you about your relationship with your mother?

___

Loving by fault-finding

Neil's mother was the victim of a family which substituted one emotion for another. This mother believed that the way a mother shows love to her son is to point out his faults; her attitude was, "I only criticize you because I love you." As a result Neil's descriptive words of his mother were: *disapproving, demanding, impatient, strong,* and *unreasonable.* Is anyone surprised that he is a driven perfectionist who feels he never can be close to or please God?

✎ **Did any extraordinary life circumstances, such as absence because of death, divorce, or military service, affect your feelings about your mother?** ❏ Yes ❏ No **If so, describe.**

___

If you were an objective observer of the relationship you have described in answering the two previous questions, how would you feel about the mother?

___

How would you feel about the child? ___

___

✎ **Does a great difference exist between what you know about God in your head and what you feel about Him?** ❏ Yes ❏ No

✎ **Would it be easier to trust God if you found that He was very different than what you feel about Him?** ❏ Yes ❏ No

> **Key Concept for Lesson 3**
> Our relationships with our parents shape our concept of God.

✎ **Please pray and ask God how this concept can apply in your life. Now please review this lesson. What has God shown you that you can use?**

___

LESSON 4

Getting to Know Your Concept of God

We increasingly believe that God can restore us to health and sanity through His Son Jesus Christ.

> *Since, then you have been raised with Christ, set your hearts on things above. . . . Set your minds on things above. . . .*
> –Colossians 3:1-2, NIV

Key Concept:
Everyone has two concepts of God—one intellectual and one emotional.

Barry was a tortured Christian when he came to the program. A pastor for 25 years, Barry was a committed believer and held a doctorate in theology. He knew all about God in his head but felt only abandonment and criticism from the god in his heart. Now that Barry is in recovery, spirituality for him means getting these two concepts together to apply to the one God.

A split-personality God

Many of us have felt very puzzled when we contemplate this God that seems to have a split personality. We never may realize that the conflict is between an emotional concept of God which probably was shaped in our minds when we were young children, and the verbal, logical God in our intellect. The difference is between what we *know* and what we *feel* about God.

✎ Explain in your own words why we benefit from seeing the difference between what you *know* and what you *feel* about God.

_____
_____
_____

Describe what happens in your life if a conflict exists between the two views of God.

_____
_____
_____

If you found the above assignment difficult, you're in good company. That's because people often have a difficult time using language to describe a feelings issue. Having these conflicts in our lives can make us miserable, can make us turn to addictive behaviors, and can keep us very confused.

Exercise About Your Concept of God

Repeat the exercise you wrote for father and mother in the last lesson. This time answer the questions about your relationships with the God of your

Remember that He is a God of love, and love "rejoices in the truth."

feelings. As you do so, select the words that reflect what you *feel* about God, not what you *know* about Him. Remember He is a God of love, and love "rejoices in the truth" (1 Corinthians 13:6). He will be pleased with your openness and honesty.

 Choose from each of the five groups of descriptive words that follow the one word that best describes how you feel about God. From the words in each line circle one that best applies.

1. gentle, harsh, loving, stern, disapproving, kind
2. distant, intimate, angry, caring, demanding, supportive
3. interested, discipliner, gracious, harsh, wise, impatient
4. unpredictable, sensitive, encouraging, passive, strong, wise
5. just, unreasonable, good, trustworthy, holy, joyful

Review the five words you circled, and get a mental picture of the type of God these five words describe. If a person has that combined view, how would you expect him or her to respond to God?

_____

_____

 Go back to Lesson 3; fill in the form below with the words describing your relationship with your parents. Use those words plus the five words you wrote above about the relationship you have with God.

My emotional relationship with my:

Father	God	Mother
_____	_____	_____
_____	_____	_____
_____	_____	_____
_____	_____	_____
_____	_____	_____

Remember: This is not about blaming parents. Not all parents have skills to show they love their children.

From an exercise like this Denise suddenly realized, "That's why I feel like I do. From my father I get the message of criticism. Nothing I do ever is good enough. From my mother I get abandonment. I was the oldest of eight kids; she was so busy with all the younger ones she never had time for me. She was never there for me. That is exactly the way I feel toward God—criticized and abandoned."

 How are your feelings about your father and your Heavenly Father alike? How are they different?

_____

_____

Feelings aren't good or bad. Feelings just are...

How are your feelings about your mother and your Heavenly Father alike? How are they different?

_____

_____

_____

Dealing with Blocked Emotions

"So what?"

You might find yourself saying, "So now I know where my feelings come from: So what?"

Jesus said, *Then render to Caesar the things that are Caesar's; and to God the things that are God's* (Matthew 22:21). We might draw from that this broad principle: Deal with different persons or things in appropriate ways. Dealing with emotions in intellectual ways is inappropriate. In the program this often is referred to as being "in your head."

Many of the problems of codependency are rooted in our feelings, but we have tried to deal with them in our heads. This approach doesn't work. Imagine trying to dig a ditch with a can opener or to paint with a saw. A major task of recovery is to deal with our emotions. We can deal with feelings, at least in part, through emotional means. Listed in the box below are some ways to get in touch with your feelings. Much of the difficult work of recovery involves using these techniques.

GET IN TOUCH WITH FEELINGS BY—

1. **Journaling**: We learn that pen and paper have almost magical qualities. Writing down feelings brings out deep emotions we have kept buried.
2. **Sharing**: Putting situations into words with a sponsor, mentor, friend, or with our group breaks through our denial.
3. **Writing letters**: Letters that express our emotions get us in touch with those feelings.
4. **Meditation on Scripture**: The Book of Psalms appeals greatly to our emotional concept of God. Meditating, with a pad and pen at hand, and writing down our feelings is a powerful way to get in touch with our emotions.
5. **Discipling relationships**: Find someone who has the character traits you desire. Ask this person to share what is working for him or her.
6. **Writing prayers**: Writing our feelings to God accesses emotion.

A bright world of joy awaits you!

All of these techniques help you to get what is buried on the inside out where you can deal with it. That may be terribly frightening for you. But it is a journey; you can take your time. A bright world of joy awaits you!

> **Key Concept for Lesson 4**
> Everyone has two concepts of God—one intellectual and one emotional.

 Please pray and ask God how this concept can apply in your life. Now please review this lesson. What has God shown you that you can use?

_____

_____

LESSON 5

Key Concept:
Changing my concept of God is a key part of my recovery.

Attributes of God

1-4- *all-knowing (omniscient)*

5-7 _____

_____

_____

13 _____

23-24 _____

_____

Experiencing God from Psalm 139

We increasingly believe that God can restore us to health and sanity through His Son Jesus Christ.

> *Thou hast enclosed me behind and before, And laid Thy hand upon me. Such knowledge is too wonderful for me; It is too high, I cannot attain to it.*
>
> –Psalm 139:5-6

We have a warped emotional picture of God. On the next page are some things we can do to aid our recovery.

- Develop an accurate understanding, or intellectual concept, of God.
- Bring our emotional concept into line with that true understanding.

When I began recovery, my sponsor made me live in Psalm 139. I didn't fully understand at the time, but now I realize why. This glorious psalm brings together our "head knowledge" of God and our emotional concept of Him.

 Read these verses from Psalm 139. In the margin write the attribute of God you find in the verse. I have done the first for you as an example.

> ¹O Lord, Thou hast searched me and known me. ²Thou dost know when I sit down and when I rise up; Thou dost understand my thought from afar. ⁴Even before there is a word on my tongue, Behold, O Lord, Thou dost know it all. ⁵Thou hast enclosed me behind and before, And laid Thy hand upon me. ⁷Where can I go from Thy Spirit? Or where can I flee from Thy presence? ¹³For Thou didst form my inward parts; Thou didst weave me in my mother's womb. ²³Search me, O God, and know my heart; Try me and know my anxious thoughts; ²⁴And see if there be any hurtful way in me, And lead me in the everlasting way.

In a personal way the psalm gives us a wonderful picture of God's majesty and power. You probably noted that verses 5 and 7 speak of God's omnipresence, or "power to be everywhere at once." Verse 13 speaks of God as our Creator, and verse 23 and 24 point to God's holiness or perfection. That exercise was "in our heads." Now let's bring it down to our emotions.

Step 2 57

✏️ **Read the following verses. Write how you *feel* about what they say.**

¹O Lord, Thou hast searched me and known me. ²Thou dost know when I sit down and when I rise up; Thou dost understand my thought from afar. ³Thou dost scrutinize my path and my lying down, And art intimately acquainted with all my ways. ⁴Even before there is a word on my tongue, Behold, O Lord, Thou dost know it all.

How thoroughly does God know you? _____

You've heard it said that "a friend is someone who knows all about you and loves you anyway." How much does God love you?

_____

How does the saying you just read about friendship relate to the psalm? How do you feel about the statement you've used to answer that question?

_____
_____

How does this make me feel—"I'm valuable to God"?

_____
_____
_____
_____

The New Testament, in Romans 5:8, tells us that *God demonstrates His own love toward us, in that while we were yet sinners, Christ died for us.* One person wrote: "Wow . . . God knows all the bad stuff about me and yet loves me deeply enough to die for me." We are great at "guilting"—the fine art of dumping guilt on ourselves. Do you guilt on yourself unmercifully? Do you feel like, "God really couldn't love me"? ❑ Yes ❑ No

Listen to what comes next in verse 5: "Thou hast enclosed me behind and before." Remember, what you love, you protect. God's perfect knowledge of you enables Him to protect you—to "hem you in." How do you feel about the statement, "God protects me because I'm valuable"? In the margin write your answer. Do you ever feel like "a holy God couldn't touch something as sinful as me"? Next the psalm says God has "laid His hand upon me."

✏️ **The passage from Luke 15 is a good illustration of a father's response to a sinful child. It tells about a son who left home, spent his father's money improperly, came to his senses, and returned to his father. The story picks up when his father spots him returning. The father runs to him, hugs him, and kisses him. If you had been the son, how would you feel as the father embraced you and gave orders for the servants to lavish gifts on you?**

_____
_____

How does it feel to realize that the father in the story is a picture of God's attitude toward you?

_____
_____

And he got up and came to his father. But while he was still a long way off, his father saw him, and felt compassion for him, and ran and embraced him, and kissed him. And the son said to him, "Father, I have sinned against heaven and in your sight; I am no longer worthy to be called your son." But the father said to his slaves, "Quickly bring out the best robe and put it on him, and put a ring on his hand and sandals on his feet; and bring the fatted calf, kill it, and let us eat and be merry; for this son of mine was dead, and has come to life again; he was lost, and has been found." And they began to be merry.

–Luke 15:20-24

Back to Psalm 139, the psalmist next says, *⁷Where can I go from Thy Spirit? Or where can I flee from Thy presence? ⁸If I ascend to heaven, Thou art there; If I make my bed in Sheol, behold, Thou art there. ⁹If I take the wings of the dawn, If I dwell in the remotest part of the sea, ¹⁰Even there Thy hand will lead me, And Thy right hand will lay hold of me. ¹¹If I say "Surely the darkness will overwhelm me, And the light around me will be night," ¹²Even the darkness is not dark to Thee, And the night is as bright as the day. Darkness and light are alike to Thee.*

When I first read those verses, I saw that "God is everywhere—judging, punishing, pursuing. No matter what I do I cannot get away from Him." What I was hearing was my emotional idea of a punishing, harsh, unloving God. I now see the passage differently. He says God loves me so much that He wants to be with me always—even in the pit if necessary.

✎ **What does the above passage—verses 7 through 12—say to you? How do you feel about what it says?**

_____

_____

God loves me so much, He wants to be in my company!

In Jesus' prayer in John 17:24, He prayed concerning you: *Father, I desire that they also, whom Thou hast given Me, be with Me where I am.* Someone explained the verse this way, "I think heaven will be heaven because Jesus will be there. Jesus thinks it will be heaven because you will be there." The passage says to me that God loves me so much, He wants to be in my company!

✎ **Verses 13-14 say you are "fearfully and wonderfully made." How would it feel to be able to look in the mirror and be very thankful that God had made you just as He wanted?**

_____

_____

Verse 16 suggests that God knew everything about you before He chose to make you and die for you. Write in the margin box how it feels to realize that He loves you that much, even when you are at your worst? After all the above, the psalmist says, *How precious also are Thy thoughts to me, O God!* (vs. 17) Do you have to make yourself pray? Would it make a difference if you felt the way about God that the psalmist did? ❑ Yes ❑ No

The psalm ends with responsibility: *Search me, O God, and know my heart; Try me and know my anxious thoughts; And see if there be any hurtful way in me, And lead me in the everlasting way.*

✎ **Would you be more willing to surrender your life to God if you felt His love as you've seen in the psalm?** ❑ Yes ❑ No

---

Key Concept for Lesson 5
Changing my concept of God is a key part of my recovery.

Step 2

Please pray and ask God how this concept can apply in your life. Now please review this lesson. What has God shown you that you can use?

_____

_____

LESSON 6

Belief Systems

We increasingly believe that God can restore us to health and sanity through His Son Jesus Christ.

And do not be conformed to this world, but be transformed by the renewing of your mind.
—Romans 12:2

Key Concept:
Four false beliefs perpetuate the power of codependency in our lives.

This unit about coming to believe has been built on the following diagram:

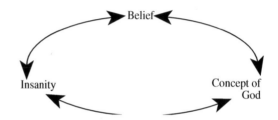

The diagram pictures the relationship of our concept of God with our need to believe and with our insanity. We can't believe in the false concept of God in our mind and emotions, so we continue trying to be God, which is insane—extremely unreasonable. We, and our entire sick society, use four false beliefs to build our lives. These false beliefs keep us sick. They are the foundation on which our destructive habits exist. In *Search for Significance* LIFE Support Edition, Robert S. McGee identifies these beliefs which distort our perception of both God and ourselves. We base these lies on the primary belief that:

$$\text{Self-Worth} = \text{Performance} + \text{Other's opinions}^{[1]}$$

In other words, we suffer from a misconception that our significance, or worth, is determined by what we do and what others think of us. Each of these four false beliefs, explained in this lesson, results in a specific fear.

> False Belief #1: *I must meet certain standards to feel good about myself.* This belief results in the fear of failure.

Don't confuse this false belief with healthy goal setting. Working toward goals is a skill healthy families teach. This false belief is that our worth is determined by living up to standards. It is performance-based self-worth.

The following are some examples of self-talk. Underline the statements that indicate this false belief.

1. I'm hopeless, I never do anything right.
2. I really blew that one.
3. Next time I'll know better.
4. I'm sure glad I don't have to be perfect.

These examples of self-talk are on a sliding scale of healthy response. One is a definite case of abusing myself over your human imperfection. Responses 3 and 4 are much healthier responses. You be the judge about number 2. Now you try out this false belief. Imagine that you have just failed at something important to you. In the first margin box write which of the above responses you most likely would use to "self-talk" yourself. Then, in the second box, write the response you truly would like to be able to say to yourself after you've failed.

I'd self-talk myself by saying:

What I'd really like to say would be:

Congratulations! You have just set a goal and taken a concrete action toward achieving it. Next time you blow it, use it!

> False Belief #2: *I must have the approval of certain others to feel good about myself. Without their approval I cannot feel good about myself.* This belief results in the fear of rejection.

Don't confuse this false belief with healthy caring for people. This belief really is part of our self-centeredness but masquerades as caring for others. What we really are doing is seeking others' approval, even if it injures them, in order to feel good about ourselves. In the margin box answer the questions about people you feel you must please.

> False Belief #3: *Those who fail (including myself) are unworthy of love and deserve to be punished.* This belief leads to the fear of punishment and the tendency to punish others.

Who are the people in your life you feel you must please?

How do you feel when you must displease them to do what's right?

Since we feel unworthy of love, we go to one or both of two extremes. We either become major self-punishers, we punish others, or we punish ourselves and others.

This is why such a range of behavior originates from the same root cause: abused codependents and abusive codependents. Both have an unwritten set of rigid rules. Since the rules are unwritten, life is like a mine field. You never know where the charges are placed; you only feel the blast.

This orientation is backward looking. Since you never defined the rules, you can't look forward and avoid them. This learned behavior comes from living with inconsistency and leads to more of the same. The behavior also leads to despair and to the final false belief, which appears on the next page.

Step 2 61

> False Belief #4: *I am what I am. I cannot change. I am hopeless.* This means I am simply a total of all my past performances, both good and bad. I am what I have done. This belief leads to a sense of shame.

God's love letter to us

The Bible is our resource for understanding God. It is His love letter to us. Understanding its truth is a key part of restoration, because codependency is a disease of habit. Our actions usually are based on our beliefs! God gives us four key truths to counteract the four false beliefs. The following chart portrays them:

False Beliefs	God's Truths
I must meet certain standards to feel good about myself. (Fear of failure)	Because of *justification* I am completely forgiven by and fully pleasing to God.
I must have the approval of certain others to feel good about myself. (Fear of rejection)	Because of *reconciliation* I am totally accepted by God.
Those who fail (including myself) are unworthy of love and deserve to be punished. (Guilt)	Because of *propitiation* I am deeply loved by God. I no longer have to fear punishment or punish others.
I am what I am. I cannot change. I am hopeless. (Shame)	Because of *regeneration* I have been made brand-new, complete in Christ.

No overnight change

Renewing our perception of God, ourselves, and others by changing our belief system will take time, study, and experience. Patterns of behavior that reflect a false belief system take years to develop. Change will not occur overnight.

Throughout this workbook we will continue to examine these beliefs. Learning to apply God's truth to our lives may be painful at times but will be rich, rewarding, and exciting! We may need months and even years to see the extent to which we operate by these deceptions.

As you grow, these Steps will become more natural and automatic.

You will use Steps 1 and 2 again and again as you encounter situations in life. As you grow, these Steps will become more natural and automatic for you. You will find yourself dealing with situations that once baffled you.

> **Key Concept for Lesson 6**
> Four false beliefs perpetuate the power of codependency in our lives.

✎ Please pray and ask God how this concept can apply in your life. Now please review this lesson. What has God shown you that you can use?

_____
_____

Step Review

✎ Please review this Step. Pray and ask God to identify the Scriptures or principles that are particularly important for your life. Underline them. Then respond to the following:

Restate Step 2 in your own words.

_____
_____

What do you have to gain by practicing this Step in your life?

_____
_____

Reword your summary into a prayer of response to God. Thank Him for this Step, and affirm your commitment to Him.

_____
_____

Memorize this Step's memory verse:
Jesus answered and said to them, 'This is the work of God, that you believe in Him whom He has sent.'
―John 6:29

Notes
[1] McGee, Robert S., *Search for Significance* LIFE Support Edition (Houston: Rapha Publishing, 1992), 26.

STEP 3

Turning It Over

We made a decision to turn our will and our lives over to God through Jesus Christ.

Step 3 Into Codependency

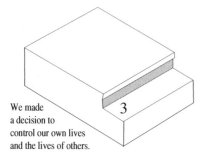

We made a decision to control our own lives and the lives of others.

Step 3 Out of Codependency

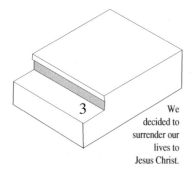

We decided to surrender our lives to Jesus Christ.

BUTCH'S CAR AND THE 12 STEPS

Butch was driving his dad's car down a country road. The road became more and more muddy. He stubbornly refused to turn back until he found himself in a lake that had swollen and covered the road.
To get out of the situation, Butch had to—
1. admit he was powerless to proceed;
2. believe the way out was to get help;
3. decide to accept outside help.

Then once he made that decision, he had to—
4. look honestly at the situation;
5. admit the truth to himself and his passenger;
6. become willing to receive help;
7. ask for that outside help;
8. list the persons his irresponsibility had harmed. This especially involved Butch's dad, since it was his car;
9. make amends to those he had harmed;
10. learn from the process and make honesty and confession a matter of life-style;
11. through the experience, cultivate a relationship with his parents and seek their guidance for his life;
12. seek to share it with friends and practice these Steps to stay out of, and when necessary to get out of, trouble (having had an awakening through the whole experience).

The Step process is like Butch's experience. In Step 1 you admit the areas in which you are powerless; in Step 2 you come to believe that God can do what you cannot; Step 3 gives you the chance to decide to let God be in charge. The rest of the Steps represent a means to help you carry out that decision.

For by grace you have been saved through faith; and that not of yourselves, it is the gift of God; not as a result of works, that no one should boast.
—Ephesians 2:8-9

Overview for Step 3

Lesson 1: Why Is Trusting So Difficult?
   Goal: You will identify and begin overcoming habits that prevent trust.

Lesson 2: Like Falling Off a Log
   Goal: You will identify the blocks that stand in the way of taking Step 3.

Lesson 3: Renewing Our Minds
   Goal: You will describe key elements of the faith as a basis for trusting Christ.

Lesson 4: Taking the Step
   Goal: You will have an opportunity to take the ultimate Step 3 by receiving Jesus Christ as your Savior.

LESSON 1

Why Is Trusting So Difficult?

We made a decision to turn our will and our lives over to God through Jesus Christ.

> *I urge you therefore, brethren, by the mercies of God, to present your bodies a living and holy sacrifice, acceptable to God, which is your spiritual service of worship.*
>
> –Romans 12:1

Key Concept:
We have difficulty turning our lives over to God because we lack the skills to trust in His grace.

"Three–Stepping It" is a slogan that means taking a problem through the first three Steps. Someone paraphrased the all-important first three Steps as: I can't. God can. I think I'll let Him.

 All people need to three-Step some issues in their lives. Can you name one of your issues and then three-Step it? An example appears below.

Issue: My reaction to my mother who criticizes me.
Step 1: I am powerless over her behavior. Her behavior is her business, not mine.
Step 2: Yes, I believe God is big enough to help me deal with my mother's critical attitude.
Step 3: I need to turn this matter over to God and please Him instead of seeking to please my mother.

Three-Stepping some issues

Your Issue: _____

Step 1: _____

Step 2: _____

Step 3: _____

Another term for "three-Stepping" a problem is "turning it over," which means working the first three Steps on the problem and then making a decision to turn it over to God.

Why Do We Have Such Difficulty?

Codependents see the gospel of Jesus Christ as oppressive, condemning, and guilt-inducing.

The gospel of Jesus Christ is a message of freedom, forgiveness, hope, love, joy, and strength. This good news is the most freeing and energizing power humankind ever will hear. As codependents we see this wonderful message as oppressive, condemning, and guilt-inducing. To us this message turns freedom to bondage, forgiveness to guilt, hope to despair, love to condemnation, joy to pessimism, and divine strength to self-sufficiency. Why is it so difficult for us as Christians to understand and apply God's grace?

Below are some of the characteristics of codependency. Circle all those that you see that cause you to have difficulty accepting God's grace.
1. fear of angry people and personal criticism
2. a warped sense of responsibility
3. self-worth based on performance
4. addiction to excitement
5. black-and-white thinking

Ought's and Should's

Codependents have a warped sense of responsibility. Since we perceive that our worth comes from our ability to perform, we are driven either to achieve as much as possible or to withdraw in hopelessness. How do you measure your performance so you can see if you have achieved value and worth? We deal with this by dividing life into categories: the "I have-to's" and the "I can't's." This outlook steals the fun and spontaneity from life and leaves you with an overactive conscience. You feel pride if you do well, despair if you don't, and a fear of failure and rejection no matter how well you do. Numbers 2, 3, and 5 in the exercise above definitely make it more difficult to "turn things over," or to accept God's grace.

We carry not only society's ought's and should's, but we also carry the ought's and should's of Christianity as well. Instead of helping to overcome oppression, a wrong perspective of Christ and the Christian life makes us feel worse about ourselves. Instead of grace, we experience guilt. Grace ultimately is what produces a "want-to" motivation, although this type of motivation may take a long time to develop.

 Reread the last sentence of the above paragraph. Now read the Scripture in the margin. What do you think the apostle Paul meant by this statement?

___

___

One way to paraphrase the verse might be: "Since Jesus loves me so much, I want to love Him and serve Him." Codependent Christians separate grace—the source of perspective and power—from the Bible's high moral and ethical expectations. We then feel obliged to meet these higher expectations, but we only have guilt motivation and our own will to achieve these expectations. The more we read the Bible, the clearer these and other expectations become. This increases our sense of guilt.

 Read the following example; then identify what is wrong with Elaine's approach.

> Elaine wanted desperately to lose weight. She read the following idea in a book and tried it. She got a photograph of herself—one that she really hated—at her highest weight ever. She then went through a farm magazine and cut out pictures of pigs. She posted the picture of herself with the pig clippings on the refrigerator door so that every time she went to the refrigerator, the pictures reminded her not to eat or else she would look like the pictures. By the end of two weeks she had gained 12 pounds.

For the love of Christ controls us.
—2 Corinthians 5:14

In your opinion, what was wrong with the method Elaine used?

_____
_____
_____
_____

Someone said that doing things like Elaine did are like "thinking the best way to run a race is to beat yourself up at the starting line." In my opinion Elaine's method doesn't work because it leads to more guilt, shame, and depression. When we get depressed, we "hug our addictions." The method made Elaine eat more, not less, because of the depression.

In the margin box at left below, describe a time in the past or present when you beat up on yourself in hopes that you would make yourself do better. You may share this example with your group or sponsor this week if you wish.

As Christians we misinterpret many commands in the Scriptures. We apply these commands in a "savior" mode to gain a sense of worth. Some of these include—
- turning the other cheek when someone hurts you;
- loving those who don't love you;
- giving cheerfully;
- denying your own desires for the sake of others;
- loving your neighbor as you love yourself;
- having a disciplined life of prayer and Bible study;
- forgiving, loving, and accepting others as Christ does.

We often believe that we are expected to perform these commands perfectly. We believe that we at all times are to have feelings of love, peace, and joy. The result is a cycle of shaming ourselves in a vain attempt at motivation.

A time I beat up on myself—

Though He scoffs at the scoffers, yet He gives grace to the afflicted.
—Proverbs 3:34

 Do you suppose the "scoffers" the Scripture at left describes would be those self-sufficient persons who stand by and ridicule, saying: "Why can't they handle their own problems?" ❑ Yes ❑ No

If so, would those who receive grace be, instead of the strong, those who have worked Steps 1 and 2? ❑ Yes ❑ No

Sometimes when we "turn an issue over," we experience relief and victory. Sometimes when we turn our lives over to God, we also have a fresh view of reality and of the pain which we have repressed for many years. Turning it over often leads to mixed emotions both of joy and of pain. Step 3 is God-centered and leads us to surrender to Him and let Him do what we can't.

Key Concept for Lesson 1
We have difficulty turning our lives over to God because we lack the skills to trust in His grace.

Step 3

✎ Please pray and ask God how the key concept you just read can apply in your life. Now please review this lesson. What has God shown you that you can use?

___

LESSON 2

Like Falling Off a Log

We made a decision to turn our will and our lives over to God through Jesus Christ.

For what does it profit a man to gain the whole world, and forfeit his soul?
—Mark 8:36

Key Concept:
Deeply ingrained habits stand in the way of our taking Step 3.

In this lesson you will describe four reasons why "turning it over" is difficult for us.
1. Failure to take Steps 1 and 2.
2. No-win situations, called "double-binds."
3. The habit of denying emotions.
4. The habit of defending God.

Back to Steps 1 and 2

Step 3 is a place where many people get stuck. They cannot bring themselves to turn their lives over to God; yet if they properly understand Steps 1 and 2, Step 3 is automatic. In the early days of Alcoholics Anonymous persons practiced Steps 1, 2, and 3 together. A person who recognized her addiction would be challenged to take Steps 1, 2, and 3 on the spot. Then the new convert immediately went to work on Step 4.

Giving control back to God

You can see how the broken addict must take these Steps in order to give control back to God. The need is more difficult for us to see. As we've emphasized earlier, codependency is addiction to controlling, which lacks the obvious harmful effects of alcoholism. People often reward codependent behaviors. Why would we need to surrender control and change behavior?

 Name some common codependent behaviors that people reward socially. I have named one.

perfectionism

___

Loss of control is a terrifying thought to most of us. That is why you have done the work on Steps 1 and 2. We must see the unhealthiness of our actions even if they are socially acceptable. You could have given many answers, including: *not standing up for ourselves, people pleasing, cleaning up after others, blaming ourselves for others' actions.*

Mark 8:36, this lesson's verse, compares gaining the world with gaining Christ. People who understand likely would choose the life Jesus offers instead of choosing self-rule. In the same way those of us who really see our powerlessness want God in charge. The decision is easy as falling off a log; carrying out the decision is the point at which we need the rest of the Steps.

Codependents who really recognize their powerlessness want God in charge.

✎ **Consider the differences in a "self-directed" life and a "turned-over" life. On the form below make lists contrasting these two approaches. To get yourself started, place in their appropriate columns these words: *forgiven, guilty, limited resources, unlimited resources, lonely, fellowship, humble, self-centered.* Then add your own words.**

Self-Directed Life	Turned-Over Life
_____	_____
_____	_____
_____	_____
_____	_____

As you read the list with the descriptions you added, is it clear that Step 3 is the sensible choice? Then why is the obvious choice so difficult?

✎ **Go back to the above list and read your choices. Then from each of the two columns—self-directed life or turned-over life—circle which word or term you choose for your own life.**

Stuck in a Double-Bind

Step 3 is difficult because we are accustomed to being stuck in lose-lose situations in which we demand the impossible of ourselves. Some people call this a double-bind.

Lisa's story

Lisa grew up in a rigid, perfectionist church. Her church leaders taught her she must be flawless to be saved. When she was a small girl, Lisa wanted a simple ring to wear, but her pastor told her she would go to hell for such an action. Lisa was in a classic double-bind. People demanded perfection of her even as they constantly reminded her that she was sinful. No matter what she did, she couldn't win.

✎ **In your own words explain a double-bind, and give an example.**

_____

_____

Codependency: A disease of sick rules.

Living with double-binds always leads to hopelessness because you can't win. Sooner or later despair catches up with codependents, and their thoughts resemble these:

- If I were walking with God, I wouldn't have these problems.
- God has deserted me.
- Nobody cares about me. I'm all alone.
- Maybe I'm not really a Christian after all. Surely nobody who feels this way can be a Christian.

The way out of this double-bind is Step 3: surrender.

Denying Emotions

In the first lesson in Step 3 we looked at how we understand a group of commands when we are in a "Savior mode." We understand those rules in black-and-white fashion, as if we must perform those rules perfectly. We think no room exists for hurt and anger in the Christian's life. This denying of emotions only complicates the problem. We stuff away hurt and anger by using such reasoning as:

A good Christian shouldn't feel this way... so I won't.

✎ **How would you respond to a friend who made the above statement?**

_____

_____

_____

Feelings neither are good nor bad. What is important is that we deal with them.

I would respond to the statement by saying that feelings neither are good nor bad. What is important is that we deal with feelings appropriately. Denying feelings is like kinking a water hose. The pressure builds up, injury results, and the hose eventually spews out anyway—usually on the wrong person.

Defending the Offender

In the codependent's eyes, the Savior needs a savior. Many of us complicate the problem still more by defending God. Just as we deny hurt and anger and excuse and defend those who hurt us, we also try to deny the hurt and anger we perceive that God has caused. We try to make sure that God doesn't get any blame. In our eyes the Savior needs a savior.

When a friend was doing his written Step work, his sponsor repeatedly said to him: "You sound to me like you are angry with God about the death of your father." With his teeth gritted for effect my friend insisted that he was not angry with God. Through writing some letters expressing his feelings, however, my friend found his sponsor was right. He also found that we really love God when we stop covering for God. God is big enough to take care of Himself.

Toward a Solution

These roadblocks to Step 3 urge us to continue to carry the load ourselves. We are frightened by the thought of surrendering to God our long-held self-sufficiency. That is why God has given us His Word, His family, and His Spirit—to help us make this step of faith.

Relax your grip

When Jason was a child, he bought at a fair a pair of Chinese handcuffs. They were simply tubes made of woven bamboo strips into which you inserted your fingers. Then the harder you pulled, the tighter the "handcuffs" held you in their grip. The solution was simple: to be free, you must relax your grip. That is the message of Step 3.

Key Concept for Lesson 2
Deeply ingrained habits stand in the way of our taking Step 3.

✎ Please pray and ask God how this concept can apply in your life. Now please review this lesson. What has God shown you that you can use?

_____

_____

_____

LESSON 3

Renewing Our Minds

Key Concept:
Codependency distorts critical parts of the faith, including: fellowship with God, unconditional love, and complete forgiveness.

We made a decision to turn our will and our lives over to God through Jesus Christ.

> *do not be conformed to this world, but be transformed by the renewing of your mind, that you may prove what the will of God is, that which is good and acceptable and perfect.*
>
> –Romans 12:2

Codependency so distorts the Christian faith that freedom becomes slavery. The Bible, the Holy Spirit, and the church are the means God has given us to get well. We must work to come out of the darkness of codependency. The truth of the Word of God, energized by the Holy Spirit, with the loving support of the people of God, enables us to be freed from bondage.

It's in the Bible!

In the beginning of my own recovery I wondered, "If codependency is such a problem, why doesn't the Bible say anything about it?" Then I realized it does! Changing warped, destructive perceptions is a key purpose of the Bible.

✏️ **Check each of the following themes of the Bible that can apply to codependency.**

❏ The character of God.
❏ The grace of God.
❏ His unconditional love and acceptance, which are not based on our performance.
❏ His declaration of our worth and value because of our identity in Christ.
❏ The importance of helping people for right reasons.

The Bible's words speak powerfully to our root needs.

The Bible does not communicate these transforming truths in the language of 20th-century psychology but in the language of the ancient writers. Still, its words speak powerfully to our root needs: the need for love, acceptance, worth, and value. You could have checked all of the themes above and even added others.

The following study is designed to help you, through Scripture, to develop a better understanding of Christ's character. The activities are designed to help you to think through each passage and to consider its meaning.

The goal is not to "fill in the blanks" but to reflect on what these passages say. This will take some time. Be thorough with the exercises. Think both about the meaning of each passage and about how it applies in your daily experience.

Important Scripture Topics

I. Fellowship with God

✏️ **As you read these Scriptures, look for the key word describing God's purpose for your life.**

1. *God is faithful, through whom you were called into fellowship with His Son, Jesus Christ our Lord* (1 Corinthians 1:9).
2. *The grace of the Lord Jesus Christ, and the love of God, and the fellowship of the Holy Spirit, be with you all* (2 Corinthians 13:14)
3. *what we have seen and heard we proclaim to you also, that you also may have fellowship with us; and indeed our fellowship is with the Father, and with His Son Jesus Christ* (1 John 1:3).

Key word reflecting God's purpose: _____

God created us so that He could love us. The Scriptures above speak of that desire on God's part. The key word is *fellowship* (companionship, friendship). When Adam sinned, he brought both the burden and penalty of sin upon all humankind. As a result, people by nature rebel against God and are separated from Him.

For as in Adam all die, so also in Christ all shall be made alive (1 Corinthians 15:22).

But your iniquities have made a separation between you and your God, And your sins have hidden His face from you (Isaiah 59:2).

But because of your stubbornness and unrepentant heart you are storing up wrath for yourself in the day of wrath and revelation of the righteous judgment of God (Romans 2:5).

✏️ **Using the first three Steps at left as a model, explain what happened to God's purpose of having a loving relationship with us. (Hint: reverse the meaning of the Steps; I have done Step 1 as an example.)**

Step 1: *We admit that we are powerless over . . . that our compulsions . . . have made our lives unmanageable.*

Step 2: *We increasingly believe that God can restore us to health and sanity through His Son Jesus Christ.*

Step 3: *We made a decision to turn our will and our lives over to God through Jesus Christ.*

Step 1. _We tried to be powerful enough to run our lives ourselves._

Step 2. _____

Step 3. _____

Our rebellion messed up God's plan to love us.

The exercise required you to think in terms of the Steps but to think of them backward. Adam reversed Step 1 by assuming what he thought was the power to run his own life. Adam reversed Step 2 by believing that he, not God, could make his decisions. We naturally are out of fellowship with God and have made the stubborn decision to run our own lives, which is Step 3 backward. God created us to love us. Our rebellion messed that up. God also created a plan to reunite us with Him. He sent His Son to die in our place. Christ took in our place the punishment we deserve.

For Christ also died for sins once for all, the just for the unjust, in order that He might bring us to God (1 Peter 3:18).

righteousness–n. the gracious gift of God whereby all who believe on the Lord Jesus Christ are brought into right relationship with God (Vine's).

Jesus literally became our sin, so that we could be the **righteousness** of God. Because we come into this right relationship, as the definition states, then we also demonstrate that righteousness in the upright, godly way we live.

God was in Christ reconciling the world to Himself, not counting their trespasses against them. . . . He made Him who knew no sin to be sin on our behalf, that we might become the righteousness of God in Him (2 Corinthians 5:19, 21).

✏️ **Respond to the following questions to summarize God's purpose for your life.**

1. Why did God create you? _____

2. What did our rejection of God do to His purpose? _____

3. Jesus is God become human. What did Jesus' death do to remedy our broken relationship with God?

God created us for fellowship because He had love to give and He wanted someone to whom He could give it (question 1). Our rejection of God broke our relationship with Him (question 2). Jesus' death paid the price so that the relationship could be restored. He showed us the Father's love, and He took the punishment we deserved (question 3).

II. Unconditional Love

God loves us purely because He loves us.

Sacrificing His only Son's life for us is proof of God's unconditional love for us. He loves us without conditions attached. He loves us purely because He loves us.

 In the following Scriptures look for evidence of God's unconditional love. In the blanks describe that evidence.

1. *By this the love of God was manifested in us, that God has sent His only begotten Son into the world so that we might live through Him. In this is love, not that we loved God, but that He loved us and sent His Son to be the propitiation for our sins* (1 John 4:9-10).

   Evidence: _____

   _____

2. *For God so loved the world, that He gave His only begotten Son, that whoever believes in Him should not perish, but have eternal life. For God did not send the Son into the world to judge the world, but that the world should be saved through Him. He who believes in Him is not judged; he who does not believe has been judged already, because he has not believed in the name of the only begotten Son of God* (John 3:16-18).

   Evidence: _____

   _____

From the passages above you may have noted: 1. God loved us first, before we could love Him. He loved us enough to send Jesus as the payment for our sin. 2. God's love is for the whole world, including me. His love is so great that all I have to do is believe or trust Him. I am not condemned if I am a believer.

III. Complete Forgiveness

Christ's death saves from the wrath of God those who believe in Him. His death also completely paid our debt of sin so that we are completely forgiven.

 In the Scriptures that follow list the evidence of God's complete forgiveness.

And when you were dead in your transgressions and the uncircumcision of your flesh, He made you alive together with Him, having forgiven us all our transgressions, having canceled out the certificate of debt consisting of decrees against us and which was hostile to us; and He has taken it out of the way, having nailed it to the cross (Colossians 2:13-14).

Evidence: _____

For while we were still helpless, at the right time Christ died for the ungodly. For one will hardly die for a righteous man; though perhaps for the good man someone would dare even to die. But God demonstrates His own love toward us, in that while we were yet sinners, Christ died for us. Much more then, having now been justified by His blood, we shall be saved from the wrath of God through Him. For if while we were enemies, we were reconciled to God through the death of His Son, much more, having been reconciled, we shall be saved by His life. And not only this, but we also exult in God through our Lord Jesus Christ, through whom we have now received the reconciliation (Romans 5:6-11).

Evidence: _____

> bearing with one another, and forgiving each other, whoever has a complaint against anyone, just as the Lord forgave you, so also should you.
> –Colossians 3:13

Because God forgives us, we can forgive others, as the Scripture in the margin shows.

Key Concept for Lesson 3
Codependency distorts critical parts of the faith, including: fellowship with God, unconditional love, and complete forgiveness.

✎ Please pray and ask God how this concept can apply in your life. Now please review this lesson. What has God shown you that you can use?

_____

LESSON 4

Taking the Step

Key Concept:
In Step 3 we turn our complete lives over to Christ; then we grow in turning over individual problems.

We made a decision to turn our will and our lives over to God through Jesus Christ.

Believe in the Lord Jesus, and you shall be saved. –Acts 16:31

God made us to have an intimate love relationship with Him. We never will be complete without that relationship.

You can try to have that relationship in one of two ways. You can trust in your own abilities to earn God's acceptance, or you can trust in the death of Christ to pay for your sins and in the resurrection of Christ to give you new life.

✎ **Mark your response to this question: On a scale of 0 to 100 percent, with 0 meaning that you are not at all sure and 100 meaning that you are very sure, how sure are you that you would spend eternity with God if you died today?**

0%_____100%

An answer of less than 100 percent may indicate that you are trusting, at least in part, in yourself. You may be thinking, "Isn't it arrogant to say that I am 100-percent sure?" Indeed, it would be arrogance if you trusted in yourself, your abilities, your actions, and your good deeds to earn your salvation. However, if you no longer trust in your own efforts but in the all-sufficient payment of Christ, then 100-percent certainty is a response of humility and thankfulness, not arrogance.

✎ **Reflect on a second question. "If you were to die today and stand before God, and He were to ask you, 'Why should I let you into heaven?', what would you tell Him?"**

_____

_____

Many of us would mention church attendance, kindness to others, Christian service, avoiding particular sin, or doing some other good deed. In the margin read what the Bible says.

> He saved us, not on the basis of deeds which we have done in righteousness, but according to His mercy.
> –Titus 3:5

✎ **What do the Scriptures at left say about why God will let you into heaven?**

_____

_____

> For by grace you have been saved through faith; and that not of yourselves, it is the gift of God; not as a result of works, that no one should boast.
> –Ephesians 2:8-9

What do they say about why God would refuse to let you into heaven?

_____

We can give up our own efforts to be good enough. Instead we can believe that Christ's death and resurrection alone are enough to pay for our sin and separation from God. The answers to the above exercise are that He will let us into heaven on the basis of His mercy and grace through faith. He will refuse us entry based on our own efforts.

> Believe in the Lord Jesus, and you shall be saved.
> –Acts 16:31
>
> I am the way, and the truth, and the life; no one comes to the Father, but through Me.
> –John 14:6

Read the bottom two verses appearing in the margin. These tell about how we can receive the Lord into our lives and what that means. For some years I knew that I was a sinner and that Jesus had died for my sin. What I did not know was how to get Him into my life. I needed to know the next truth: We receive Jesus by invitation. Boundaries are important to recovery. Remember, boundaries keep us from imposing on others while these boundaries also protect us from these persons. God has good boundaries. Though He loves you more than you can imagine, He will not force Himself on you.

John wrote: "But as many as received Him, to them He gave the right to become children of God, even to those who believe in His name" (John 1:12).

If you are not 100-percent sure that you would spend eternity with God if you died today, and if you are willing to trust in Christ and accept His payment for your sins, you may use this prayer to express your faith:

> "Lord Jesus, I admit I am powerless to save myself. I believe that you died on the cross for my sin. I now surrender my life and my will to you. I accept Your death on the cross as payment for my sins. Thank You for forgiving me and giving me a new life. Thank You for the new life that is now mine through You. Please help me grow in my understanding of Your love and power so that my life will bring glory and honor to You. Amen."

_____   _____
(date)   (signature)

If before you read this you already had placed your trust in Jesus Christ, consider reaffirming your faith and commitment to serve Him. You may do so by using this prayer:

> "Lord Jesus, I need You and thank You that I am Yours. I confess that I have sinned against You and ask You to 'create in me a clean heart, and renew a steadfast spirit within me' (Psalm 51:10). I renew my commitment to serve You. Thank You for loving me and for forgiving me. Please give me Your strength and wisdom to continue growing in You so that my life can bring glory and honor to You. Amen."

_____   _____
(date)   (signature)

Trusting in Christ does not guarantee that we are free instantly from codependent behavior or from any other problem. Receiving Christ is the culmination of the first three Steps. You are forgiven for rebelling against God; you are restored to a relationship with Him that will last throughout eternity; and you will receive His unconditional love and acceptance as well as His strength and wisdom as you continue to grow in recovery.

Baptism

Identifying with Christ

Water baptism is the biblical way of showing on the outside what Christ has done for you on the inside. The act of baptism symbolizes being dead, buried, and raised with Christ. Through baptism we identify ourselves publicly with Christ and with His people. I encourage you to go to a Bible-believing church, make a public profession of your faith in Christ, and demonstrate that faith through water baptism.

Be honest about your feelings and thoughts. Admit them to yourself. Tell them to the Lord and to someone else who understands and cares about you. The deep wounds of codependency—the shame, the hurt, the anger, and the unfulfilled longing to be loved—will not heal quickly. Surface solutions sound so good. They seem to help so many people. But in the long run, quick and easy answers only prolong our problems. People need real answers that speak to the real issues of one's worth and identity. People can experience these solutions during a long process so these ideas will sink in deeply and profoundly.

This is not the end but the beginning of a new way of life.

You now have worked Steps 1, 2, and 3. This is not the end but the beginning of a new way of life. You will continue to "three-Step" until turning over your problems becomes natural. As you work the rest of the Steps, you will grow in your ability to turn over to our loving God each area of your life.

Key Concept for Lesson 4
In Step 3 we turn our complete lives over to Christ; then we grow in turning over individual problems.

✎ Please pray and ask God how this concept can apply in your life. Now please review this lesson. What has God shown you that you can use?

_____
_____

Step Review

✎ Please review this Step. Pray and ask God to identify the Scriptures or principles that are particularly important for your life. Underline them. Then respond to the following:

Restate Step 3 in your own words.

_____
_____

What do you have to gain by practicing this Step in your life?

_____
_____

Reword your summary into a prayer of response to God. Thank Him for this Step, and affirm your commitment to Him.

_____
_____

Memorize this Step's memory verse:
For by grace you have been saved through faith; and that not of yourselves, it is the gift of God; not as a result of works, that no one should boast.
–Ephesians 2:8-9

STEP 4

Honesty at Work

We make a searching and fearless moral inventory of ourselves.

Step 4 Into Codependency

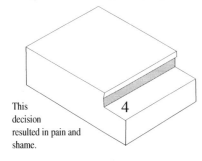

This decision resulted in pain and shame.

Step 4 Out of Codependency

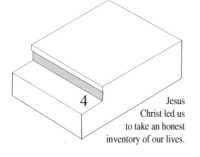

Jesus Christ led us to take an honest inventory of our lives.

Overview for Step 4

THE TWINS' DECISIONS

The Sanders twins were loyal church members. At every revival and after every challenging sermon, these boys would "walk the aisle" and "make a decision." This happened so regularly, you could set your watch by it. In the years since, I see those boys as being typical of many people. They really wanted to be right with God and to serve. In 12-Step terms, they just kept taking the first three Steps over and over, and it never seemed to work for them. In a real sense you can say working the 12 Steps really begins with Step 4. Steps 1, 2, and 3 are essential, but they aren't *doing* anything. They are an admission, a coming to believe, and a decision. With Step 4 we begin to put into action the decision we have made.

The Sanders twins needed to know how to put into practice what they had learned. They admitted their sin, came to believe in Jesus, and made a decision to give their lives to Him. What they didn't know was how to carry out the decision. That process is called discipleship. In 12-Step terms, the process is called "working the Steps." The Steps teach us to put our decision into action by: 4) making a moral inventory, 5) confessing, 6-7) allowing God to change our lives, 8-10) clearing our consciences, 11) cultivating a relationship with God, and 12) sharing what God has done with others. The following pages will launch you into that process.

But let each one examine his own work, and then he will have reason for boasting in regard to himself alone, and not in regard to another. –Galatians 6:4

Lesson 1: Welcome to Step 4
  Goal: You will describe the three stages of beginning the healing process.
Lesson 2: A Lack of Objectivity
  Goal: You will write an objectivity inventory.
Lesson 3: A Warped Sense of Responsibility
  Goal: You will write a responsibility inventory.
Lesson 4: Controlled/Controlling
  Goal: You will do a self-study on controlling yourself and others.
Lesson 5: Hurt and Anger
  Goal: You will write an inventory on hurt and anger in your life.
Lesson 6: Guilt
  Goal: You will distinguish between godly sorrow and guilt and write an inventory about the effects of guilt in your life.
Lesson 7: Loneliness
  Goal: You will identify some of the habitual feelings and actions that lead to your sense of loneliness.
Lesson 8: The Need to Detach
  Goal: You will describe the detaching process and will identify some aids to detaching.

LESSON 1

Welcome to Step Four

We make a searching and fearless moral inventory of ourselves.

Let us examine and probe our ways, And let us return to the Lord.
—Lamentations 3:40

Key Concept:
A written fourth Step enables us to identify our behaviors so we can detach and then decide on better alternatives.

Gary was almost in tears. His wife Sara, to whom he had been married 47 years, was making one of her regular threats to leave him. When Sara was a child, her parents constantly pampered her because she was ill. At age eight Sara finally recovered from her illness, and at that point, her parents stopped paying so much attention to her. She felt abandoned. Throughout the time Sara and Gary were married, Sara accused Gary of abandoning her. Sara often felt traumatized when Gary left the house. Sara did not understand that the abandonment feelings probably began in childhood. Sara's fear of abandonment had stolen her life and her marriage. If she could learn to identify those feelings and detach from them, she could decide on some new, more healthy actions. Doing a written fourth Step, which we will learn about here, is a key to that process.

As we learn more about how dysfunctional relationships have affected us, we also learn how to respond in new and more positive ways. This part of the healing process involves three stages: *identify*, *detach*, and *decide*.

1. No relief is possible until we first *identify* the behaviors, feelings, thoughts, words, and actions that become the habits of codependency. Until we identify our behaviors, we usually choose to blame others for our difficulties.

Responding differently

2. As we identify these habits in our lives, we can *detach* (disconnect) from the behaviors. We can reflect on the situation and on how we can stop responding in the usual way.

3. After that reflection we can *decide* on a course of action. This can be a response based on objective reality, not a reaction based on codependent reflexes. Identify. Detach. Decide. See it. Analyze it. Choose your response.

✎ **In the descriptions below fill in the three key stages to the healing process.**

1. Once I am aware of the habits which are running my life, the next stage is to _____.
2. When habitual feelings, thoughts, and actions are running my life, I first must _____ them.
3. One by one I identify patterns working in my life. I then must _____ from them before I can choose a different course of action.
4. When I recognize a destructive pattern at work and emotionally separate myself from it, I then must _____ on my new course of action.
5. The stages of dealing with a these powerful learned behaviors in my life are: _____, _____, and _____.

By writing the stages in the blanks on the previous page you are building skills you will need to change your life. The answers were: 1. detach, 2. identify, 3. detach, 4. decide, and 5. identify, detach, decide.

✎ **Consider the story of Gary and Sara you just read. How might Sara apply in her life the principles of identify, detach, and decide?**

_____

_____

Some elements in Sara's recovery might include:
- *Identify*. She can recognize that the feelings she experiences are abandonment feelings from the past.
- *Detach*. She can work on dealing with those old feelings. She can do this by writing and sharing the feelings and by forgiving herself and others.
- *Decide*. She then becomes free enough to choose new courses of action.

Identify

The first stage is to identify the specific things we say and do. Some persons can identify self-defeating behavior fairly easily. Others will have a more difficult time. Some may see a few instances, but they don't see the patterns of behavior very clearly. Still others lack objectivity so that they don't see any characteristics of their codependency at all. They just don't get the picture, and healing can't begin until the Holy Spirit begins to overcome their denial. Until this realization begins, however, most of us think our situations are normal.

Some people just don't get the picture, and healing can't begin.

✎ **Below is a list of some of the ways we overcome our denial and identify self-defeating behavior. Read the list carefully. Then rank the items (with 1 being the highest and 8 being the lowest) in the order of how they have impacted your life.**

_____ 1. Reading books on codependency.
_____ 2. Sitting in a group and hearing others share their struggle with their problems.
_____ 3. Journaling; reflecting on my life experiences.
_____ 4. A "Damascus Road" experience, in which God powerfully communicates through events or circumstances.
_____ 5. Talking with a friend and identifying my own struggles and feelings as I listen to his or her experiences.
_____ 6. Hearing a speaker at church or a conference.
_____ 7. Reading about a biblical character who struggles with hurt, control, or grief.
_____ 8. Other _____

Salvation is a lifelong, growing relationship.

Identifying our behaviors is an ongoing process. Recovery is just like our relationship with the Lord Jesus. Regeneration, or being born again, is an instant experience, but salvation is a lifelong, growing relationship.

What Is "Normal?"

The "don't talk" rule in families destroys objectivity. As a result, we believe our lives are fairly normal. If we compare our lives to whoever in the family

> The newcomers guide for the group said: "We needed to go through an identification process and come out of our dreamlike state, dropping layers of denial at whatever level was comfortable for us."

seems "really messed up," we think we are doing pretty well. We fail to recognize our own sick behavior. Most of us have a difficult time knowing what is normal. Even though we diligently try to help others, we often believe that we are terrible people. We see the dominating, manipulating, abusive people in our lives as good and right and wonderful, because seeing them objectively is too threatening to us. Others of us rationalize that we are very good people with no wrong motives or hidden faults. At one point, a young man I know told me that he didn't think he ever had sinned; yet at other times in his life, this same man was overcome with guilt and morbid introspection. This illustrates how strongly people can be deceived about themselves.

The truth is that our responses to life have not been "normal." We have felt guilty even when we've tried to help. We have felt lonely even though we wanted intimacy badly. We have controlled, been controlled, and rescued people from the consequences of their choices. We haven't allowed ourselves to feel normal hurt and normal anger when these people have condemned, used, and ignored us. We haven't been "normal" at all! Reality demands that we open our eyes to the truth—good and bad—and recognize the evil in all people—even ourselves. In the long run blindness never helps. It only lessens our ability to recover from our behavior. Step 4 can be a turning point. We don't have to remain bound to these self-defeating behaviors. We can change! Growth and healing begin with an honest look at our behavior. Reviewing our behavior often helps us understand why we act in certain ways at certain times. With this understanding, we gain a new acceptance of ourselves. A positive sense of self-respect begins to emerge. With it comes a new tolerance for other people.

 Read the proverb in the margin. Below describe how working Step 4 can help you be patient in dealing with others.

_____

_____

> A man's wisdom gives him patience; it is to his glory to overlook an offense.
> –Proverbs 19:11, NIV

The proverb seems to suggest that when I have wisdom—when I know what makes me tick—I will find it easier to understand others. I begin to see that others struggle with the same problems. Not only does it become easier to forgive others, it becomes easier to forgive myself. As you move into a deeper awareness of reality, you may experience a sense of hurt, loss, and grief. These feelings are normal and vital to healthy recovery. Step 4 is not designed to increase your sense of guilt and shame, but it is designed to bring the hidden areas of your life into God's light so that you may experience His grace more fully (1 John 1:5-10).

Experiencing His grace

MAJOR ISSUE ALERT!

Don was in recovery for about a year and a half when he told his wife, "I feel like recovery has saved my life." She said, "That's good. For a while I thought it was making things worse for you." What she saw was the fact that as he opened some "cans of worms" in his life and began to feel some feelings he long had denied, he experienced pain.

Seeing an important pattern here is crucial. We see that we usually walk through some pain on the way to real joy. Jesus warned against "putting our hand to the plow and looking back." In the same way many people give up just before they begin to enjoy the benefits of recovery.

> Search me, O God, and know my heart; Try me and know my anxious thoughts; And see if there be any hurtful way in me, And lead me in the everlasting way.
> –Psalm 139:23-24

You often will have a temporary increase in pain on the way to real healing. You may feel worse as you work on an issue. Do you suppose the psalmist could have had that concept in mind when he wrote the passage appearing in the margin? This verse seems to say to me, "God, I know it will be painful for me when You point out the garbage in my life, but the relief I feel when I get rid of the garbage will be worth the pain." You will work Step 4 by doing an inventory on each of the six symptoms of codependency.

> **Key Concept for Lesson 1**
> A written fourth Step enables us to identify our behaviors so we can detach and then decide on better alternatives.

 Please pray and ask God how this concept can apply in your life. Now please review this lesson. What has God shown you that you can use?

LESSON 2

A Lack of Objectivity

Key Concept:
For healing to occur, we must begin to see our lives as they really are.

We make a searching and fearless moral inventory of ourselves.

you shall know the truth, and the truth shall make you free. –John 8:32

Many of us are unable to see reality clearly for two primary reasons. They: 1) lack the skills to see the truth, and 2) fear reality.

A friend began to have headaches. He went to see an optometrist. When he fitted my friend with his very first pair of glasses, a whole new world appeared. He had absolutely no idea he was seeing so poorly and missing so much; the problem developed too slowly to notice. Codependents have the same problem, except they have trouble seeing reality.

 Stop and pray, asking God to open your eyes to help you understand this concept. Then circle any of the examples here and on the next page that apply to you.

Seeing poorly, missing much

- Jan's parents told her she never could do anything that required thinking because she was not smart enough.
- Earl's family rule was never to upset anybody, so family members didn't tell the truth.
- Steve was taught that he was better and smarter than anybody else. This positive comparison made him feel prideful.

Step 4 83

- Mary learned never to talk about what was going on at her house; her family's rule was "we don't air our dirty laundry in public."
- Shelley's mother constantly criticized Shelley and others. Her mother did this in an attempt to make herself look important.
- Don's father said to him, "You'll never be a man."
- Some common shaming statements in your family were _____

Children believe the way their parents treat them is how life really is.

If we live with constant deception and denial, we think it is normal. Children believe their parents are godlike. They think that the way their parents treat them is how life really is. If their parents are loving, children imagine that they themselves are lovable. If their parents are manipulative, condemning, or neglectful, children conclude that everything is their own fault. They see themselves as unlovable and unworthy of love and attention, but they still believe that their parents always are good and right. Marrying or being in any strong relationship with a person who has a compulsive disorder has the same effect. The dysfunctional person lives a lie and expects you to live it, too! In the margin box explain why we lack the skills to understand reality clearly.

Why do we lack skills to understand reality?

To answer this question, you may have written that many of us have experienced families in which we either were forbidden to tell the truth, or we simply never heard anyone telling it. Therefore, we did not develop the skills to see reality objectively.

The second reason why we lack objectivity is that we fear reality. Life comes with pain and anger. We have turned to concentrating on others' pain to keep from dealing with our own. The result is greater pain and anger. Now the prospect of any more pain and anger simply is too much to bear.

This fear is at least partially reasonable. Seeing the truth often brings great pain and anger. Reality, with its hurt and anger, is absolutely necessary for healing to occur. Crawling inside an emotional turtle shell may provide temporary relief, but this approach will bring more long-term pain and will prevent the process of healing.

A part of this fear of reality is the fear of losing our frail sense of identity. However broken and painful our self-concept may be, it is all that we've got! The fear of losing that morsel of identity is very threatening. Strangely, that leaves us clinging to another dysfunctional person who brings pain, abuse, and neglect, instead of going through the healing process, and experiencing love, freedom, and strength. Denial, or lack of objectivity, may sound fairly harmless, but it is powerful and destructive.

✎ **In what ways do you see fear of reality working in your life? In what areas is it easier to crawl into your emotional shell?**

_____

_____

_____

Be prepared to share with your group or sponsor your response. We will look at two ways we avoid painful reality: exaggerating and daydreaming.

84   Step 4

Ways we avoid painful reality:

1. exaggerating
2. daydreaming

Exaggerating

Many of us exaggerate. Making people or situations seem a little worse than they really are gives a sense of identity or importance. It causes others to be more concerned than they might be if they knew the truth. In the same way, making people or situations seem a little better than they really are makes us look better and more impressive. Our goal in relationships either is to impress people or to cause them to feel sorry for us.

Objective people are more balanced because they see life as being good and bad at the same time. They realize that these two views exist in tension with each other. A codependent, however, gives up one view to embrace the other. This leads to extreme thinking and causes wide emotional swings. Sometimes these swings occur very quickly, and sometimes they occur when our situation hasn't changed at all!

✎ **In what ways do you see exaggeration occur during the different stages of your life?**

When you were a child: _____

_____

As a teenager: _____

_____

As an adult: _____

_____

In the margin box answer the question about situations in which you use extreme thinking.

When and with whom do you tend to use extreme thinking?

_____
_____
_____
_____

MAJOR ISSUE ALERT!

Many of us are experts at the art of beating ourselves up. Notice that this Step is a moral inventory, not an immoral or amoral inventory. The purpose is not to see how bad we are but honestly to see what is in our lives—the good and the bad!

Daydreaming

Daydreaming—the second way we avoid reality—is a reflection of our extreme perspective. These daydreams reflect either the negative thoughts of the worst-possible thing that could happen or glorious thoughts of the best-possible thing that could occur. We can have fantasies about making millions of dollars, being praised and respected, and having all the things we've ever wanted. These things may include a sense of worth and love, especially the love of the dysfunctional person in our lives. These images can be quite detailed and emotional. They can conjure up all of the dreams and/or self-pity that hides deep in our hearts. In one moment, we may feel elated. In the next

Reflecting the best or worst

instant, an ambulance may roar by, and we may assume that a spouse, child, or parent is lying critically injured and helpless. We then often assume that the accident is our fault, and intense guilt compounds our fear.

Many of these daydreams also include escaping from the abuse and neglect of needy persons in our lives. Often, we daydream about escaping from a painful relationship to a lover who is tender, strong, wise, and comforting. Daydreams about killing the one who is hurting us so deeply may reflect our deep anguish. Reason has little to do with these dreams and fears. The fantasies reflect our hurt, desire for affirmation, and fear of being hurt again.

 Do you have any recurring daydreams? If so, describe them here.

_____

_____

What need in your life does daydreaming attempt to fill?

_____

A common theme for many of us is a fantasy where we "save the day" at great personal cost. After we save the day, everyone finally recognizes, applauds, and loves us.

> **Key Concept for Lesson 2**
> For healing to occur, we must begin to see our lives as they really are.

 Please pray and ask God how this concept can apply in your life. Now please review this lesson. What has God shown you that you can use?

_____

_____

LESSON 3

A Warped Sense of Responsibility

We make a searching and fearless moral inventory of ourselves.

> *Peter said to Jesus, "Lord, and what about this man?" Jesus said to him, "... what is that to you? You follow Me!"*
>
> —John 21:21-22

Key Concept:
Serenity occurs as we take responsibility for our own lives and allow others to be responsible for theirs.

Many people feel like either saviors or Judases—rescuers or betrayers. Often, these extreme perceptions change in a heartbeat, depending on whether others are happy or angry with us. In our savior mode we may believe that we can do no wrong and may rescue everyone who is in need. Our creed is:

- If someone has a need, I'll meet it!
- If a need doesn't exist, I'll find one and then I'll meet it!
- If a small need exists, I'll make it a large one. Then I'll feel even better when I meet it!
- Even if nobody wants help, I'll help anyway! Then when I've helped, I'll feel good about myself!

✎ **Check all the possible reasons for the savior complex.**

❏ 1. Our self-esteem is based on rescuing others.
❏ 2. People can't take care of themselves.
❏ 3. People in our lives are irresponsible.
❏ 4. We feel better when we are in control.
❏ 5. We are trying to meet our own needs at their expense.

Our savior mode

When we are in our savior mode, we think no one can do without us. We believe that whatever we are doing is absolutely the most important thing in the world! Nobody else's role even comes close. Answers 1, 4, and 5 were correct; they reflect the selfish motives for rescuing. Answers 2 and 3 were the excuses we make for keeping others dependent on us to meet our own needs.

Our Judas mode

When we change into the Judas mode, the outlook is one of failure and despair. One man explained, "I feel like I have to rescue people, but I'm so afraid of failing that I'm paralyzed." He lives with tremendous tension and heartache. Paralyzing fear and withdrawal prevent the person with a Judas complex from rescuing actively. Therefore, we may not see ourselves as codependent even though we are. We desperately want to rescue others just like a codependent in the savior mode, but our creed now sounds like this:

- People need me, but I can't help them.
- Their needs are enormous, and I feel awful that I can't help.
- Every time I try to help, I mess up.
- No matter what I do, it's wrong.
- If I try, I fail. If I don't try, I fail. I am a miserable failure.

When we are in the Judas mode, we believe that our family would say about us: "We thought we could count on you, but I guess we can't."

If we have a savior complex, we can nosedive into a Judas complex in three basic ways, which these statements illustrate:

1. I try to help, but I fail.
2. I try to help, but I'm not appreciated.
3. I don't even try because I'm sure I will fail.

In any of these situations, our response usually is withdrawal, guilt, loneliness, anger, self-condemnation, and hopelessness.

The savior and Judas complexes are flip sides of the same coin: the need for a sense of worth and the need to be loved and accepted. The savior feels that he is accomplishing that goal. The Judas fears that he can't.

Step 4

Results of a Warped Sense of Responsibility

Pain results from trying to rescue people. We will examine this process by looking at these typical stages: 1) rescuing others; 2) neglecting ourselves; 3) collecting resentments; 4) wallowing in self-pity; 5) taking ourselves too seriously. The process leads us back to feeling like a savior, a Judas, or both.

Stages of a rescue:
1. **rescuing others**
2. **neglecting ourselves**
3. **collecting resentments**
4. **wallowing in self-pity**
5. **taking ourselves too seriously**

1. Rescuing others

Codependents prevent others from developing responsibility. By constantly solving, fixing, helping, and rescuing, codependents deprive others of the opportunity to become capable people. That keeps others dependent on us, and the cycle continues.

✎ What is the difference between rescuing and legitimate helping?

_____

_____

Beyond legitimate helping

Rescuing is not simply helping others. It is attempting to help others by taking over their responsibilities. It goes beyond legitimately helping others, in which we help out of a desire for loving service instead helping to make ourselves feel important. Rescuing keeps people from facing the consequences of their own actions or lack of actions.

✎ In what ways have you kept others dependent by rescuing them?

_____

_____

What has happened because you rescued them? _____

_____

_____

> Let others do things for themselves!

2. Neglecting ourselves

By focusing on others' needs, we fail to see our own. We derive our self-worth from others' opinions. We use all of our resources to please them. We neglect our own identity, opinions, time, friends, and feelings.

✎ In what ways have you neglected yourself while you have tried to rescue others?

_____

_____

What have been the results of neglecting yourself?

> If you treated others with the same kindness that you show yourself, what kind of friend would you be?

You shall love your neighbor as yourself.
—Matthew 22:39

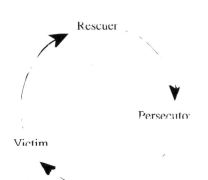

3. Collecting resentments

We resent being saviors. We rescue others in order to feel good about ourselves, but this feeling often vanishes quickly. We rescue; then we get angry that someone has taken advantage of us; then we feel sorry for ourselves. This cycle of rescue–anger–self-pity, or rescuer–persecutor–victim is the insight of Stephen B. Karpman and is called the Karpman Drama Triangle.[1] This drawing appears in the margin at left.

✎ **Write the name of the person or persons with whom you see this cycle repeated in your life.**

Do you ever threaten to stop rescuing, only to continue doing so? Name some results of these threats.

We threaten but continue rescuing. When we feel anger and self-pity, we threaten to stop "helping." We say, "That's the limit! That's as far as I go! You have to change your behavior!" But when we consistently follow these threats with more fixing, solving, and rescuing, they become meaningless. The persons we threaten know we always will rescue them.

4. Wallowing in self-pity

Because we spend so much of our lives helping others, we see ourselves as humble (or abused) servants. But a great difference exists between helping people because you want to and feeling that you must help others to gain a sense of your own worth. One is loving service, the other is codependency.

✎ **Check the situations in which you feel sorry for yourself.**

❏ Nobody notices the sacrifices I make.
❏ I do all the work; they get all the credit.
❏ Nobody appreciates me around here.
❏ They just take me for granted.
❏ Other _____

Step 4 89

Here's what I learned about myself:

_____
_____
_____
_____

Self-pity tells us that we are not the humble servants we would like to think. Rather, we are helping others for what we can get out of it. When we don't get our rewards, we feel sorry for ourselves. In the margin box describe what your responses to the activity you just did tell you about yourself.

4. Taking ourselves too seriously

We think the universe can't run without us! Several years ago a co-worker told me, "Pat, you take yourself too seriously. Lighten up!" *Fine,* I thought. *I'll just give up trying to have a sense of self-worth by accomplishing enough to win the respect and approval of other people. That will help!* He was right, of course. I was much too serious (and probably still am), but telling me not to take myself seriously doesn't solve the problem.

 What are some results of taking yourself too seriously?

_____
_____

How would your self-concept, your time, your values, and your relationships be affected if you weren't compelled to fix and rescue?

_____
_____

> **Key Concept for Lesson 3**
> Serenity occurs as we take responsibility for our own lives and allow others to be responsible for theirs.

 Please pray and ask God how this concept can apply in your life. Now please review this lesson. What has God shown you that you can use?

_____
_____

LESSON 3

Controlled/Controlling

We make a searching and fearless moral inventory of ourselves.

> *For whoever wishes to save his life shall lose it; but whoever loses his life for My sake shall find it.*
> —Matthew 16:25

Key Concept:
Seeking to control ourselves and others brings us pain and chaos.

Why do we allow others to control us? Why do we abuse ourselves? Without the security of love and acceptance, we feel responsible for everything but

Like puppets

confident in nothing. We try to find security by pleasing people, by being right and by doing right things in the right way. We become like puppets. We dance on the strings of praise and condemnation. Others' desires easily control us. We want to be in absolute control of our own lives so we won't fail, and we want to control others' behavior.

Codependents Are Easily Controlled

We need love and respect, but since we've been deprived of them, we will do anything to win the approval and value we crave. Our means to this end is to make people happy. We fear that people will be unhappy with us. Others use praise and shame to control us with statements like:

Control statements

- "95 on an exam isn't good enough."
- "I wish you'd get that promotion. I'd be so proud of you!"
- "Why do you drive that piece of junk?"
- "I'm proud of you for doing so well. I can't wait to tell my friends!"
- "You are so wonderful to help me. I wish your sister were as kind as you are."
- "You wouldn't be stupid enough to vote for somebody like that, would you?"
- "I wish you had come; I really needed you."
- "My goodness, what an unusual hair style; I'm sure it will look better when it grows out."

✎ Circle all of the above statements that you have heard or used. What is the underlying message of the statement(s)? For example, if you chose the first statement, the words in the margin show what its underlying message might be.

"You have to be perfect to please me, but you aren't perfect, so it's my job to inform you."

_____
_____

The trouble with these statements is simple: they are controlling and manipulative. The one who controls you probably believes she is doing you a great favor. She justifies her control over you by making statements such as:

- "I'm only saying this for your own good . . . because I love you."
- "I know what's best for you. In fact, I know you better than you know yourself."
- "I'm your father. If I can't say this to you, who can?"
- "If it weren't for me, there's no telling what a mess you'd make of your life!"

✎ How do you FEEL when you hear statements like these?

_____
_____

All these are methods of manipulation. By itself each way may sound harmless. But when we feel worthless and desperate for love and affirmation, it constitutes an attack to maintain control.

Guilt, the Great Manipulator

Appropriate guilt is a sense of conviction which tells us when we have done wrong and prompts us to take corrective action. This kind of guilt represents godly sorrow for our sins. Codependent guilt says you have to obey to be loved. No freedom to fail exists without risking loss of love and/or respect. We become driven. We have to be perfect. (That's not asking too much, is it?) With a smile we will do anything for anybody at any time—at least for a while. In the margin box describe the proper function of guilt, or godly sorrow, in our lives. You will study these matters in depth in Step 10.

The proper function of godly sorrow in our lives—

✏️ **What is the difference between godly sorrow and codependent guilt we're talking about?**

_____
_____
_____

Healthy guilt leads to confession. Codependent guilt leads to slavery.

This type of godly sorrow is a wonderful gift God has given us. It tells us when we have done wrong against ourselves, others, or God. It leads us to confess and make amends, which brings freedom. Codependent guilt is manipulative and leads to more slavery. Others use it to manipulate us. We use it to motivate ourselves, but we end up abusing ourselves.

✏️ **Describe some ways you use guilt in an attempt to control yourself or others.**

_____
_____
_____

Comparison Used to Control

A friend told me what her mother tells her, "My friends' children always do nice things for them. They buy them clothes, take them on vacations, and buy them jewelry and nice furniture. Their children are there whenever they are needed, but I guess I'll just have to take care of myself."

Manipulation is not harmless. It is evil, seductive, and destructive.

Was that a neutral statement of fact—a statement of independence? No way! The friend's mother used comparison to manipulate her daughter! Manipulation is not harmless. It is evil, seductive, and destructive.

✏️ **How did (does) your family try to control you? In what ways is this like or unlike how you try to control others?**

_____
_____

Describe a time in which someone's use of comparison controlled you.

_____

Have you tried to control by comparison? Below describe the situation.

_____

_____

_____

The control abusive people use on their families is almost unbelievable, but we who are codependent can't see it. No matter how much abuse and neglect we endure, the overwhelming thirst for the abuser's acceptance keeps us coming back for more.

Lack of Self-Confidence

Balls in a pinball machine

Many of us have so little self-confidence that we seldom have our own ideas and desires. We react only to the ideas and desires of others. We are like balls in a pinball machine, being forced in one direction, then another. We always do what the outside force demands. We learn to react to the slightest hint of praise or condemnation. In fact, we don't even wait for a hint. We anticipate what others might want from us and act accordingly.

✎ **Do you ever find yourself doing for someone else what you really want someone to do for you. (Perhaps the other person doesn't even care about what you do.)** ❏ Yes ❏ No

If so, what effect does this have on you and on your relationships?

_____

_____

_____

objectivity–n. seeing our situation from an impartial, unbiased perspective. That is why we so desperately need a group of fellow disciples, so we can see through their eyes.

The Development of Passive-Aggression

We become angry as we see how we are being controlled and used but also how we lack the **objectivity** to change our behavior. We hate ourselves for giving in, and we hate others for using us; but because this is the only game we know, we keep playing. Our desperate need for approval keeps us on the endless treadmill of need-manipulation-anger. We may become openly hostile or passive-aggressive.

Passive-aggression is the most dishonest form of anger. We may appear to be passive, but the real goal is to hurt the one who has been controlling us.

How do people-pleasing and anger create passive-aggression?
_____
_____
_____

We are afraid to express our anger openly, so we express it through gossip, sarcasm, or withdrawal. Or, when the people we hurt with our passive-aggressive behavior confront us, we say, "I was just kidding," or "I didn't mean it," or "You're just paranoid." Sometimes we act as though we resent their confronting us. We act as though we are dismissing their pain. In the margin box explain how anger and people-pleasing can create passive-aggressive behavior.

Step 4

Do you ever use passive aggression? Below describe how this occurs.

_____

_____

> *The Codie Passive-Aggressive Game: I'm terribly unhappy. Try to guess what's wrong with me.*

When we feel angry but our people-pleasing habits keep us from dealing with the anger appropriately, we express the anger in dishonest ways. A woman once stopped making up her husband's side of the bed. She never told him why she was angry; she just acted out her anger in a goofy way.

✎ **Check below all the passive-aggressive ways of dealing with anger.**

❑ 1. Cook the meals that he/she hates.
❑ 2. Refuse to talk to him/her.
❑ 3. Criticize other things about him/her.
❑ 4. Talk to someone else about how badly you are treated.

All the answers are indirect and harmful ways of dealing with a matter.

✎ **What is a better approach to the problem?**

_____

_____

> **The basic honesty approach:**
> 1. Talk honestly to the person
> 2. Talk to a counselor, sponsor, or friend
> 3. Talk to God

The basic course of honesty is best. Honesty can be used three ways. 1) Talk honestly to the person with whom you are angry. 2) Talk to a counselor, sponsor, or friend about your anger. 3) Talk to God about your anger.

Imitation Independence

Those around us give the impression of encouraging freedom, but it is only an impression. If we go too far in setting boundaries, the person may explode in anger and say, "How could you be so selfish?" Or, he may take a subtle approach by saying, "We need to talk." What he really means is, "We need to talk so I can convince you to go back to being dependent on me, submissive to me, and manipulated by me. No limits should be placed on what you will do for me. After all, pleasing me is the way you gain self-worth."

✎ **Describe three situations in which you felt pressured to perform. Who pressured you? How did he/she pressure you? What would you have lost if you hadn't performed? How did you respond?**

1. _____

_____

2. _____

_____

3. _____

_____

Controlling Ourselves

We often define ourselves by what we do, how we look, and how well we accomplish tasks. We don't perceive failure as an option. We feel we must be in control of our lives, because the rest of our lives are so chaotic that we need to find an area of our lives that we can control. We go to extremes: being compulsive to gain control of life, dominating others, or even partying to excess. Or we give up or withdraw.

✎ **Name the areas of your life that you can point out to show you are in great shape.**

_____

_____

What areas are you covering up because they really are out of control?

_____

_____

Rigid control of emotions

Compulsive people usually rigidly control their emotions—neither too much crying nor laughing. Anger is forbidden. Anger means you are really out of control. Their relationship with God is highly controlled, too. It often is rigid and ritualistic, with good activities but with little spontaneity and warmth.

✎ **Rate yourself on the following scale of 1 to 10, where 1 represents rigid, controlled, and unemotional and 10 represents spontaneous, expressive, and joyful.**

In my private emotional life I am more nearly:

Rigid   1   2   3   4   5   6   7   8   9   10   Joyful

In my relationships with others I am more nearly:

Controlled   1   2   3   4   5   6   7   8   9   10   Spontaneous

In my relationship with God I am more nearly:

Unemotional   1   2   3   4   5   6   7   8   9   10   Expressive

What does working this exercise tell you about yourself?

_____

_____

You may want to share your insights with your group or sponsor this week. No one can be in complete control all of the time, so we are forced to choose the areas on which we will concentrate (and get our self-worth from) and which areas to let slide (and say we don't care about). For some people, being in complete control at all times is simply too much. They appear to be irresponsible, when in truth, they are really compulsives who have broken under the strain of striving for perfection. They've given up, but they still have no feeling of freedom or relief.

Controlling Others

We dominate with the same methods that others use to control us. We may hate the way others have treated us, but it is the only model we have to follow. We use our wit and humor to impress people. We may have excellent minds and develop strong communication skills to win acceptance. We use sarcasm to cut people to ribbons. We also use praise, anger, and withdrawal to get people to do what we want them to do. These techniques worked on us; they work on others most of the time, too.

Some of us become dictators—barking orders and exercising our real or imagined authority. Others give up in withdrawal. We are tired of trying to control others. We feel inadequate and worthless. We believe no one will do what we want. Our poor self-concept overcomes our desire to manipulate. We give up.

The paradox is that while we try to control others, they are controlling us. We get our self-worth from their approval. One man tried to get his wife, who was addicted to prescription drugs, to pull her act together. She had him on a string. She could be happy when she wanted or angry or sad when she chose, but he had to be responsible. She could get him to do almost anything for her. The rabbit was chasing the dog.

The rabbit chasing the dog—it means:

_____
_____
_____
_____

In the margin box write your explanation of the above statement about the rabbit and the dog.

You might write in the margin box something like this: When I try to run someone else's life, that person winds up running my life. My life gets more and more out of control.

✎ Is there a person you are trying to control, who is actually controlling you? Below name the individual and describe how this is occurring in your life.

_____
_____
_____
_____

We can cut the strings!

We can learn to take our controls off of others. We can learn to let them make their own decisions and live with consequences. We can learn to gain our self-worth from something other than their approval of us. We can cut the strings!

Key Concept for Lesson 4
Seeking to control ourselves and others brings us pain and chaos.

Please pray and ask God how the concept you just read can apply in your life. Now please review this lesson. What has God shown you that you can use?

LESSON 5

Key Concept:
Anger is an emotion that becomes damaging when we deny it or express it inappropriately.

Defense mechanisms:
1. **denying reality**
2. **pleasing people**
3. **being in control**
4. **keeping people at a distance**
5. **being numb to feelings**
6. **displacing anger**
7. **excusing people**

Hurt and Anger

We make a searching and fearless moral inventory of ourselves.

Be angry, and yet do not sin; do not let the sun go down on your anger.
–Ephesians 4:26

Anger is a God-given emotional response. Feeling angry is OK. What we do with that anger is something else. Many of us use our anger destructively rather than constructively. We can express destructive anger outwardly or inwardly; either way, depression and a low sense of self-worth result.

Destructive anger can destroy recovery. Expressed outwardly, it can keep us away from others and God. When we turn it inward, we harm ourselves. We increase our sense of guilt and shame and destroy our self-worth. Hurt and anger go together. Hurt is the result of not being loved and valued. It comes from feeling abandoned, used, and condemned. Anger is our reaction toward the hurt. If healing doesn't occur, we carry these painful emotions everywhere.

The pain seems overwhelming, so we set up defense mechanisms to block pain and control anger. Some of these mechanisms appear in the margin. Most of us develop layers of denial to make sure we're protected. These methods numb pain and help us control anger but do so at a huge cost. They prevent us from beginning the healing process. We need to peel away these layers to expose our pain and anger so that we can deal with it. We start by seeing the truth. Here are some destructive ways we cope with hurt and anger.

Numbing Anger

"I don't want to feel this way, so I won't," is a philosophy for some of us. Our pain is too great, so we block it. Our anger is too frightening, so we act like it's not there. We live life at the surface emotionally because what's underneath is too much to bear. We have surface emotions and surface relationships.

 Read the following case study; then describe what you believe happened in this woman's life.

> A woman's parents divorced when she was seven. Her father remarried and moved away. For several years after he left, her father sent her gifts, but he later faded from her life. Her mother was frazzled and frantic as an abandoned single parent. I asked the woman how her parents' divorce affected her. "Not much at all," she replied. I asked her if she missed her father. She replied, "No, not really."

Step 4 97

I asked whether she felt especially close to her mother since her mother had taken care of her so well. "Yeah, I guess so, but we're not that close," she replied. She seemed a bit detached from her situation, so I asked a different question. "What makes you really happy? What do you really enjoy?" She thought for a minute. "I can't think of anything." She said nothing made her angry or upset. "I don't feel much of anything," she said.

✎ **Why was she feeling nothing?** _____

_____

Since feelings are sometimes painful, we suppress them. The problem is, when we repress the painful feelings, we stifle the enjoyable ones, too. As a friend says, "It is as if there were a breaker panel in my head, and one by one I had turned the breakers off because it hurt so much. Now I'm learning to turn them back on." In the margin box write what switches you identify that you have turned off to numb the pain.

Switches I use to numb the pain:

_____
_____
_____
_____

Staying Busy

We avoid pain by staying so busy that we don't have time to feel. We can stay numb. We fill our lives with activities and superficial relationships; we don't have time to feel pain or joy.

✎ **Describe how "the busies," a deliberate frenzy of activities, keep you from feeling pain or joy.**

_____

_____

Stuck in the Pain

Some of us may wish we were numb, but we aren't. We hurt so badly we can hardly stand it. We feel as though we've been broken into a million pieces and no glue can fix us. No healing; only hurt. We can't go through life admitting this kind of hurt to others, so we pretend to be happy and in charge. Few people ever realize the darkness that lurks beneath the neon outside.

Peeling away layers

 In the following case study, underline the feelings with which you identify; then answer the question at the end.

A woman came to see me. She said she felt she was going crazy. She looked good on the outside but was dying on the inside. She described her home life. On the surface it seemed normal enough: no violence, no divorce, no addictions. Yet she described her parents' relationship like an armed truce. She was left an emotional orphan and lacked the love, protection, and support that every child needs. She wept, "My father never held me. He never told me that I was his special little girl or anything. I want to be loved, but no matter what I've done to please him, I've never felt that he loves me." What would you suspect about this woman's current relationships? Answer this question in the margin box.

I suspect this individual's relationships are—

_____
_____
_____
_____

This dear woman is afraid to be loved. She is afraid that if she experiences love, she may lose it, and the pain would be unbearable. She wants to be loved so badly, but she's afraid of being hurt even worse than she hurts now. That is hurt with no hope, hurt with no healing.

✎ **Does your life contain areas in which you are afraid to accept love?**
❑ Yes ❑ No If so, in what areas?

_____

_____

Abusive Self-Talk

Some of us think and say terrible things about ourselves. In this "self-talk" we call ourselves horrible, degrading names. If we heard someone saying those same things to another person, we would describe this as hatred and abuse. We don't call it abuse when we call ourselves these names, however, because we believe that we deserve that kind of treatment.

✎ **Are you aware of your self-talk?** ❑ Yes ❑ No

When his sponsor first discussed self-talk with him, Ron said, "I don't talk to myself." Then he began to listen and realized he was talking to himself in ways he never would talk to another person. In the margin box identify what kinds of abusive things you say to yourself.

> **Abusive things I say to myself:**
> _____
> _____
> _____
> _____

Excusing the Offender/Blaming Ourselves

Often, when hurt exists without healing, the anger at the offender is displaced, but we excuse the offender for her offense. Instead of blaming her, we blame ourselves.

✎ **Describe situations where you defend the offender and blame yourself.**

_____

_____

Displaced Anger

We often express repressed anger at people or things that have nothing to do with the cause of the anger. Their anger surfaces at odd times and in odd ways.

✎ **In what situations have you been the object of someone else's displaced anger?**

_____

_____

_____

Step 4

How do you displace your anger? On whom or what do you displace it?

Outbursts of Anger

Codependents also become angry to a degree that's out of proportion to the incident. Their suppressed anger may explode like a tube of toothpaste that is squeezed until it pops and toothpaste squirts in all directions. Debbie's father was an alcoholic who beat his wife and children. Debbie's mother was quiet and stoic, but after years of neglect and abuse, Debbie's mother committed suicide when Debbie was 12. When Debbie grew up, she treated her three children in the same mixed way her parents treated her. She tried to be gentle and protective of her children, but when they misbehaved Debbie flew into angry rages and threatened them.

Describe a time in which your buried anger emerged in an outburst.

Using Self-Pity and Anger to Manipulate Others

Hurt and anger are powerful emotions. We have learned to use them to get others to care about us and dance to our tune. A raised eyebrow or a raised tone of voice can mean that a person had better agree with us—or else! We often are the recipients of manipulation, neglect, and abuse, and we can use these powerful forces on others as well.

Below describe ways you use anger or self-pity to try to get your way.

How well does it work at obtaining real love?

Painful Memories

When a person begins to get in touch with the pain of his past, often he will remember events that have long been buried in his mind and heart. The hurt and anger that these memories evoke are painful, and some people may interpret this pain as going backward. But it is progress. Read the verse at left.

Weeping may last for the night,
But a shout of joy (comes) in the morning.
—Psalm 30:5

Constructive Anger

In recovery, we begin to discover ways we can channel anger into positive action. Because we release our grip on denial, we more often can admit feelings of anger. We can admit them first to ourselves and then to God.

Many of us fear that if we ever lessen our grip for a moment, we will: go crazy, kill someone, or start to cry and never stop. We who have been there have been just as afraid. Listen to one woman's comment on pain: "Facing the reality of pain and recovery is not the end but is the beginning of happiness."

 MAJOR OUTSIDE ASSIGNMENT. (By now, you probably have a sponsor with whom to share your Step work. If not, now is a good time to seek one out.) Write an angry letter to God. Express whatever anger you have uncovered in your recovery process to this point. Then read your letter to your sponsor or to a trustworthy person.

The momentum we need

Constructive anger can give us the momentum we need to detach from a manipulative person or a harmful situation. It can give us the incentive to confront someone in love; it can motivate us to stop acting compulsively. As we progress, we gradually learn that anger is a gift from God. It can lead us to provide loving correction and to confront the evils which threaten His purposes in our lives. We need His direction before we respond.

> **Key Concept for Lesson 5**
> Anger is an emotion that can become damaging when we deny it or express it inappropriately.

 Please pray and ask God how this concept can apply in your life. Now please review this lesson. What has God shown you that you can use?

_____

_____

LESSON 6

Guilt

We make a searching and fearless moral inventory of ourselves.

> *I acknowledged my sin to Thee, And my iniquity I did not hide; I said, "I will confess my transgressions to the L*ORD*," And Thou didst forgive the guilt of my sin.*
>
> –Psalm 32:5

Key Concept:
Healthy guilt is essential to our relationships, but false guilt is subtle and destructive.

Many of us feel guilty. We feel guilty for what we've done and haven't done. We feel guilty for what we've said, haven't said, felt, and haven't felt. We feel guilty for just about everything. Often such guilt produces feelings of worthlessness and shame. We can understand the model on the next page to learn the difference between godly sorrow for our sins and destructive guilt. The two diagrams show the two possible ways we build our self-concept.

Step 4

Self-concept based upon:

When my self-concept is based on who I am in Christ, my value is determined by what God says about me. My base is unshakable. When I sin or fail, I still am secure and can deal with my actions in a healthy way. The remorse that I feel for my sins is God's caring way of correcting me so that I may live happy and free. If my self-concept is based on myself, my value is based on my performance. When I sense that I have failed, the very foundation of my life is attacked. Learning to distinguish between godly sorrow for our sins and destructive guilt is a major life skill. Dysfunctional families don't teach this life skill. We have learned to get our worth from what we do for other people. We rescue, help, and enable, but no matter how much we do for others, it's never enough. We don't even recognize that we are trying to earn our self-worth.

A major life skill

All people stand guilty before God and need forgiveness and the acceptance of the cross. That is healthy guilt. But the guilt that we look at here is different. It is the painful, gnawing perception that we are worthless, unacceptable, and never can do enough to be acceptable no matter how hard we try. Godly sorrow for our sins leads to positive life change called **repentance**. Oppressive guilt just dumps shame on us.

repentance–n. a change of mind

✎ **In the Scripture at left, underline with one line phrases that represent godly sorrow and with two lines phrases that represent oppressive guilt.**

I now rejoice, not that you were made sorrowful, but that you were made sorrowful to the point of repentance; for you were made sorrowful according to the will of God, in order that you might not suffer loss in anything through us. For the sorrow that is according to the will of God produces a repentance without regret, leading to salvation; but the sorrow of the world produces death.
 –2 Corinthians 7:9-10

The apostle Paul called this the *sorrow* of God and of the world, which is a good description. For godly sorrow you might underline *to the point of repentance* and *produces repentance without regret, leading to salvation*; for oppressive guilt you might underline *produces death*.

✎ **Name an occasion when you have experienced godly sorrow for something you did. Write what you did about it and how you felt. Be prepared to share your insights with your group or sponsor.**

_____

_____

_____

_____

Name an occasion or circumstance where you experienced destructive, oppressive guilt. Write what you did about it and how you felt.

___

Crushing guilt

This oppressive guilt crushes a person. If your worth comes only from helping others, then you can't say no. If you do say no, if you say yes and fail, or if you succeed but others don't appreciate you, your worth is shattered. Even success and praise bring only short-term relief. The nagging fear of losing that approval always exists. To please people you take on their dreams and desires—not your own—and you lose your personality in the process.

Guilt Motivates: The hope of gaining acceptance and the threat of losing it are powerful motivators. They lead us to rescue people who take advantage of us and to help people who don't appreciate us. We perform because we think we have to, not because we want to. The ability to say no, to make our own decisions, to relax, and to enjoy life are foreign to us because they don't contribute to our consuming goal in life: earning worth.

✏️ What things do you do out of a sense of guilt? (Hint: Think about the things you do but resent.)

___

What is your true motive in doing these things you resent?

___

Constantly looking inside

Guilt and shame make us look inside ourselves. With our worth based on our performance, we keep checking to see how we are doing. We become introspective; we constantly look inside ourselves to take our own spiritual temperature.

Using Guilt on Others

Barbara says she first came to a recovery group because of a pledge she made many years ago. She said she never would treat her children the way her mother treated her. She said she never would lecture them in the same way. Then one day Barbara said: "I found my mother's voice and words coming out of my mouth."

If someone used guilt to motivate and manipulate you, you probably will use

Step 4

Even if you despise the way others treated you, you may find yourself treating others the same way.

Out of balance either way

it on others. Even if you despise the way others treated you, that model is so strong that you may find yourself treating others the same way. The same words of praise and condemnation; the same actions, tone of voice and expressions; the same aggressive, angry behavior; and the same withdrawal and passivity that others use to manipulate us are the ingredients we tend to use with others. Or we may go the opposite extreme. Instead of condemning, we withdraw; instead of being passive and neglectful, we smother. We may be a duplicate or an opposite, but we will be out of balance either way.

 What ways have you identified that you use guilt to control others?

_____

_____

Guilt is a way of life for many of us. The nagging pain of believing, *Something is wrong with me, and I must fix it* is a powerful, harmful force. We can learn to see this force for what it is: evil and destructive.

 What would your life be like if you had a strong sense of worth and were not plagued by guilt?

_____

_____

Key Concept for Lesson 6
Godly sorrow and repentance are essential to our relationships, but oppressive guilt is subtle and destructive.

Please pray and ask God how this concept can apply in your life. Now please review this lesson. What has God shown you that you can use?

_____

LESSON 7

Loneliness

We make a searching and fearless moral inventory of ourselves.

Key Concept:
Feeling abandoned is a habit that plagues us. Until we realize that fact and begin to change the habit, these feelings will be with us always.

God makes a home for the lonely; He leads out the prisoners into prosperity, Only the rebellious dwell in a parched land.
—Psalm 68:6

If we spend our lives taking care of others, we will look on the outside like the most social of people. Inside loneliness and fear of abandonment fills us. We are afraid that God and persons in authority will abandon us. We build a false front to hide the pain in our lives.

Fear of Abandonment—by People

We have felt the pain of abandonment in the past. Incidents in the present trigger those old feelings. We feel condemned. We feel controlled. We feel confused. We feel lonely. We feel angry, but we can't say anything about that anger, or we might experience even more condemnation, manipulation, and loneliness.

Joyce's story

Every fall Joyce felt horribly abandoned when her husband Stan went for his annual hunting trip. By working the Steps she began to realize the source of her feelings. The next year Stan went hunting as usual, but for the first time Joyce did not wallow in hurt feelings. She used the period with Stan away to spend time with her daughters instead of as a time to feel rejected and angry.

✎ What instances of abandonment have you experienced in your life? (For example, you might write, "the death of my father when I was nine.")

_____

_____

What did that abandonment feel like? _____

_____

_____

What present-day happenings trigger your feelings of abandonment, in the same way Stan's hunting triggered Joyce's feeling abandoned?

_____

_____

family-of-origin–a study of one's background in order to understand and detach from the past.

Joyce worked through the Steps and **family-of-origin** issues enough to identify reasons from her past that caused her to feel abandoned. Studying family-of-origin issues involves looking at one's background in order to understand and detach from the past. By identifying these issues and by doing some appropriate grieving and forgiving, she has detached and found freedom. As long as we fear our emotions, we stuff them and act as if nothing is wrong. Because we fear abandonment, we are unwilling to say how we feel. We are desperate for intimacy, but we don't feel lovable. We're afraid we will be left alone. We feel paralyzed. We feel confused.

Fear of Abandonment—by God

If our parents neglected us, we may feel that God doesn't care.

The way out of our pain is the unconditional love, forgiveness, and acceptance of God, but most of us feel distant from Him. We feel that He doesn't approve of us and that we can't do enough to please Him no matter how hard we try.

Our relationship with our parents greatly influences our view of God. If our parents neglected us, we may feel that God doesn't care. If our parents condemned us, we may feel that God is harsh and demanding.

As codependent Christians we usually tend to feel one of two extremes. We either feel that God is cool, distant, and harsh, or we sense the love of God to an extreme depth, and we become "hyper-mystical." As with every other area of our lives we lack objectivity and balance, and we react as extremists.

Fear of Abandonment—by Authority

We view authority figures with extreme mixed feelings. We have been victims of misused and abusive authority, so we react with fear. We believe that the person in authority must be right. Often we are intensely loyal to parents, bosses, pastors, or other authorities. In our extreme way of thinking we sometimes believe that the person in authority can do no wrong. In our minds others seem all-powerful because we feel so inadequate.

In our extreme way of thinking we believe that the person in authority can do no wrong.

We will put up with all kinds of mistakes until, at last, the pendulum swings. The authority figure who could do no wrong suddenly can do no right.

✎ **Do you feel that a pastor is closer to God than are persons in the pews?**
❑ Yes ❑ No
Have you attended a church and been very impressed with the pastor, church staff members, deacons, or church members, only to be let down later? ❑ Yes ❑ No
Have you trusted someone often, only to have that person let you down later? ❑ Yes ❑ No

Extreme loyalty—even when the other person doesn't deserve it—is a characteristic of codependents. Yes answers to any of the above questions may indicate that your extreme thinking leads you to see authority figures in an unrealistic way. The truth is that we all make mistakes. Bonnie said, "Part of my destructive behavior is taking responsibility for others' mistakes and giving away my sense of authority. A server once brought the wrong food order for my son. Before I knew it, I was apologizing to her for *her* mistake."

✎ **Can you describe an instance in which you have given your authority away inappropriately?**

_____

_____

For at least two reasons many of us make authorities out of others. At some time in our lives we have been led to accept others' decisions instead of making our own. We also make authorities out of them because we feel so inadequate.

The Result of Fear of Abandonment—False Fronts

We fear being abandoned, so when someone asks us a question, we respond the way we think others want to hear. We want to feel close, but we're afraid.

106 Step 4

We're afraid to risk trusting because others might reject us. Then we would hurt even more. To avoid more pain we protect ourselves by appearing to be happy even when we are dying inside. We build false fronts.

 In the following paragraphs circle the words or phrases that describe the way you put up false fronts in your life.

"As a child I learned that looking calm, cheerful, or tough allowed me to shield my feelings. My false fronts protected me for a while, but they hurt in the long run because I can't have honest relationships."

"Hiding behind my false fronts, I don't say what I mean or mean what I say. To put it bluntly, I lie a lot. I say yes when I want to say no. I say I'm fine even though I'm feeling just a step away from suicide. I say I want to go somewhere because I think it will make someone else happy so they'll like me even though I really don't want to go there at all. I get so wrapped up in other people's desires and in making other people happy that I get numb and confused and don't even know what I want or feel."

"I offer to help with a friendly smile even when I'm so angry with that person I could spit nails. I try to make people believe I really am doing well, but I feel that what I've said is a lie and that my false front is a lie. As a result, I often feel dirty, guilty, and alone."

"My motto is: 'The truth hurts, so avoid it.' If people knew me, they'd reject me. So I have complex defenses to avoid the truth, and I keep people from knowing how much I hurt."

These false fronts may protect us from the risks of intimacy, but they leave us lonely. When we lock others out, we lock ourselves in.

 Check all the answers that describe what is wrong with the false fronts in our lives. Then in the margin box describe some of the false fronts you put up in your life.

❑ 1. They leave us feeling guilty and dishonest.
❑ 2. They prevent us from forming real relationships.
❑ 3. Christians always should be kind.
❑ 4. We lose ourselves in the process.
❑ 5. Standing up for ourselves is selfish.

False fronts I put up in my life:

The false fronts we put up leave us feeling guilty and dishonest because they *are* dishonest. They prevent us from forming deep and meaningful relationships, and we lose ourselves in the process. Answers 1, 2, and 4 are correct.

Grief Work

Grieving is a necessary part of healing. Grief begins with shock and denial. If the process is completed, it reaches acceptance. In between we go through periods of anger and bargaining with God. We do not need to become an expert in this process. It is enough to know that the process is normal and has an end. We grieve over our lost dreams, childhoods, relationships. We grieve over our past abandonments and present loneliness. We can work through the process to get to the peace on the other side.

> **Key Concept for Lesson 7**
> Feeling abandoned is a habit that plagues us. Until we realize that fact and begin to change the habit, these feelings will be with us always.

 Please pray and ask God how this concept can apply in your life. Now please review this lesson. What has God shown you that you can use?

_____

_____

LESSON 8

The Need to Detach

We make a searching and fearless moral inventory of ourselves.

> *You thought that I was just like you; I will reprove you, and state the case in order before your eyes.*
>
> –Psalm 50:21

Key Concept:
Detaching from sick situations is the path to serenity and healthy relationships.

Jill invited her mother for a visit. Jill cleaned the house, planned the schedule, and prepared her guest room meticulously. Soon after arriving however, Jill's mother began throwing some subtle barbs, such as: "So, I see you still have those curtains." "It is hard to get dishes like that really clean, isn't it?" "Is that the same dress I gave you seven years ago?" "Oh, I'll just have to give you my recipe for this sometime!"

Jill's feelings of guilt and shame mounted as her mother made each comment. Because Jill was in recovery, however, she realized what was happening in the interaction with her mother. Stepping away briefly to her bedroom, Jill wrote about how she felt and how she had responded to her mother. She realized that she didn't have to agree with her mother's accusations about her house, her cooking, her clothes, or herself. She considered the difference between her codependent identity (I'm a bad person, etc.) and her identity in Christ (unconditionally loved, forgiven, accepted, secure).

Jill returned to the living room with a new sense of confidence. During the next several days Jill found herself needing to detach like this quite a few times. It wasn't an instant or perfect response, but for the first time Jill began to feel a security and strength.

Some people use the word *detach* to describe the act of isolating ourselves in a negative, harmful way. We use the word to describe a positive healthy action: stepping back to obtain objectivity about a person or situation. Detaching is not the same as withdrawal. Withdrawal is a defensive reaction to block pain and to avoid reality. Detaching involves becoming objective, dealing with reality, feeling our emotions, and determining the best course of action.

108   Step 4

✎ **Write *D* beside each of the following statements describing healthy detaching; write *I* beside those describing unhealthy isolating.**

_____ 1. Block pain and avoid reality.
_____ 2. Feel our feelings.
_____ 3. See the situation objectively.
_____ 4. Escape reality.
_____ 5. Deal with reality.

The purpose of unhealthy isolation is to avoid pain and reality—numbers 1 and 4. The purpose of detaching is to 2. feel our feelings, 3. see objectively, and 5. deal with reality. Detaching involves three elements: time, objectivity, and distance. We remove ourselves from the situation—emotionally, physically, or both—and gain some insight into our feelings and actions. This process takes time. No simple formula exists, but we can ask ourselves this question: "What do I need (time, space, objectivity) so that I can reflect on this situation?"

With practice we can act more readily to identify, detach, and decide. In the beginning, however, we need to remove ourselves from the offending person or situation in order to be more objective. The pressure simply is too strong. Go to another room. Take a drive in the country. Go away for a weekend. Do whatever you must do in order to feel and think. A distraction may help you gain a sense of calm before you reflect. Read a book or magazine. Watch a television show. Take a walk. Do whatever helps you. Remember the three elements of detachment: time, objectivity, and distance. If necessary, go back to the above paragraphs and review the purpose of each.

> Acquire wisdom! Acquire understanding! Do not forget, nor turn away from the words of my mouth. Do not forsake her, and she will guard you; Love her, and she will watch over you. The beginning of wisdom is: Acquire wisdom; And with all your acquiring, get understanding.
> –Proverbs 4:5-7

The Scriptures have a lot to say about reflecting on reality and truth so that we can respond wisely instead of reacting. The Scriptures instruct us to take time to acquire wisdom. Read what the Scripture at left says about this. We need each other in this process. Call a sponsor or friend: ". . . in abundance of counselors there is victory" (Proverbs 24:6).

✎ **What does the passage at left say about our right to choose not to stay in certain people's company?**

_____

_____

> Do not associate with a man given to anger; Or go with a hot-tempered man.
> –Proverbs 22:24

Proverbs makes plain that not detaching is foolish. I not only have the right but the duty to detach. Proverbs 22:24 teaches me to beware of an abusive person and to stay away. These verses represent just a sampling of the rich instructions the Scriptures offer about detaching and reflecting.

Detaching is a new skill for us. Here are some ideas to help with the process.

✎ **Please pray and ask God how each of these principles apply to your life. Then write in the margin what you believe God wants to help you do with the principle. I have done the first one for you.**

I need to have a group and a sponsor or mentor in recovery.

Maintain a support system. Detaching is difficult. It is almost impossible to do alone. A slogan in the program is: "We use the telephone." It means we reach out and seek an objective viewpoint. Look for at least one friend to help you be objective, to encourage you, and to model a healthy lifestyle for you.

Whether in love or in anger, do it. This may seem selfish, but being controlled by someone and pleasing that person above all else is not a good thing. It is idolatry. If you have the choice either to detach in anger or in love, by all means do it in love. But by all means, detach.

Important new skills

God gave us anger so we can protect ourselves. Anger is a strong motivation to develop our independence and identity. We can see constructive anger in such thoughts as: *I refuse to be manipulated again, I'm not going to take this anymore,* or *I'm going to detach so I can develop my own identity and make my own decisions.*

Don't wait to detach perfectly. Some of us are such perfectionists that we think we have to detach perfectly. One woman told me that she was afraid to detach because she "might not do it just right, and what would my father say if I made a mistake?" After a few minutes, she realized that this perfectionism and fear were the very reasons she needed to detach!

Be realistic. Detaching requires a major change in thoughts, feelings, and emotions. Changes like these are not computerized. We are not robots. We are people, and people need time, practice, and patience to change deeply ingrained habits.

Expect conflict. Don't expect everybody to applaud you when you stop being their doormat. They have lived their lives by having you rescue them as they controlled you. As they realize that you no longer are controllable, they probably will step up the pressure and use stronger manipulation: more guilt, more condemnation, and more withdrawal. They may accuse by saying, "You are so selfish!"

As the family re-forms its boundaries, family members may leave you on the outside. Objectivity and courage are necessary to take these bold steps. Remember, you are doing this for their good as well as your own. Everyone benefits from healthy boundaries.

Expect confusion and pain. Don't despair if you feel awkward and afraid as you learn to detach. These feelings simply represent a part of the reality of change. Accept them for now. They will change as your confidence grows. Increasingly you will enjoy your independence and freedom.

Regarding the option of divorce—You may be considering divorce because of pain in your marriage. Many a hurting codependent leaves one spouse only to find another to control and rescue, and the cycle continues. The scope of this workbook doesn't include an adequate treatment of divorce, separation, and remarriage. I encourage you to read *Jesus and Divorce* by Bill Heth and Gordon Wenham or *Love Must Be Tough* by James Dobson. Before you make any decisions about divorce, consult a competent, qualified Christian counselor or pastor.

Develop the habit of detaching. Don't be too discouraged if your first attempts at detaching are painful and awkward. Drastic change takes time, patience, practice, and courage. The more you try to detach, the more confident you can become. Eventually, detaching can become a very constructive habit for you.

Attach to the Lord. As we detach from the habits of codependency, we find a new joy and freedom in becoming attached to the Lord.

Build your relationship with God. Our relationship with Jesus will deepen as we realize that He is all we have longed for. He is loving and kind, strong, and wise. He is not condemning, aloof, and manipulative. He can be trusted.

> **Key Concept for Lesson 8**
> Detaching from sick situations is the path to serenity and healthy relationships.

✎ Please pray and ask God how this concept can apply in your life. Now please review this lesson. What has God shown you that you can use?

Step Review

✎ Please review this Step. Pray and ask God to identify the Scriptures or principles that are particularly important for your life. Underline them. Then respond to the following:

Restate Step 4 in your own words.

What do you have to gain by practicing this Step in your life?

Reword your summary into a prayer of response to God. Thank Him for this Step, and affirm your commitment to Him.

Memorize this Step's memory verse:
But let each one examine his own work, and then he will have reason for boasting in regard to himself alone, and not in regard to another.
—Galatians 6:4

Notes
[1] Claude M. Steiner, *Scripts People Live* (New York: Grove Press, 1974), quoted in Melody Beattie, *Codependent No More*, 77. This cycle of rescue-anger-self-pity, or rescuer-persecutor-victim, is the insight of Stephen B. Karpman and is called the Karpman Drama Triangle.

STEP 5

Out of the Darkness

We admit to God, to ourselves, and to another person the exact nature of our wrongs.

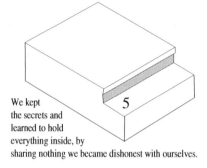

Step 5 Into Codependency

We kept the secrets and learned to hold everything inside, by sharing nothing we became dishonest with ourselves.

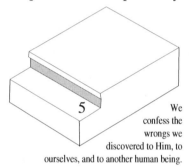

Step 5 Out of Codependency

We confess the wrongs we discovered to Him, to ourselves, and to another human being.

FINDING A FRIEND

Amanda's motto could have been, "Just the facts, ma'am." That phrase summed up the way Amanda related to others—totally factually. When she returned from her grandfather's funeral, she described in great detail the service. She described the color of each flower arrangement sent and the dress that each woman in the family wore to the service. But when someone asked her, "But how did you *feel*, Amanda? How did it feel to lose your grandfather, who was very special to you?", Amanda reacted as though she were hearing a foreign language. She could not identify her feelings.

Amanda began to learn some things about why she related to people in this factual manner. She grew up in a home in which her mother had a drug addiction. Much of Amanda's early life was spent covering up for her mother—telling friends that her mother was sick when the effects of her addiction kept her from getting out of bed. Amanda often telephoned her mother's boss when her mother couldn't go to her job.

As an adult Amanda never told anyone about these incidents in her childhood. She kept a tight lid on her emotions. She believed that if people ever really knew her and her secret, they would stop being friends. She related to everyone in a highly factual way to try to keep a lid on her feelings.

As Amanda learned about codependency. she began to share some of these details with Phyllis, an older woman who through her support-group experience Amanda came to trust. By breaking the "no-talk" rule and confessing these matters to Phyllis, Amanda began breaking free from her denial and began expressing how she felt about her pain. Read in these lessons how a process like Amanda experienced is possible.

If we say that we have no sin, we are deceiving ourselves, and the truth is not in us. If we confess our sins, He is faithful and righteous to forgive us our sins and to cleanse us from all unrighteousness.

—1 John 1:8-9

Overview for Step 5

Lesson 1: Breaking the "No Talk" Rule
   Goal: You will describe the process and benefits of confession.
Lesson 2: You Don't Have to Do it Alone
   Goal: You will describe the ways the Holy Spirit will help you to take Step 5.
Lesson 3: Taking the Step
   Goal: You will make final preparations to take Step 5.

LESSON 1

Breaking the "No Talk" Rule

We admit to God, to ourselves, and to another person the exact nature of our wrongs.

> *Therefore, confess your sins to one another and pray for one another, so that you may be healed.*
>
> –James 5:16

Key Concept:
Keeping the secrets keeps us in slavery to our destructive habits, while confession opens the door for release and healing.

Many of us have been have been keeping secrets almost all of our lives. Every day those secrets take their toll from us. We pay in loss of self-respect, in drained energy, and in bondage to old codependent habits. We are a little squeamish when we hear that we need to admit our wrongs to another person. We reason, "Isn't it enough that I tell God?" No, it isn't. Something about our human nature keeps us from change until we have confessed our struggles to another person.

Letting secrets be known

If we reveal ourselves to another human being, we may feel like we have everything to lose and nothing to gain. What will we lose?

- **We will lose our sense of isolation.** Because Step 5 is intended to be a dialogue, not a monologue, we will discover that we are not alone in our sinful deeds and desires. Our sense of aloneness then will begin to vanish.

- **We will lose our unwillingness to forgive.** When people accept and forgive us, we realize that we can forgive others.

- **We will lose our inflated pride.** As we see and accept who we are, we begin to gain humility. Humility involves seeing ourselves as we really are and seeing who God really is.

- **We will lose our sense of denial.** Honesty with another person tears away denial. We will begin to feel clean and honest.

 Circle any of the following that you want to keep in your life:

isolation   unwillingness to forgive   inflated pride   denial

Confession

As Christians we can understand that confessing the wrong things that we have done does not make us forgiven. We are forgiven because Christ died to pay for our sins. Confession is a means by which we can experience our forgiveness, not obtain it.

Confession is a means by which we can experience our forgiveness, not obtain it.

 Explain in your own words the last sentence of the paragraph you just read.

_____

_____

Step 5 113

We work Step 5 not to be forgiven of sin but so we can enjoy the benefits of the forgiveness God already has given us. A person confesses with an attitude of repentance. Repentance is not a matter of feeling sorry for ourselves because we've been caught. Repentance is turning away from sin and turning instead to God. Look at what happened to one of God's mightiest men when this person turned to God under the weight of unconfessed sin.

David: A Man After God's Heart

God called David, the shepherd, psalmist, and king of Israel, a man after His own heart (1 Samuel 13:14). But, like each of us, David was a sinner. David's sin was that of committing adultery. Then, to cover that sin, he resorted to murder! (See 2 Samuel 11.) David not only felt remorse about his sin, but he confessed it and then repented of it. David's attitude made him a man after God's heart. Look in Psalm 32 at the process of David's reconciliation to God.

David's confession

> How blessed is he whose transgression is forgiven, whose sin is covered. How blessed is the man whom the Lord does not impute iniquity, and in whose spirit there is no deceit.
> —Psalm 32:1-2

✎ **In Psalm 32:1-2 at left, David describes the one whose sin is forgiven as** _____.

What does the term *blessed* mean to you? _____

To bless means to give the power for success. To me it means that when God forgives my sin I can live the way God planned.

> When I kept silent about my sin, my body wasted away through my groaning all day long. For day and night Thy hand was heavy upon me; my vitality was drained away as with the fever heat of summer.
> —Psalm 32:3-4

✎ **In Psalm 32:3-4 at left, what happened to David's body when he kept silent about his sin?**

_____

Have you felt the same kind of effects in your life? Explain.

_____

_____

_____

> I acknowledged my sin to Thee, And my iniquity I did not hide; I said, I will confess my transgressions to the Lord; And Thou didst forgive the guilt of my sin.
> —Psalm 32:5

✎ **In Psalm 32:5 at left, what did David do about his sin?** _____

_____

What was God's response? _____

_____

David not only confessed his sin to God, he confessed it on paper. We don't all need to publish our confession, but David's example certainly makes plain that breaking secrecy is valid and valuable. God's response was forgiveness and restored fellowship.

A disease of sick rules

Codependency has a lot of sick rules. Many of us grew up with this rule: "We don't air our dirty laundry in public." It is a rule designed to keep us in slavery to our destructive habits. Break it! But break it at the right time with trustworthy people.

> **Key Concept for Lesson 1**
> Keeping the secrets keeps us in slavery to our destructive habits, while confession opens the door for release and healing.

 Please pray and ask God how this concept can apply in your life. Now please review this lesson. What has God shown you that you can use?

_____

_____

LESSON 2

Not Alone

We admit to God, to ourselves, and to another person the exact nature of our wrongs.

> *And I will ask the Father, and He will give you another Helper, that He may be with you forever. . . . I will not leave you as orphans; I will come to you.*
>
> –John 14:16,18

Key Concept:
The Holy Spirit gives us the power and encouragement to take Step 5.

Admitting our wrongs to another person is a terrifying task. God does not ask us to do it alone. As believers we have received the Spirit of Christ within us.

The following exercise will help you identify the working of the Holy Spirit. The Holy Spirit, our helper, will provide the strength to work Step 5.

What the Holy Spirit does

In the Scriptures below, look for ways that the Holy Spirit acts on your behalf. Then match the passage to the descriptions that follow.

> A. "But the Helper, the Holy Spirit, whom the Father will send in My name, He will teach you all things, and bring to your remembrance all that I said to you" (John 14:26).
> B. "But when He, the Spirit of truth, comes, He will guide you into all the truth; for He will not speak on His own initiative, but whatever He hears, He will speak; and He will disclose to you what is to come" (John 16:13).
> C. ". . . the thoughts of God no one knows except the Spirit of God. Now we have received, not the spirit of the world, but the Spirit who is from God that we might know the things freely given to us by God" (1 Corinthians 2:11-12).
> D. "And He, when He comes, will convict the world concerning sin, and righteousness, and judgment" (John 16:8).

✏️ **Match the Scriptures that you just read with the following. The Holy Spirit . . .**

_____ 1. points out my need of confession.
_____ 2. reveals the truth to me.
_____ 3. teaches me what I need to know.
_____ 4. reminds me of the teaching and example of Jesus.
_____ 5. tells me of my identity and other gifts in Christ.
_____ 6. convicts me of my need for Christ and of specific sins.

The presence of the Holy Spirit breaks through our denial and shows us that we need to confess and change. He then supplies both the instruction and power to accomplish that transformation. Your answers could include: 1. d; 2. b; 3. a; 4. a; 5. c; 6. d.

The last Scripture in the exercise you just completed speaks about how the Holy Spirit convicts us of sin, righteousness, and judgment.

✏️ **Read the following Bible story and consider the importance of conviction in our lives. Then answer the questions that follow.**

Read the story of David, Bathsheba, Uriah, and Nathan in 2 Samuel 11-12. King David committed at least four of the most damaging sins in life. He committed adultery, he lied, he betrayed a friend who trusted him, and he resorted to cold-blooded murder. Nathan, the prophet, confronted David to convict him of his crimes. David was convicted in his heart and repented. In repenting he confessed his sin publicly. I don't mean he told everybody. He would have demonstrated unhealthy boundaries if he had done that. Confessing publicly means breaking the secrecy to the appropriate person.

✏️ **In the following list write C by the things that might have occurred as a result of David's experience of conviction. Put an X by those that might have resulted had he not been convicted.**

_____ 1. A premature death from carrying secret guilt.
_____ 2. Turning away from God over the shame in his life.
_____ 3. Becoming a more compassionate person and king.
_____ 4. Becoming hard and callous and therefore an evil ruler.
_____ 5. Great relief and joy from experiencing forgiveness.
_____ 6. A deeper love relationship with God.
_____ 7. A growing denial, stuffing his emotions.

Look at your responses. Would you prefer the results of conviction or of avoiding it in your life? Conviction seldom is a pleasant thing to experience, but it is valuable. I hope you responded that answers 1, 2, 4, and 7 would result from lack of conviction. Answers 3, 5, and 6 would result from experiencing conviction.

✏️ **Read the verse appearing in the margin. Can you name a time in your life in which God convicted you of a wrong and you confessed it? How did you feel afterward?**

_____

_____

> All discipline for the moment seems not to be joyful, but sorrowful; yet to those who have been trained by it, afterwards it yields the peaceful fruit of righteousness.
> –Hebrews 12:11

> If we confess our sins, He is faithful and righteous to forgive us our sins and to cleanse us from all unrighteousness.
> –1 John 1:9

This discussion helps me to see that even though working Step 5 is difficult and painful, it produces good results in my life. Conviction allows me to deal with sin in my life so I can continue to experience God's love, power, and wisdom. Read the verse at left to see what 1 John 1:9 says about this.

The Purpose of Confession

Some of us are so good at putting ourselves down and punishing ourselves that we will see confession as a means of paying for our sins. Remember that confession is not payment for our sin. It is the means God has given us so that we can experience the forgiveness He already has extended to His children. Jesus' death on the cross paid for our sins completely.

✎ What is confession? _____

_____

Does confession make you forgiven? Why or why not? _____

_____

If necessary review this unit for the answers.

You may be preparing to confess your sins to God for the first time. If you need some help, you might use as a guide the prayer below.

> Dear Father,
> The Holy Spirit has shown me that I sinned when I (name sins of thoughts and actions as specifically as possible). Thank You that I am completely forgiven and that You choose not to remember my sins. I realize that You have declared me to be deeply loved, completely forgiven, fully pleasing, totally accepted, and a new creature—complete in Christ. Amen.

Here are some more helpful insights on confession.

Sinning against God

All sin is against God.
In Psalm 51:4, as David confessed his sin of adultery and murder, he said: "Against Thee, Thee only, I have sinned, And done what is evil in Thy sight." Although his sin affected others, David recognized that his sin primarily was against God. Nathan the prophet asked, "Why have you despised the word of the LORD by doing evil in His sight?" (2 Samuel 12:9). Notice that the focus is on God, not David or others. When we have the truth of God's Word to guide us and still choose to sin, we are devaluing Him.

Perhaps if before choosing to sin we said to God, "I don't value You and Your Word," we would be more aware of how sin grieves our Heavenly Father.

Making excuses

Confession recognizes the full scope of sin.
By confessing we realize that not only is a specific act sinful, the ungodly thoughts and false beliefs behind it are sinful as well. The excuses we use to

Step 5 117

justify our sins are part of those ungodly thoughts. When we deal with sin, we must deal with the root of our actions.

Confession includes accepting forgiveness.

Many Christians construct a penance cycle that they believe they must put themselves through before they can feel forgiven. Once God convicts them of a sin, they plead with God for forgiveness. Then they feel depressed for a couple of days just to show that they really are sorry and deserve to be forgiven. The truth is that Jesus Christ died on the cross for our sins and has declared us justified by the cross. We cannot earn forgiveness by punishing ourselves. Confession simply is an application of the forgiveness we already have in Christ. Accepting our forgiveness allows us to move on in our fellowship with the Lord and to serve Him joyfully.

Moving on in fellowship

Confession includes repentance.

Repentance means turning away from sin and turning instead to God. When we truly repent, we have a change of attitude about sin. If we recognize what our sin has cost Jesus, that sin will grieve us just as it grieves God.

Changing our attitudes

Confession may include restitution.

Righting a wrong

You may need to go to a specific person you have wronged and ask for his or her forgiveness. You may need to return something that you stole, or fix or replace something that you damaged. Step 5 prepares us for our restitution in Steps 8 and 9. It is important for codependents to work the Steps in order at this point. Many of us think we owe restitution to the whole world. Working the Steps gets us healthy enough to make sane decisions about Steps 8 and 9.

Finally, as we come before God to confess our sins, we can do this knowing that our Savior and Lord, Jesus Christ, was tempted in all areas of life just as we are. Read the verses appearing in the margin to see what the writer of Hebrews tells us about these temptations.

✎ **What confidence do these passages give you as you prepare to share your confession with God and another human being?**

_____

_____

Therefore, He had to be made like His brethren in all things, that He might become a merciful and faithful high priest in things pertaining to God, to make propitiation for the sins of the people. For since He Himself was tempted in that which He has suffered, He is able to come to the aid of those who are tempted.
—Hebrews 2:17-18

For we do not have a high priest who cannot sympathize with our weaknesses, but one who has been tempted in all things as we are, yet without sin. Let us therefore draw near with confidence to the throne of grace, that we may receive mercy and may find grace to help in time of need.
—Hebrews 4:15-16

These verses might reassure you that since Jesus defeated temptation before, He can lead you to victory over temptation. The verses also promise that when we fail, Jesus will help us to get up and to continue to fight.

> ### Key Concept for Lesson 2
> The Holy Spirit gives us the power and encouragement to take Step 5.

✎ **Please pray and ask God how this concept can apply in your life. Now please review this lesson. What has God shown you that you can use?**

_____

_____

LESSON 3

Taking the Step

We admit to God, to ourselves, and to another person the exact nature of our wrongs.

> But prove yourselves doers of the word, and not merely hearers who delude themselves.
>
> –James 1:22

Key Concept:
It's not knowing but actually *doing* Step 5 that brings healing and relief.

Choosing a Good Listener

With a better understanding of what it means to confess our wrongs, we are ready to analyze the best way to work Step 5. We begin by determining who will be the best person to help us share. Choosing the right listener is important for an effective Step 5. Please make this choice only after you consider it prayerfully.

The following suggestions may help you in your selection process. Keep these guidelines in mind as you pray about this person.

- Choose someone who has been growing spiritually for several years or who is very familiar with both Step 5 and the issues of codependency. A person who is familiar with this Step, with recovery, or with dependency issues will understand this Step's importance for you and your recovery.

- Choose someone who can keep a confidence. The information you are preparing to disclose is very personal. The person with whom you talk should be completely trustworthy.

- Choose an objective listener. This is not yet the time, and the time never may come, when we can talk openly with those who are emotionally involved with us. They may find what we have to say to be more than they can bear. Be considerate. Sharing is a responsibility.

- Choose someone who may be willing to share with you personal examples from his or her life. The fact that a person with whom you talk is a good listener is highly important, but having someone who also can share in a healthy back-and-forth exchange of feelings and experiences may help you find the acceptance you especially need right now.

⇨ **Stop and pray, asking God for His leadership in this decision. Review the guidelines above. Don't wait to make a perfect decision. Make your first selection, and then in the margin box write the person's name.**

To share my progress in recovery, I will share with—
_____

Beware of perfectionism. You can't make a perfect selection with only imperfect people from which to choose. Beware of fear of rejection. The person you choose may not be available for a variety of reasons such as schedule or for reasons that have nothing to do with you.

I have had to learn that if I reach out to someone and find that he or she is busy or unavailable to me, the person's response does not represent rejection of me, though it may feel like it at first. If necessary, pray and go on to the next name.

✎ **Write how and when you will talk to this person.** _____

_____

Telling Your Story

Taking notes

Once you have found a good listener, you are ready to get on with telling your story. Perhaps the best way to begin is by taking some notes. Start from the very beginning and write down a list of those persons, circumstances, and events that affected you most along the way.

You of course can refer to Step 4 to insert other significant things you have done—positive and negative—over the years. When you do finally sit down with the person you've chosen—your sponsor, pastor, counselor, physician, or trusted friend—you may want to read from your notes or refer back to them as an outline. This is up to you. The point is that you get it ALL out: everything that is significant about your life that you never have told.

> BOUNDARY ISSUE: Getting it all out does not mean all the lurid details. Notice carefully the wording of the Step: We admit *the exact nature of our wrongs*. The nature of our wrongs refers to their character or qualities.

As you write your story, read these final words of caution: Some people who take Step 5 seriously and act on it are disappointed because they experienced no immediate feelings of relief. Feelings of relief do not determine the success of Step 5. You work the Step successfully by disclosing the significant events in your life which you need to share with another human being. We urge you to think about this before you take this Step; be realistic in your expectations.

Finally, remember that this Step is for you. Regardless of who we choose to share ourselves with, we need to realize that our purpose in taking this Step is NOT to please the listener but is to gain healing for ourselves.

Story Outline

Following this story outline will help you focus on important details as you prepare to share. You almost certainly will need to use extra paper or the margin for more room to write.

✎ **What was your life like when you were a child? (Describe your relationships with your parents, brothers, and sisters):**

_____

_____

_____

_____

How has your home life affected you?

How has rescuing and controlling others given you a sense of self-esteem and power?

✏️ **Explain in detail how codependency has affected—**
your self-esteem:

your relationships with your friends:

your job:

your values:

your relationship with God:

How has a lack of objectivity shown itself in your life?

How have you demonstrated a warped sense of responsibility?

How have you been controlled? . . . controlling?

_____
_____

How has your life been characterized by hurt and anger?

_____
_____

How has codependent, habitual guilt shaped your life?

_____
_____

In what ways has this all resulted in feelings of loneliness?

_____

Keep in mind that confession brings relief and joy.

> **Key Concept for Lesson 3**
> It's not knowing, but actually *doing* Step 5 that brings healing and relief.

✎ **Please review this Step. Ask God to identify the Scriptures or principles that are particularly important for your life. Underline them. Then respond to the following:**

Restate the Step in your own words. _____
_____

What do you have to gain by practicing this Step in your life?

_____
_____

Reword your summary into a prayer of response to God. Thank Him for this Step, and affirm your commitment to Him.

_____
_____

Memorize this Step's memory verse:
If we say that we have no sin, we are deceiving ourselves, and the truth is not in us. If we confess our sins, He is faithful and righteous to forgive us our sins and to cleanse us from all unrighteousness.   —1 John 1:8-9

STEP 6

Willing to Be Willing

We commit ourselves to obey God and desire that He will remove patterns of sin from our lives.

Step 6 Into Codependency

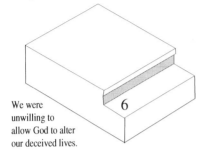

We were unwilling to allow God to alter our deceived lives.

Step 6 Out of Codependency

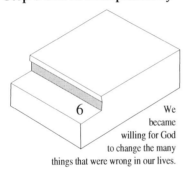

We became willing for God to change the many things that were wrong in our lives.

LEARNING TO ENJOY LIFE

Any time someone offered Jim a gift—even ice cream—Jim's first response was to refuse it. If Jim and a friend went to lunch and the friend offered to pay half the bill, Jim muttered, "No, I insist," even if he were running short of funds that week.

"I guess I just didn't think I was worthy of receiving a gift or of having fun," Jim later said in describing why he refused such offers.

After studying about codependency and about what causes individuals to deny themselves in unhealthy ways, Jim is learning to value himself, to give freely, and to receive with freedom and gratitude. He's beginning to enjoy life.

Now when someone offers to do something nice for Jim, he graciously accepts. If he wants to go to lunch with someone but can afford only to pay for his own meal, he uses good boundaries by saying in advance, "Let's go out for lunch—Dutch treat."

Furthermore, Jim is learning to do things that he enjoys. He's taken up woodworking. At one time in his life Jim would have felt selfish doing things for himself. Now he understands how important having fun is to his emotional health. Read in these lessons about why persons like Jim need to value themselves more highly.

For it is God who is at work in you, both to will and to work for His good pleasure.
–Philippians 2:13

Overview for Step 6

Lesson 1: **The Motivation for Lordship**
   Goal: You will distinguish between the positive motivations of lordship and the motivations of self-centered codependency.
Lesson 2: **The Idol Connection**
   Goal: You will describe an idolatrous reason and six healthy reasons to obey God and to serve others.
Lesson 3: **Improper Motivations for Obedience**
   Goal: You will examine four common dysfunctional motives for obedience.
Lesson 4: **Time to Stop Being a Victim**
   Goal: You will describe four elements of making a decision to follow Jesus as a disciple.

LESSON 1

The Motivation for Lordship

We commit ourselves to obey God and desire that He will remove patterns of sin from our lives.

> *Humble yourselves, therefore, under the mighty hand of God, that He may exalt you at the proper time, casting all your anxiety upon Him, because He cares for you.*
>
> –1 Peter 5:6-7

Key Concept:
A relationship of secure love and healthy respect is the basis for obedience.

Caution! This Step can easily be taken lightly or overlooked. This Step focuses on the fact that I cannot force myself to obey God. I need to learn to love and trust Him enough to want to have Him in charge of my life. In the Steps of Alcoholics Anonymous, Step 6 is phrased to say we "were entirely ready to have God remove all these defects of character." Step 6 is about becoming "entirely willing" to have Jesus as our Lord. Most of us are afraid to trust Him with our lives because we have a mistaken picture of lordship.

A Biblical Picture of Lordship

The Scriptures present a beautiful picture of the lordship of Christ. They describe our opportunity to be bond-servants to God. Paul, James, and Peter all described themselves as bond-servants. The term comes from Exodus 21. Some verses from this biblical passage appear in the margin.

Becoming a bond-servant involved two things: the master's character and the slave's new identity. When it was time to gain his freedom, the slave had a choice. If the master had been harsh, the slave could go free, but if the slave had experienced his master's love and care, he could choose to remain with his master in a new relationship. The master put a hole in the slave's ear. This showed that the slave freely had chosen to remain.

> *Now these are the ordinances which you are to set before them. If you buy a Hebrew slave, he shall serve for six years, but on the seventh he shall go out as a free man without payment. . . . But if the slave plainly says, I love my master, my wife and my children, I will not go out as a free man, then his master shall bring him to God, then he shall bring him to the door or the doorpost. And his master shall pierce his ear with an awl, and he shall serve him permanently.*
>
> –Exodus 21:1-2,5-6

The slave became a bond-servant. His identity changed. His relationship with the master changed. His motivations changed. Instead of being *forced* to serve, he had *chosen* to serve. The master's love caused him to remain and to serve with joy, love, and respect. The new "want-to," not "have-to," motivation was based on the character of the master.

 What is the difference between a bond-servant and a regular slave?

_____

_____

A frightening idea

The idea of obeying the Lord can be frightening to many of us. The lenses of overresponsibility, perfectionism, repressed emotions, and guilt motivation can distort the beauty of an intimate relationship with Christ.

Instead of gaining a sense of belonging, trust, and affirmation, we often see the Christian message as involving demands, condemnation, and guilt. The difference is in motivation. A slave serves out of obligation. A bond-servant serves out of love.

Four basic misconceptions about God exist: 1) a warped emotional concept of God, discussed in Step 2; 2) an inability to understand God's free grace; 3) the failure to grasp the matter of lordship; and 4) the improper basis of our self-worth performance.

✎ **Carefully study the explanation below. Then match one of the basic misconceptions to each of the seven examples that follow.**

A. Concept of God: If we fear God and see Him as unloving and unreliable, we will have difficulty being willing to surrender to Him.

B. Grace: If we never have experienced unconditional love, we will have difficulty accepting God's grace. We will continue trying to earn love. God's grace is totally undeserved.

C. Lordship: We may go to the opposite extreme and not feel guilt because we don't feel accountable. We then think God is a pushover who makes no demands on our lives.

D. Performance-Based Self-Worth: If our value is based on performance, we can't surrender to God. We are too busy proving our worth, even to Him.

Below are seven common distorted attitudes. Each grows out of one or more of the basic misconceptions above. In the margin write the letter and the description behind each attitude. I have done the first as an example:

A. *Concept of God*

1. God is mean. Many of us do not believe that God has our best interests at heart. We think He only wants to use us. We may "serve" Him with many activities, but we do that service out of fear that He will punish us if we don't do exactly what He wants.

2. The Lord demands too much of me. We may fear that we can't measure up to our unrealistically high expectations of the Christian life. We give lip service to grace and forgiveness but experience little of the freedom and positive motivation.

3. I'm trying as hard as I can; what more can I do? We may feel anger as well as guilt at what we see as the demanding nature of God. Many of us channel this anger toward a person, church, or organization because we don't feel like we can be angry with God.

4. I don't want to lose control of my life. Living their lives by controlling every detail, activity, and emotion, codependent believers find it extremely difficult to turn over that control to another person—even to God.

5. God will make me weird. Many of us already are lonely. We already feel distant from others. The stories of those who take a stand for Christ and who suffer ridicule do not entice many people to sign up!

6. I can gain worth by serving God. Some see Christian service as a means of gaining security and worth. They plunge headlong into Christian activities in the hope of gaining others' recognition. Though they experience feelings of fear and guilt, their thirst for approval drives them to take the risks of performing for acceptance.

Step 6 125

7. If God loves me, He won't ask me to do anything difficult. We are people of extremes. Some of us only can see messages demanding more than we can do. Others of us read the Scriptures selectively. We pick out only the passages that soothe. As a reaction to the fear and guilt we have felt in our lives, some of us focus only on God's love. We create a grandfatherly God—one without justice or discipline.

The result of these misguided perceptions is destructive for believers who are in the grip of codependency. We make inaccurate conclusions about God—that He is demanding, harsh, or distant—and about ourselves. We feel that we can never measure up, or that we can gain a sense of worth by serving Him. In answering the previous exercise, you may have discovered that more than one of the misconceptions applied to the examples that followed. I found that possible answers were: 1. A, B; 2. A, B; 3. A, B, D; 4. A, B, D; 5. A,C; 6. D; 7. C.

 On the following line 0 represents serving out of such reasons as guilt or fear, 100 represents serving out of love and respect. Put a *small* mark on the spot indicating your motivation for serving Christ.

0 _____ 100

Now put a *big* mark at the spot on the line where you desire to be. This is the point of Step 6. We desire to arrive at that place where we are willing for Jesus to be Lord because we love and trust Him.

Key Concept for Lesson 1
A relationship of secure love and healthy respect is the basis for obedience.

 Please pray and ask God how this concept can apply in your life. Now please review this lesson. What has God shown you that you can use?

_____

_____

LESSON 2

The Idol Connection

We commit ourselves to obey God and desire that He will remove patterns of sin from our lives.

You shall have no other gods before Me. –Exodus 20:3

Idolatry: A Major Roadblock

Many of us have a major roadblock to experiencing the love and power of God. We try to get a sense of worth from rescuing, controlling, and serving others. We value the approval, the affection, and the respect of people because we believe that their affirmation will give us the security and worth we desire.

Key Concept:
Attempts to gain self-worth from any source other than God are idolatrous.

idolatry–n. worship of something that is not God.

We are guilty of the same sin as were the Pharisees. Jesus rebuked them, "for they loved the approval of men rather than the approval of God" (John 12:43). We need to call this what it is—**idolatry**. The material in Lessons 2 and 3 on proper and improper motivations for obedience is adapted from *Search for Significance* LIFE Support Edition. Idolatry occurs any time a person tries to get security and value from someone or something other than the Lord. When we attempt to control other people or to gain power and approval by serving, we put ourselves in God's place.

✏️ **Below check the types of service that show unhealthy motivations— serving—**
❑ 1. to be in control;
❑ 2. out of gratitude to the Lord;
❑ 3. because of the needs of others;
❑ 4. to prove my self-worth;
❑ 5. to gain approval;
❑ 6. to glorify God.

Healthy service is directed toward God and others; the sick type of service is self-centered. Answers 2, 3, and 6 are healthy reasons to serve. Answers 1, 4, and 5 are unhealthy motivations.

Ways I serve for wrong reasons—

✏️ **Stop and pray, asking God how idolatry applies in your life. Then in the margin box describe ways that you are driven to serve to prove your worth or to maintain control.**

Some people may become confused at this point and ask, If I serve because of others' needs, am I codependent? To explain: The act of serving is not the problem. Controlling, self-centered, and manipulative serving is a problem. Jesus was the greatest servant of all time. He was not codependent.

✏️ **In the next paragraph circle the words and phrases that demonstrate that Jesus' service was healthy rather than codependent.**

> Jesus served more than anyone ever has or ever will, but definitely He was not codependent. He offered His help, but He let people make their own decisions. He let them walk away. At one point all of the multitude, except for the twelve disciples, abandoned Him. He spoke the truth and let people respond however they chose. In the garden of Gethsemane, He was completely objective about His ordeal of suffering. He didn't repress His emotions. Even when the twelve disciples abandoned Him, He continued to do the Father's will.

Two main motivations to serve exist. One is to gain a sense of worth; that is idolatry. The second is serving because you appreciate God's grace and your worth in Him. The first motivation causes fear, guilt, withdrawal, and drivenness; the second results in love, trust, and joyful obedience. You may have circled *let people make their own decisions, let them walk away, spoke the truth, was objective, didn't repress His emotions,* and *continued to do the Father's will.*

Healthy Motivations for Obedience

God loves and accepts us based on His grace—His unmerited favor—not on our ability to impress Him by our good deeds. If we do not obey God to be accepted, what are good reasons for obeying God? Here is a list of them:

Step 6

Jesus: service for right reasons

If you love Me, you will keep My commandments... He who has My commandments and keeps them, he it is who loves Me; and he who loves Me shall be loved by My Father, and I will love him, and will disclose Myself to him.

–John 14:15,21

For the love of Christ controls us, having concluded this, that one died for all, therefore all died; and He died for all, that they who live should no longer live for themselves, but for Him who died and rose again on their behalf.

–2 Corinthians 5:14-15

1. Christ's love motivates us. Our obedience to God expresses our love for Him. It comes from what Christ has done for us on the cross:

We love because He first loved us and clearly demonstrated His love for us at the cross. (See the verses at left.) This great motivation is missing in many of our lives because we really don't believe that God loves us unconditionally. We expect His love to be based on our ability to earn it.

✎ **Does the love of Christ motivate you to obey Him? Why or why not?**

_____

_____

2. Sin is destructive. God's plans for my life always are for my good. Disobeying God always causes pain and hurt, although the pain may be delayed or disguised. Satan has blinded us to the painful, damaging consequences of sin. Sooner or later sin always will result in some form of destruction.

Sin is destructive in many ways. Emotionally, it brings guilt, shame, and fear of failure or punishment. Mentally, we spend our time and energy thinking about our sins and rationalizing our guilt. Physically, it contributes to a number of illnesses. Relationally, it separates us from others. Spiritually, we grieve the Holy Spirit, lose our testimony, and break our fellowship with God.

✎ **Think of a time you have disobeyed God and experienced painful consequences. Below write a summary of that experience. In your summary include what you can learn from the experience.**

_____

_____

Satan is the master deceiver. He whispers promising suggestions to us. When these thoughts first enter the mind, they speak only about pleasure and never about sin's devastating consequences. When such an occasion happens to you, would it help to remember the example you wrote above?

❏ Yes ❏ No If so, how? _____

_____

My son, do not regard lightly the discipline of the Lord, nor faint when you are reproved by Him; for those whom the Lord loves He disciplines.

–Hebrews 12:5-6

3. The Father's discipline trains us. If sin is so destructive, why doesn't God do something about it? The answer is, He does. He lovingly but firmly disciplines His children. See what the verse at left says about disobeying God. Discipline is not punishment. Punishment is venting one's anger about an offense. Discipline is training. God is training us to live effectively and to obey Him for His glory and our good. That God disciplines us is a proof that we belong to Him.

Jesus took all our punishment on the cross; we no longer have to fear punishment from God for our sins. We seek to obey out of love and wisdom. When we sin and are disciplined, we can remember that God corrects us in love so that we may be like Christ.

4. God's commands for us are good. God gives us His commands to protect us from the harm of sin and to lead us to a life of joy and victory. Many people view God's commands only as restrictions on their lives. We need to see these commands as guidelines which God gives us so that we may enjoy life to the fullest. God's commands are holy, right, and good. They have value in themselves. To choose to obey God and follow His commands always is best.

✎ **Check all the reasons why God's commands for you are good.**

❏ 1. He knows the complete results of an action.
❏ 2. He loves me and has my best interest at heart.
❏ 3. He doesn't want me to have any fun.
❏ 4. He wants to protect me from harm.
❏ 5. Only He knows what joys await my faithfulness.
❏ 6. His purpose is to develop my character.

Avoid trying to keep God's commands by legalism and self-effort. That leads to bitterness, condemnation, and rigidity. The Holy Spirit will give you power, joy, and creativity as you trust Him to fulfill the commands of God's Word through you. All the answers above were correct—except answer 3.

5. God will reward our obedience. Our self-worth is not based on our performance and obedience, but our actions make a huge difference in the quality of our lives and in our impact on others. Disobedience results in spiritual poverty; it short-circuits intimate fellowship with God, causes confusion and guilt, and robs us of spiritual power and the desire to see people won to Christ. Obedience enables us to experience His love, joy, and strength. It also enables us to minister to others, to endure difficulties, and to live for Him. We are completely loved, forgiven, and accepted apart from our performance, but how we live is very important! In the margin box write which of the results of disobedience described here that you have experienced in your life and which were the most painful.

> **Results of disobedience I have experienced—**
>
> _____
> _____
> _____
>
> **Which were the most painful?**
>
> _____
> _____
> _____

6. Christ is worthy. Our most noble reason for serving Christ simply is that He is worthy of our love and obedience. Read at left what the Bible says about His worthiness. Each time we choose to obey, we express the righteousness of Christ. Our performance, then, reflects who we are in Him. We draw on His power and wisdom so that we can honor Him.

Worthy art Thou, our Lord and our God, to receive glory and honor and power.
—Revelation 4:11

✎ **Write the six reasons you have just read for being willing to have Christ as Lord of our lives. If necessary review the chapter.**

1. _____
2. _____
3. _____
4. _____
5. _____
6. _____

Now go back and rank your list from the most important to the least important. Be prepared to share with your group or sponsor your results.

> **Key Concept for Lesson 2**
> Attempts to gain self-worth from any source other than God are idolatrous.

 Please pray and ask God how this concept can apply in your life. Now please review this lesson. What has God shown you that you can use?

LESSON 3

Improper Motivations for Obedience

We commit ourselves to obey God and desire that He will remove patterns of sin from our lives.

> *Some, to be sure, are preaching Christ even from envy and strife, but some also from good will.*
>
> –Philippians 1:15

Key Concept:
Obedience for selfish motives is disobedience.

Jesus repeatedly emphasized that He not only is concerned about what we do but also about why we do it. The Pharisees obeyed many rules, but their hearts were far from God. Motives are important! The following represent poor motivations for obeying God and their possible results:

1. Someone may find out. We may obey God because we fear what others will think of us if we don't. Allen visited prospects for his church because he feared what his Sunday School class would think if he didn't. Barbara was married but wanted to date a man with whom she worked. She didn't because of what others might think.

Basing our behavior on others' opinions is not wise. Times will occur when no one is watching. Our desire to disobey eventually may exceed the peer pressure to obey. Once someone finds out we've sinned, we no longer may have a reason to obey. The biggest problem with this type of obedience is that it isn't obedience at all. It is purely self-interest.

 Is the fear of someone's finding out a motivation for you to obey God? If it is, identify what you are trying to avoid; then go back to the last lesson and review the six reasons to obey Him. Which of these proper motives seems to encourage you most in regard to your specific temptation?

---

2. God will be angry with me. We sometimes obey God because we think He will get angry with us if we don't. We have discussed the difference in God's

130   Step 6

discipline and punishment, but to state this again: God disciplines us in love, not anger. His response to our sin is grief, not condemnation.

Hank was afraid that God would "zap" him if he did anything wrong, so he performed for God. He lived each day fearing God's anger. As you might expect, Hank's relationship with the Lord was cold and mechanical. God doesn't want us to live in fear of His anger but in response to His love. Living in response to His love produces joyful obedience instead of fear.

God doesn't want us to live in fear of His anger but in response to His love.

 Pray and ask God to show you ways you can change this feeling of unhealthy fear. Take time to recall what you have learned in recovery. Now write as many ways as possible that you can change your attitude toward God to a relationship based on healthy love and respect.

_____

_____

You may have written such things as: *I can be honest and voice my feelings and complaints to God; I can meditate on Scripture and on Jesus' love and sacrifice for me; I can write about my feelings; I can share feelings honestly with another person.*

3. I couldn't approve of myself if I didn't obey. Some people obey rules in an attempt to live up to standards they've set for themselves. In doing this they are not yielding their lives to a loving Lord. They are trying to avoid the feeling of shame that occurs when they don't meet their own standards. These people primarily are concerned with do's and don'ts. Instead of seeing it as an intimate relationship with God, they see the Christian life as a ritual—as a life emphasizing rules. If they succeed in keeping the rules, they become prideful. They compare themselves with others. They hope others will accept them because they are a little bit better than someone else.

Phillip's story

Philip was reared in a strict church family. His family taught him that cursing is a terrible sin. All of Philip's friends cursed, but he never did. He secretly thought that he was better than his friends. The fact that God wants pure language is not the reason Philip refrained from cursing. He refrained from cursing because he was compelled to live up to his own standards. Philip needed to base his behavior on God and His Word, not on his own standards.

 What things are you, like Philip, doing to obey God with the motivation to meet your own standards?

_____

God gave us His commands because He loves us. As we obey Him, we are protected and freed to enjoy life more fully.

4. I'll obey to be blessed. God doesn't make bargains. If our only motive to obey is to be blessed, we simply are attempting to manipulate God. Our underlying assumption is: "I've been good, so bless me." It's true that we will reap what we sow, but when we obey in order to get rewards, we are disobedient. Brian went to church so that God would bless his business, not because he wanted to worship God. Penny chose not to spread gossip about Diane because she told God that she wouldn't tell anybody about Diane if He would get her the promotion she wanted.

Step 6

> My grace is sufficient for you, for power is perfected in weakness. Most gladly, therefore, I will rather boast about my weaknesses, that the power of Christ may dwell in me. Therefore I am well content with weaknesses, with insults, with distresses, with persecutions, with difficulties, for Christ's sake, for when I am weak, then I am strong.
> —2 Corinthians 12:9-10

✏️ **Have you ever bargained with God and said, "I'll obey You if You'll 'fix' me?"** ❏ Yes ❏ No

We reason that if we are "fixed," we will be able to serve God and be freed from having to deal with a particular problem or temptation. God sometimes has something important to teach us through our weakness. The apostle Paul three times begged the Lord to remove a "thorn," or difficulty, from him. Read the Scripture appearing in the margin about how the Lord responded to him.

✏️ **Christ has freed us from the bondage of sin so that we can respond to Him in obedience. We have discussed six reasons the Bible says we are to be involved in good works. As a review, fill in the key words from those reasons.**

1. Christ's _____ motivates us to obey Him.

2. Sin is _____.

3. The Father's _____ trains us.

4. God's commands for us are _____.

5. God will reward our _____.

6. Christ is _____.

If necessary, check your responses against information you learned in the previous lesson on page 128-129.

The Lord never said everything had to be perfect in our lives for us to follow Him. He said, "If anyone wishes to come after Me, let him deny himself," (and that denial may mean being denied the right to be free of difficulties) "take up his cross daily, and follow Me" (Luke 9:23). This doesn't mean we should stop working to rid ourselves of our difficulties. We can express our feelings about them to the Lord and with others as appropriate. Then we are to act in faith on His Word.

We don't have to deny the difficulties we have in life, but spiritual growth, character development, and Christian service must not be held hostage by them. God has given each of us a will, and we can choose to honor the Lord in spite of our difficulties.

As you become aware of your motives, you may think, "I've never done anything purely for the Lord in my whole life!" You may feel a sense of pain and remorse because you've had inappropriate motives.

Try not to shame yourself for your past attitudes—we all have them. Instead, realize that the Lord wants you to make godly choices today so that you can enjoy the benefits of those decisions in the future. Then ask the Holy Spirit to help you develop an intensity about these choices.

As the verse at left indicates, your motives won't become totally pure until you see the Lord face to face. The more you grow in your understanding and relationship with Him, the more you will desire to honor Him with your love, loyalty, and obedience.

> Beloved, now we are children of God, and it has not appeared as yet what we shall be. We know that, when He appears, we shall be like Him, because we shall see Him just as He is.
> —1 John 3:2

✏️ Recognizing the great reasons for obedience, will you write your own statement showing that you intend to grow in your willingness to follow Christ? It will provide you with direction and will be your own "pledge of allegiance to Jesus."

_____

_____

> **Key Concept for Lesson 3**
> Obeying because of selfish motives is disobedience.

✏️ Please pray and ask God how this concept can apply in your life. Now please review this lesson. What has God shown you that you can use?

_____

_____

LESSON 4

Key Concept:
We must choose between committing ourselves to God or continuing in our codependency.

We change habits by acting in positive, healthy ways.

Time to Stop Being a Victim

We commit ourselves to obey God and desire that He will remove patterns of sin from our lives.

And if it is disagreeable in your sight to serve the LORD, choose for yourselves today whom you will serve: whether the gods which your fathers served which were beyond the River, or the gods of the Amorites in whose land you are living; but as for me and my house, we will serve the LORD.

–Joshua 24:15

Deciding

Obeying God boils down to an act of your will. You can detach, feel, and consider your options without making any decisions at all. Codependency is a condition of habit. We change habit by acting in positive, healthy ways. We stop rescuing and controlling. We start saying and doing things that reflect independence, security, strength, and health. This is extremely important—for ourselves and for our victims.

In this lesson you will describe the process of taking charge of your life. The process has four parts: 1) making independent choices, 2) setting limits, 3) giving up control of others and 4) enjoying life.

1. Making independent choices—We are not accustomed to making choices and standing up for ourselves. By detaching and becoming objective, we can

Admitting how we feel

admit how we feel. We can be angry, sad, glad, or afraid. We can consider our options and make choices. We can act in confidence and stand up for ourselves. When we aren't sure of ourselves, or when we feel pressured, we often use evasive language. My friend Michael caught me in this bad habit. Someone asked me to go to a party which I had no desire to attend. To be polite, (that is, to avoid offending and risking rejection), I said, "We'll see." Overhearing me, Michael spoke up and said, "When Pat says, 'We'll see,' he really means 'no.'"

Making independent choices also means making honest statements and not using evasive language or double-talk. We need to say what we mean and mean what we say.

✎ In what situations do you find yourself lying, or using evasive language like I did in the example of the party invitation?

_____

_____

2. Setting limits—Good boundaries are vital to healthy living. The analogy below about limits is from a friend.

Guarding it with your life!

> All people receive pieces of land when they are born. Codependents allow people to take water from their property, cut down trees, and trample their pastures. They even encourage people to take advantage of their land, in the hope of winning others' approval. When their houses have been burned, their crops and pastures trampled, and everything has been stolen, they finally get angry and decide to set limits. At first, they don't let anyone even set foot on their property. They guard it with rifles to be sure no one takes advantage of them again. After they have rebuilt their homes, planted new crops, and become established again, they will be more willing to let people on their land. Even then, they will make sure that others do not take advantage of them.

Often our destructive behavior has very few limits. In most cases we feel responsible for everyone and everything. We try to help everybody. We feel guilty about everything. With recovery, we realize that we need boundaries. When we set limits clearly and firmly, we will make statements such as:
- This is what I will do. This is what I won't do.
- I will not take this kind of behavior anymore.
- I refuse to be manipulated.
- I'm sorry, I wish I could help you, but I can't.
- I want to talk about this.

Instead of anticipating others' needs and jumping in to rescue, you can listen patiently and wait for others to ask for help. You then can make a decision whether or not to help. People often explain their troubles and wait for us to volunteer without even being asked. That's what we've done before! If others want help, let them ask for it; then make an objective decision.

Are you so indispensable that you feel you must take God's place?

Kathy, who struggled to develop more healthy relationships, said: "This seems so selfish! These people need me! What about going the extra mile?" The question to ask ourselves is, Is what I'm doing for this person a rescuing, compulsive, codependent reaction to this person's needs, and or is it a healthy, independent, loving response? Sick responses are based on the idea that "If I don't help her, who will?" Can the Almighty, Omnipotent, Sovereign Lord take care of that person you are determined to rescue? Are you so indispensable that you feel you must take God's place? Sometimes helping is appropriate, but other times we need to get out of the way.

We rescue others and keep them from developing responsibility and independence. We keep them and ourselves from depending on God. It's not up to you! The Lord can take care of that person, and He can take care of you as you learn to identify, detach, and decide to stop compulsive rescuing.

✎ **Ask God what limits you need to set. Then write at least four boundaries you need to establish. In the margin is an example.**

> *I need to allow people to ask for help if they need it instead of jumping to rescue.*

_____

_____

_____

_____

3. Stop controlling others. Make your own decisions. Give others the same freedom. Stop trying to control them. We have tried to control others' attitudes and behavior by praise or condemnation. Since most people live for acceptance, it often has worked. Now, as you are learning to make your own decisions, you can help others to do the same. Calmly and clearly let people know what the consequences of their decisions will be. Love these people, encourage them, but let them know that their choices make a difference. Instead of yelling or withdrawing say something like, "I felt hurt when you said that. I feel it will hurt our relationship if you say things like that to me." We attempt to control children by using praise and condemnation, anger and withdrawal. It works at first, but it takes more as the child tests his limits and gets used to each level of manipulation. Calm, loving discipline is far better than manipulation. It helps children develop responsibility and learn the consequences of behavior. Trying to control by praising and condemning keeps children from seeing situations clearly and from making objective decisions. When these children are adults, they will probably treat their children the same way. The cycle then will continue.

✎ **Study carefully parts 2 and 3 about setting limits and controlling others. In your own words write the difference between healthy boundaries and controlling others.**

_____

_____

That was a difficult assignment. You may have written that the biggest difference is honesty. We can communicate honestly and clearly our wishes and feelings instead of focusing on getting others to do what we want.

4. **Enjoying life**—As we grow in recovery, we begin to feel free and spontaneous. Instead of being driven to please others and feeling disappointed by their responses, we begin to experience unconditional love from God and from a new set of friends. We begin to enjoy life! Many of the things that seemed so vital fade in importance. Love, intimacy, spontaneity, and new dreams take their places. What do you enjoy? What have you withheld from yourself because you weren't "worthy?" What goals have you neglected? What can you do just for the fun of it? Go out to dinner. Play a game. Go to a movie. Buy a canoe. (I did!) Tell a joke. Help somebody because you "want" to. Make new friends. This may sound like selfishness, but it's not. Having fun gives balance to life for a guilt-riddled, overly responsible person.

Love, intimacy, spontaneity, and new dreams can take the places of old, sick habits.

 On a three-by-five-inch card, write several statements that will help you to act in a strong, healthy way. Consider having one statement from each of the four parts of the decision-making process this Step describes. Here are some examples.

- Give my opinion (without hesitating) to my mother.
- If John asks me to lend him more money, I will say no.
- I am not going to tell Suzanne how to act. She can make her own choices.
- I'm going to treat myself to lunch.

Keep the card with you to remind you to act in a strong, healthy way.

Key Concept for Lesson 4
We must choose between committing ourselves to God or continuing in our self-defeating behavior.

Please review this Step. Pray and ask God to identify the Scriptures or principles that are particularly important for your life. Underline them. Then respond to the following:

Restate the Step in your own words. _____

_____

What do you have to gain by practicing this Step in your life?

_____

Reword your summary into a prayer of response to God. Thank Him for this Step, and affirm your commitment to Him.

_____

_____

Memorize this Step's memory verse:
For it is God who is at work in you, both to will and to work for His good pleasure.

–Philippians 2:13

STEP 7

Ready for Change

We humbly ask God to renew our minds so that our codependent patterns can be transformed into patterns of righteousness.

Step 7 Into Codependency

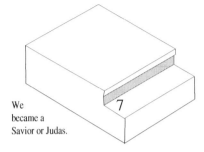

We became a Savior or Judas.

Step 7 Out of Codependency

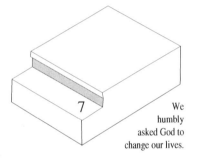

We humbly asked God to change our lives.

RUINING HIS CHANCES

When he was a child, James never could please his father, who was rigid and demanding. Now James is a successful business executive, a deacon in his church, and a classic victim of low self-esteem.

James offends his fellow church members by his seemingly egotistical statements. His statements seem to be full of pride, but they actually reflect his lack of a sense of self-worth. He says of his new position in the church, "I'm going to straighten this church out now that I'm running it." His statements imply that he thinks the previous leaders have done a terrible job.

Everything James does is an attempt to prove himself to others. In the process he ruins his own chances to experience what makes life worthwhile—loving relationships. James never would identify himself as a victim of shame, but those who know him would. Read on pages 155-156 about what contributes to this shame-based identity.

And do not be conformed to this world, but be transformed by the renewing of your mind, that you may prove what the will of God is, that which is good and acceptable and perfect.

–Romans 12:2

Overview for Step 7

Lesson 1: The Grace Step
Goal: You will identify why you need a renewed mind.

Lesson 2: The Performance Trap
Goal: You will determine the effect of performance-based worth on your life, and you will describe the solution.

Lesson 3: The Approval Addict
Goal: You will evaluate the effect of addiction to approval on your life, and you will describe the solution.

Lesson 4: The Blame Game
Goal: You will estimate the effect of habitual blaming on your life, and you will describe the solution.

Lesson 5: Shame
Goal: You will estimate the effect of low self-esteem on your life, and you will describe the solution.

Lesson 6: Taking the Step
Goal: You will describe three practical actions necessary to work this Step.

LESSON 1

The Grace Step

We humbly ask God to renew our minds so that our codependent patterns can be transformed into patterns of righteousness.

> *for it is God who is at work in you, both to will and to work for His good pleasure.*
>
> –Philippians 2:13

Key Concept:
A solid, biblical, belief system is the key to healthy behavior.

In Step 1 we discovered that we are powerless. In Step 7 we begin to apply God's power to our situation. Philippians 2:13 above describes grace as God's giving us both the desire and the power to do His will. That requires having a renewed mind so we can be rid of our self-destructive patterns.

✎ **Read Philippians 2:13 again. Why is it important that God give us the will (desire) as well as the work (ability) to follow Him?**

_____

_____

_____

We often define *grace* as God's unmerited favor. It is His free, undeserved gift of loving and accepting us. I would say that God's gift of the desire and the power to follow Him is important because I do not naturally desire what is best and because I do not, on my own, have the ability to do God's will.

Why Do I Need My Mind Renewed?

Distorted thinking

I need my mind renewed because I think in a distorted manner. Theology tells us that sin has damaged every aspect of life—thinking, feeling, and acting. This is called depravity. This Step is designed to help us see that damage and to ask God to correct it.

Sin in our lives occurs largely because of our distorted belief system. The following diagram shows this process:

Most of the time we act because of habit rather than because of clear choices. Our thoughts, feelings, and actions mostly are habit. They result from learned behavior. We all must deal with a variety of situations in life. Between our situation and our thoughts, emotions, and actions is a filtering system—our beliefs.

As (a man) thinks within himself, so he is.
—Proverbs 23:7

Our beliefs represent our deepest, most basic thoughts. They affect the way we feel, the way we perceive others and ourselves, and ultimately, the way we act. They determine whether we will live according to God's functional truth or according to the world's dysfunctional value system.

✎ **Check all of the following that are basic false beliefs:**

❏ 1. I must gain the approval of others to feel good about myself.
❏ 2. I cannot change, I am hopeless.
❏ 3. I am feeling depressed because I failed to meet expectations.
❏ 4. I must meet certain standards to feel good about myself.
❏ 5. Those who fail are unworthy of love and deserve to be punished.

✎ **Which approach is more likely to succeed: confronting and replacing the basic false belief, or continually battling with the behaviors? Why?**

_____

_____

In your opinion, upon which do we usually concentrate most, the dysfunctional beliefs or the behaviors they produce?

_____

If you checked numbers 1, 2, 4, and 5, you were correct. Answer 3 is a feeling that grows out of the false belief that my performance determines my worth. In my opinion people usually concentrate on the habitual thoughts, feelings, and actions. They seldom deal with the genuine problem—a false belief system.

How False Beliefs Run and Ruin Our Lives

How our filters work

Our beliefs represent the filters through which we interpret the situations we encounter. Some of these interpretations are conscious reflections; most, however, are based on unconscious habits. These beliefs trigger thoughts, which in turn lead to emotions, which drive actions.

False Beliefs

If what we believe about ourselves is founded on the truth of God's Word, we likely will have a positive sense of self-esteem. However, as we mentioned in Step 2, Satan has deceived most of humankind by convincing us that:

Our Self-Worth = Performance + Others' Opinions

In your work on this Step you will examine how each of those false belief systems operates in your life. Remember from Step 2 that for each of the false beliefs God has a life-changing truth.

Beliefs, consequences

✎ Below read the list of the four basic false beliefs and the list of God's truths. Before each false belief write the letter of the appropriate truth.

_____ 1. *I must meet certain standards to feel good about myself*: results in fear of failure; perfectionism; being driven to succeed; manipulating others to succeed; withdrawing from healthy risks for fear of failing.

_____ 2. *I must have the approval of certain others to feel good about myself*: results in fear of rejection; becoming a people-pleaser; being overly sensitive to criticism; withdrawing from others to avoid disapproval.

_____ 3. *Those who fail, including me, are unworthy of love and deserve to be punished*: results in fear of punishment; a tendency to punish others; blaming self and others for personal failure; withdrawing from God and fellow believers; being driven to avoid punishment.

_____ 4. *I am what I am. I cannot change. I am hopeless*: results in feelings of shame, hopelessness, apathy, inferiority; passivity; loss of creativity; isolation, withdrawing from others.

A. Propitiation, which means we have the capacity to experience God's love deeply because we no longer will fear punishment or punish others. Results include: increasing freedom from the fear of punishment; patience and kindness toward others; being quick to forgive; deep love for Christ.

B. Justification, which means we are completely forgiven and fully pleasing to God. Results include: increasing freedom from the fear of failure; desire to pursue the right things: Christ and His kingdom; love for Christ.

C. Regeneration, which means we have been made brand new, complete in Christ. Results include: no longer experiencing the pain of shame; Christ-centered self-confidence; joy, courage, peace; desire to know Christ.

D. Reconciliation, which means we are totally accepted by God. Results include: increasing freedom from the fear of rejection; willingness to be open and vulnerable; ability to relax around others; willingness to take criticism; a desire to please God no matter what others think.

These four basic truths become the foundation on which to build an effective, Christ-honoring life. The responses were 1. B, 2. D, 3. A, 4. C.

Key Concept for Lesson 1
A solid, biblical, belief system is the key to healthy behavior.

✎ Please pray and ask God how this concept an apply in your life. Now please review this lesson. What has God shown you that you can use?

_____

_____

_____

_____

Step 7

LESSON 2

The Performance Trap

We humbly ask God to renew our minds so that our codependent patterns can be transformed into patterns of righteousness.

> *nevertheless knowing that a man is not justified by the works of the Law but through faith in Christ Jesus, even we have believed in Christ Jesus, that we may be justified by faith in Christ, and not by the works of the Law; since by the works of the Law shall no flesh be justified.*
> –Galatians 2:16

Key Concept:
I am completely forgiven by God and am fully pleasing to Him.

The false belief that I must meet certain standards in order to feel good about myself results in a fear of failure. Take the following test to determine how strongly this belief affects you.

Fear of Failure Test

 Read the statements below. Then, from the top of the test, choose the term which best describes your response. Put in the blank beside each statement the number above that term you chose.

1	2	3	4
Always	Sometimes	Seldom	Never

_____ 1. I avoid participating in some activities because I am afraid I will not be good enough.
_____ 2. I become anxious when I sense I may fail.
_____ 3. I worry.
_____ 4. I have unexplained anxiety.
_____ 5. I am a perfectionist.
_____ 6. I feel I must justify my mistakes.
_____ 7. I feel I must succeed in some areas.
_____ 8. I become depressed when I fail.
_____ 9. I become angry with people who interfere with my success and who make me appear incompetent.
_____ 10. I am self-critical.
_____ Total (Add up the numbers you placed in the blanks.)

My score means—

Interpreting Your Score
If your score is . . .

34-40
God apparently has given you a very strong appreciation for His love and unconditional acceptance. You seem to be free of the fear of failure that plagues most people. (Some exceptions exist: Some people who score this high either are greatly deceived or have turned off their emotions as a way to suppress pain. Examine your heart and talk to your group members to see if these exceptions apply to you.)

28-33
The fear of failure rarely controls your responses or does so only in certain situations. Again, people who are not honest with themselves represent the major exceptions to this statement.

22-27
A sense of failure and fear of criticism is a cause of pain in your life. As you reflect on many of your previous decisions, you probably will find that you can relate many of them to this fear. The fear of failure also will affect many of your future decisions unless you act directly to overcome this fear.

16-21
The fear of failure forms a general backdrop to your life. Probably, few days exist in which this fear does not affect you in some way. Unfortunately, this fear robs you of the joy and peace your salvation is meant to bring.

10-15
Experiences of failure dominate your memory. They probably have caused you to experience a great deal of depression. These problems will remain until you take action. In other words, this condition will not simply disappear. You need to experience deep healing in your self-concept, in your relationship with God, and in your relationships with others.

Effects of the Fear of Failure

We interpret situations through our belief system. This results in a cycle of thoughts, feelings, and actions. The key beliefs behind the fear of failure are our self-imposed standards. Fear of failure stems from the false belief, "I must meet certain standards in order to feel good about myself."

✏️ Think of a situation in which your performance did not measure up to the standard you had set for yourself. Try to remember what thoughts and emotions arose because of that situation. What action did you take in response to those emotions? Read the example below; then write your thoughts.

Example:
Situation: I failed to make a sale.
Standard: I must meet my quota to feel good about myself.
Thoughts: I'm a failure. I'll never make my quota. I'll never get promoted. I'll probably be fired any day now.
Emotions: Fear, anger, depression.
Actions: I avoided my boss for three days. I yelled at my wife and kids. I took out my anger on them.

Situation: _____

Standard: _____

Thoughts: _____

Emotions: _____

Actions: _____

✎ **Do you see any of the following patterns at work in your emotions and actions? Check all that apply:**
- ❑ avoiding failure at all costs by only attempting things in which I feel have a limited risk of failure.
- ❑ spending time around those who are not a threat to me.
- ❑ avoiding people who by their greater success make me feel like a failure.
- ❑ feeling angry at those who stand in the way of my meeting my standards and goals.
- ❑ blaming myself or others for my inability to meet my standards.
- ❑ others _____

If we believe that our self-worth is based on our success, we will try at all costs to avoid failure. Most of us have become experts at avoiding failure. We attempt only things in which we are confident of success. We avoid activities in which the risk of failure is too great. We spend time around persons who are not a threat to us. We avoid people who, either by their greater success or by their disapproval, make us feel like failures. We have trained ourselves very well!

Most of us have become experts at avoiding failure.

✎ **Do you have to be successful in order to feel good about yourself?**
❑ Yes   ❑ No

What would you have to be or do to feel like you are a success?

_____

When we evaluate ourselves by our performance, we ultimately lose, no matter how successful we are. As we answer the last question, many of us discover that even reaching our goals would not make us feel successful.

✎ **In the following paragraph underline two additional dangers of living by the lie of performance-based self-worth.**

Meeting certain standards in order to feel good about ourselves also causes us to live a rules-dominated life. We know people who have a set of rules for everything and who always place their attention on their performance. They miss the joy of walking with God. The gospel is about relationships, not regulations. The opposite danger is feeling good about ourselves because we are winning the performance game. We can't afford to mistake this pride for positive self-worth. God can bring about circumstances to stop us from trusting in ourselves.

The gospel is about relationships, not regulations.

God intends to bring us to Himself through prayer and through studying His Word so that we can know, love, and serve Him. Sometimes He will allow us to fail so that we will look to Him instead of to ourselves for our security and significance. Before becoming upset that God would allow you to experience failure, remember that any life less than God intended is a second-class existence. He loves you too much to let you continue to obtain your self-esteem from the empty promise of success.

✎ **What do you think the writer of the verse appearing in the margin meant? Write your own version of the verse:**

_____

It is good for me that I was afflicted, That I may learn Thy statutes.
   –Psalm 119:71

The two dangers that appear in the paragraphs you just read are: a rules-dominated life and pride in our seeming success. My own version of the psalm read: "God loves me so much that He knows I can learn from experiencing my failure and inadequacy. Failure can lead me to the joy of a love and trust relationship with Him."

God's Answer: Justification

Impute means to credit something to one's account. My sins were imputed to Jesus, and His righteousness was imputed to me. God loves us and has provided a solution to the nightmare of the performance trap. That solution is called justification. Someone explained the meaning of justified very simply. God makes me "JUST as IF I'D" never sinned. As a result of Christ's death on the cross, our sins are forgiven, and God has imputed Christ's righteousness to believers. Christ has justified us. Therefore, we are fully pleasing to God. Some people have trouble thinking of themselves as being pleasing to God because they link pleasing so strongly with performance. They tend to be displeased with anything short of perfection in themselves, and they suspect that God has the same standard. The point of justification is that we never can achieve perfection on this earth. Yet God loves us so much that He appointed His Son to pay for our sins. God credited to us His own righteousness, His perfect status before God.

> Therefore having been justified by faith, we have peace with God through our Lord Jesus Christ.
> –Romans 5:1

> There is therefore now no condemnation for those who are in Christ Jesus.
> –Romans 8:1

> . . . but you were washed, but you were sanctified, but you were justified in the name of the Lord Jesus Christ, and in the Spirit of our God.
> –1 Corinthians 6:11

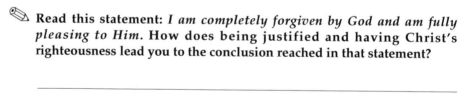 **What does it mean to be justified?** _____

> He made Him who knew no sin to be sin on our behalf, that we might become the righteousness of God in Him.
> –2 Corinthians 5:21

Justification is one of the central messages of Scripture. Second Corinthians 5:21 at left is an example. We have not pulled out a couple of isolated passages to prove a point. Literally hundreds of passages all through the Bible teach this liberating truth. If you are in Christ, God considers you just as holy and righteous as the Lord Jesus Himself because He has taken your sins and placed His righteousness in its place.

Read this statement: *I am completely forgiven by God and am fully pleasing to Him.* **How does being justified and having Christ's righteousness lead you to the conclusion reached in that statement?**

This doesn't mean that our actions don't matter and that we can sin all we want. Our sinful actions, words, and attitudes make the Lord sad, but our status as beloved children remains intact.

Some people may read these statements and become uneasy. They may believe that I am not taking sin seriously. As you will see, I am not minimizing the destructive nature of sin. I simply am trying to make sure we see Christ's payment on the cross as very, very important.

Visualize two ledgers, like the ones appearing on the next page. On one is a list of all your sins; on the other, a list of the righteousness of Christ. In the left column write your name and list some of your sins.

144   Step 7

All _____'s (your name) Sins	All Christ's Righteousness

God transferred our sin to Christ and His righteousness to us.

Now go back to the right column and list some of Christ's wonderful characteristics, such as His love, faithfulness, holiness, and kindness. Now exchange names on the ledgers. Write your name in place of Christ's and write His name in place of yours. This represents an example of justification: transferring our sin to Christ and His righteousness to us. In 1 Corinthians 5:21 Paul wrote "He (God) made Him (Jesus) who knew no sin to be sin on our behalf, that we might become the righteousness of God in Him."

> **Key Concept for Lesson 2**
> I am completely forgiven by God and am fully pleasing to Him.

✎ Please pray and ask God how this concept you just read can apply in your life. Now please review this lesson. What has God shown you that you can use?

_____

LESSON 3

The Approval Addict

We humbly ask God to renew our minds so that our codependent patterns can be transformed into patterns of righteousness.

> *For am I now seeking the favor of men, or of God? Or am I striving to please men? If I were still trying to please men, I would not be a bondservant of Christ.*
>
> –Galatians 1:10

Key Concept:
I am totally accepted by God.

Living by the false belief that I must be approved by certain others to feel good about myself causes fear of rejection. We cannot be free to serve Christ as long as this fear makes us conform our attitudes and actions to others' expectations. Take the test that follows to determine how strongly you fear rejection.

Fear of Rejection Test

✎ Read each of the statements below. Then, from the top of the test, choose the term that best describes your response. Put in the blank beside each statement the number above that term you chose.

1	2	3	4
Always	Sometimes	Seldom	Never

_____ 1. When I sense that someone might reject me, I become anxious.
_____ 2. I spend lots of time analyzing why someone was critical or sarcastic to me or ignored me.
_____ 3. I am uncomfortable around those who are different from me.
_____ 4. It bothers me when someone is unfriendly to me.
_____ 5. I am basically shy and unsocial.
_____ 6. I am critical of others.
_____ 7. I find myself trying to impress others.
_____ 8. I become depressed when someone criticizes me.
_____ 9. I try to determine what people think of me.
_____ 10. I don't understand people and what motivates them.

_____ Total (Add up the numbers you have placed in the blanks.)

My score means—

Interpreting Your Score
If your score is...

34-40
God apparently has given you a very strong appreciation for His love and unconditional acceptance. You seem to be free of the fear of rejection that plagues most people. (Some exceptions exist: Some people who score this high either are greatly deceived or have turned off their emotions as a way to suppress pain. Examine your heart and talk to your group members to see if these exceptions apply to you.)

28-33
The fear of rejection controls your responses rarely or only in certain situations. Again, the only major exceptions are those who are not honest with themselves.

22-27
Emotional problems you experience may relate to a sense of rejection. Upon reflection you probably will relate many of your previous decisions to this fear. The fear of rejection also will affect many of your future decisions unless you take direct action to overcome that fear.

16-21
The fear of rejection forms a general backdrop to your life. Probably few days go by in which this fear does not affect you in some way. Unfortunately, this robs you of the joy and peace your salvation is meant to bring.

10-15
Experiences of rejection dominate your memory and probably cause you to experience a great deal of depression. These problems will persist until you take definitive action. In other words, this condition will not simply disappear; time alone cannot heal your pain. You need to experience deep healing in your self-concept, in your relationship with God, and in your relationships with others.

> **I felt rejection when—**
>
> _____
> _____
> _____
>
> **How I felt when it happened:**
>
> _____
> _____
> _____
> _____

In the margin list a specific instance in which a relative, friend, or boss withheld approval or used criticism, silence, or sarcasm to make you do what this person wanted you to do. Then describe how you felt in this situation.

 We need great courage to face the results of fear of rejection in our lives. In the following paragraph circle the words or phrases that describe patterns you identify in your life:

When we have felt the pain of rejection, our fear of going through it again can affect us profoundly. Sometimes people see emotional pain as a sign of weakness, and since we have not learned how to deal with it, we avoid it. We deny our pain by stuffing or ignoring it. To try to gain approval, we do tasks we hate. Some of us can't say no for fear others will reject us. Others of us become passive. We withdraw from people and avoid decisions or actions which others might criticize. Our goal usually is to avoid rejection by not doing anything which might be objectionable.

Evaluating our self-worth by what we and others think about our performance leads us to believe that any time our performance is unacceptable, we are unacceptable as well.

 Do you identify in your life any of the following results of fear of rejection? Check all that apply:

- ❏ being easily manipulated
- ❏ being hypersensitive to criticism
- ❏ defensiveness
- ❏ hostility toward others who disagree with me
- ❏ superficial relationships
- ❏ exaggerating or minimizing the truth to impress people
- ❏ shyness
- ❏ passivity
- ❏ nervous breakdown
- ❏ other _____

Virtually all of us have made the following sentence a part of our belief system. We hold to it with amazing strength:

> *I must have acceptance, respect, and approval in order to have self-worth.*

This is the basic false belief behind all peer pressure. Several of the characteristics in the checklist and paragraph above have affected my life. Underlying all of them is the idea in the sentence above. That sentence is so powerful because it is partly true. I do need acceptance from outside myself. We make the mistake of trying to get this acceptance from people who don't have what we need and wouldn't give it if they did. Marty's mother was cold, aloof, and critical, yet Marty exhausted himself trying to get his mother to praise his accomplishments on his job. Every year when his mother visited him at Christmas, Marty took his mother to his office and showed her his latest project, but his mother looked bored and disinterested.

We try to get acceptance from people who don't have what we need and wouldn't give it if they did.

Marty was miserable constantly because he was unable to get his mother's affirmation. We need to learn to get our acceptance, respect, and approval from our loving Lord and then from healthy believers.

God's Answer: Reconciliation

reconcile-v. to restore to friendship or harmony; to settle or resolve something (Webster's)

namely, that God was in Christ reconciling the world to Himself, not counting their trespasses against them, and He has committed to us the word of reconciliation.
—2 Corinthians 5:19

And although you were formerly alienated and hostile in mind, engaged in evil deeds, yet He has now reconciled you in His fleshly body through death, in order to present you before Him holy and blameless and beyond reproach.
—Colossians 1:21-22

He saved us, not on the basis of deeds which we have done in righteousness, but according to His mercy.
—Titus 3:5

God's answer to the pain of rejection is **reconciliation**. Christ died for our sins and restored us to a proper relationship with God. We are both acceptable to Him and accepted by Him. We are not rejected! We are His. The verse from 2 Corinthians at left explains this.

When God chose to redeem us He did not go part way. He did not make us partially righteous due to our poor performance. The blood of Christ is sufficient to pay for all sin. Because of His blood, we are holy and righteous before God, even in the midst of sin. This does not minimize the destructiveness of sin. It glorifies the sacrifice of Christ. We are restored to a complete and pure love relationship with God.

We may neglect this teaching more than we do any other in Scripture. The passage from Colossians at left says it plainly. Relish those last words. God sees us as holy and blameless and beyond reproach at this very moment. This is not merely a reference to our future standing; it describes our present status as well. We are totally accepted by God. God received us into a loving, intimate, personal relationship the moment we placed our faith in Christ. We are united with God in an eternal and unbreakable bond (Romans 8:38-39). Knowing that no sin can make a Christian unacceptable to God is faith in a pledge sealed with the Holy Spirit (Ephesians 1:14).

Since our relationship with God was bought entirely by the blood of Christ, no amount of good works can make us more acceptable to Him. Read what Titus 3:5, which appears in the margin, says. Because Christ has reconciled us to God, we can experience the incredible truth that we are totally accepted by and acceptable to God.

✎ **Review the last two paragraphs and look for reasons to thank God for reconciling you to Himself. Write a prayer thanking Him for totally accepting you.**

_____

_____

_____

As in the last lesson, this truth is a central theme of Scripture. What can we do when we have failed or when someone disapproves of us? A practical way of summarizing the truth we've examined is:

> "It would be nice if _____ (my boss liked me, I could fix the refrigerator, my complexion were clear, James had picked me up on time, or _____), but I'm still deeply loved, completely forgiven, fully pleasing, totally accepted and complete in Christ."

This statement doesn't mean that we won't feel pain or anger. We can be honest about our feelings. The statement simply is a quick way to gain God's perspective on what we experience. It is not magic, but it enables us to reflect on the truth. We can apply this truth in every difficult situation, whether it involves someone's disapproval, our own failure to accomplish something, or another person's failure.

✎ On the lines below, write the following statement: **I am deeply loved, completely forgiven, fully pleasing, totally accepted, and complete in Christ.**

_____

_____

_____

_____

Now go back and read the statement aloud three times. Patti's sponsor assigned her to look in the mirror and read that truth to herself each day for a month. Patti said it was the most difficult thing she ever did. Today Patti gratefully acknowledges that this statement was a key to changing her life.

⇨ Memorize the truth in the above statement and begin to apply it in your situations and relationships.

Key Concept for Lesson 3
I am totally accepted by God.

✎ Please pray and ask God how this concept can apply in your life. Now please review this lesson. What has God shown you that you can use?

_____

_____

_____

LESSON 4

The Blame Game

We humbly ask God to renew our minds so that our codependent patterns can be transformed into patterns of righteousness.

> *He has not dealt with us according to our sins, Nor rewarded us according to our iniquities.*
> —Psalm 103:10

Key Concept:
I am deeply loved by God.

The false belief that those who fail, including me, are unworthy of love and deserve to be punished, is at the root of our fear of punishment and our tendency to punish others.

Take the following test to determine how much this lie influences you.

Fear of Punishment/Punishing Others Test

✎ Read each of the following statements. Then, from the top of the test, choose the term that best describes your response. Put in the blank beside each statement the number above that term you chose.

1	2	3	4
Always	Sometimes	Seldom	Never

_____ 1. I fear what God might do to me.
_____ 2. After I fail, I worry about God's response.
_____ 3. When I see someone in a difficult situation, I wonder what he or she did to deserve that situation.
_____ 4. When something goes wrong, I tend to think that God must be punishing me.
_____ 5. I am very hard on myself when I fail.
_____ 6. I find myself wanting to blame others when they fail.
_____ 7. I get angry with God when someone who is immoral or dishonest prospers.
_____ 8. I am determined to make sure others know about it when I see them doing wrong.
_____ 9. I tend to focus on the faults and failures of others.
_____ 10. God seems harsh to me.
_____ Total (Add the numbers you have placed in the blanks.)

My score means—

Interpreting Your Score
If your score is. . .

34-40
God apparently has given you a very strong appreciation for His unconditional love and acceptance. You seem to be freed from the fear of punishment that plagues most people. (Some exceptions exist: Some people who score this high either are greatly deceived or have turned off their emotions as a way to suppress pain. Examine your heart and talk to your group members to see if these exceptions apply to you.)

28-33
The fear of punishment and the compulsion to punish others control your responses rarely or only in certain situations. Again, the only exceptions are those who are not honest about how strongly these matters affect them.

22-27
When you experience emotional problems, they may have to do with a fear of punishment or to an inner urge to punish others. Upon reflection you probably can relate many of your previous responses to this fear. The fear of punishment and/or the determination to punish others also will affect many of your future responses unless you take direct action to overcome these tendencies.

16-21
The fear of punishment forms a general backdrop to your life. Probably few days go by that the fear of punishment and the tendency to blame others do

not affect you. Unfortunately, this robs you of the joy and peace your salvation is meant to bring.

10-15
Experiences of punishment dominate your memory. You probably have suffered a great deal of depression as a result. This condition will not simply disappear; time alone cannot heal your pain. You need to experience deep healing in your self-concept, in your relationship with God, and in your relationships with others.

The Fear of Punishment and Tendency to Punish Others

A wife spent her hour in the counselor's office attempting to show that a marital problem was all her husband's fault. When it was time for her husband's appointment, he tried to prove that she was to blame. People often are more interested in avoiding blame and pinning it on someone else than they are in solving problems.

 Using the example of the couple above, explain the meaning of the slogan in the margin.

_____

_____

> *An addict is someone who would rather be in control than be happy.*

We seem to believe that we deserve to be blamed for our shortcomings and that others deserve the same. You may have written that we would rather be in control by proving something isn't our fault than by solving the problems and have the pain taken away.

 Pretend that you are captain of the school debate team. Your subject is "Why blaming doesn't work." Draw from the paragraphs below and from your own knowledge and experience to list all the facts you can to support your argument. As you read, mark items you can use.

We have been conditioned either to accept personal blame or to blame somebody else when our performance is unsatisfactory. You may think that this false belief does not affect you at all—but it probably does. Do you generally have an urge to find out who is at fault when something fails?

Rather than evaluating our problems objectively, we tend to defend ourselves. We sometimes do this by attacking others. The more we criticize other people, the more defensive they become, and the less likely they are to admit their errors, especially to us. Criticism can lead to a counterattack from both sides, and pretty soon it's like a volleyball game, with each person intensifying the pace while returning blame to the other person's side.

The blame debate

Points for the debate—Why blaming doesn't work: _____

_____

_____

_____

Step 7 151

Tom's story

Some of us have learned to accept blame without defending ourselves. Under his wife's constant condemnation Tom was becoming an emotional zombie. Instead of fighting back he kept thinking, "Yes, Suzanne's right. I am an incompetent fool." He was like a worn-out punching bag. I listed some of the following as arguments why blaming doesn't work:
- It leads to defensiveness.
- It builds walls instead of solving problems.
- It creates more denial because I can't risk being wrong.

Both self-inflicted punishment and the compulsion to punish others result from the false belief: Those who fail are unworthy of love and deserve to be blamed and condemned.

God's Answer: Propitiation

propitiation–n. describes what happened when Christ, through His death, became the means by which God's wrath was satisfied and God's mercy was granted to the sinner who believes on Christ

God's plan for us is centered in the cross. At the cross, God poured out His wrath against sin. To understand His plan we must understand what **propitiation** means. Propitiation is difficult to define because it brings together four concepts:
1. God is holy.
2. His holiness leads to the necessity of justice—His actions must be expressions of justice, He must punish sin.
3. God lovingly chose to provide a substitute—His beloved Son took the punishment our sins deserved.
4. As a result, God's justice is satisfied—no more punishment is required.

✎ **Write the number of the appropriate part of propitiation in the blanks following the parts of the following paragraphs. I have done the first one for you.**

a. # __1__ The problem with our sinfulness is that God is absolutely holy, pure, and perfect. Absolutely nothing is unholy in Him.
b. # _____ Therefore, since God is holy, He can't overlook or compromise with sin.
c. # _____ It took one sin to separate Adam from God. For God to condone even "one" sin would instantly defile His holiness.
d. # _____ The Father did not escape witnessing His Son's mistreatment: the mocking, the scourging, and the cross. He could have spoken and ended the whole ordeal, yet He kept silent.
e. # _____ Confronted with the suffering of His Son, God chose to let it continue so that we could be saved. What an expression of love!
f. # _____ God loves you, and He enjoys revealing His love to you. He enjoys being loved by you, but He knows you can love Him only if you are experiencing His love for you.
g. # _____ Propitiation means that His wrath has been removed and that you are deeply loved!
h. # _____ God is holy, and therefore He must punish sin. But He loves us and provided a substitute to take the punishment we deserve.

Jesus has completely satisfied the righteousness of God so God's only response to us is in love. The answers are: a. 1, b. 1, c. 2, d. 2, e. 3, f. 3, g. 3, h. 4.

✎ **Read the verse at left. Does the Father love you?** ❑ Yes ❑ No
How do you know He loves you?

By this the love of God was manifested in us, that God has sent His only begotten Son into the world so that we might live through Him. In this is love, not that we loved God, but that He loved us and sent His Son to be the propitiation for our sins.
–1 John 4:9-10

Do you feel loved? ❏ Yes ❏ No

Explain _____

Try to recall an experience in which you felt someone else loved you. That person cared about you and wanted to be with you. You didn't have to perform; just being you was enough. The thought of that person selecting you to love was intoxicating. He or she loved you, and that love was soothing to you and satisfied many of your inner longings. If a person's love can make us feel this way, consider how much greater fulfillment the heavenly Father's love can bring. We can't truly appreciate the Father's love unless we realize that it goes beyond any experience of being loved by another man or woman.

Many of us have a distorted concept of the heavenly Father. We believe that God is thrilled when we accept Christ and are born into His family. But many of us also believe that He is proud of us for only as long as we perform well, and that the better we perform, the happier He is with us. In reality, as the Scripture at left indicates, not a moment goes by that God isn't thinking loving thoughts about us. We are His children, and we are special to Him because of Christ! Propitiation, then, means Jesus Christ satisfied the Father's righteous condemnation of sin by His death. The Scriptures give only one reason to explain this incredible fact: God loves you!

> Many, O LORD my God, are the wonders which Thou hast done, And Thy thoughts toward us.
> –Psalm 40:5

Applying the Principle to Others

The more we understand God's love and forgiveness, the more we will be willing and able to forgive others. If we think about it, the things that others do to us are unimportant compared to our sin of rebellion against God that He graciously has forgiven. This is why Paul encouraged the Ephesian Christians to forgive each other just as God in Christ also has forgiven you—completely and willingly (Ephesians 4:32).

✎ **Do you have trouble forgiving some sins, or even personality differences, in others? If so, list them and confess to God your lack of forgiveness.**

_____

_____

How do these compare to your sins that deserved God's wrath but that received the payment of Christ's substitutionary death?

Key Concept for Lesson 4
I am deeply loved by God.

✎ **Stop and pray. Ask God how this concept can apply in your life. Now please review this lesson. What has God shown you that you can use?**

_____

_____

LESSON 5

Shame

We humbly ask God to renew our minds so that our codependent patterns can be transformed into patterns of righteousness.

> *And now, little children, abide in Him, so that when He appears, we may have confidence and not shrink away from Him in shame at His coming.*
> –1 John 2:28

Key Concept:
I am complete in Christ.

Read again the story of James, the business executive, on page 137. When we base our self-worth on performance, our failures and dissatisfaction with our personal appearance lead us to a fourth false belief: "I am what I am. I cannot change. I am hopeless." This lie binds people to the hopeless pessimism of poor self-esteem. Take the following test to establish how strongly you experience shame.

Shame Test

 Read each of the following statements. Then, from the top of the test, choose the term that best describes your response. Put in the blank beside each statement the number above the term you chose.

1	2	3	4
Always	Sometimes	Seldom	Never

_____ 1. I often think about past failures or experiences of rejection that have occurred in my life.

_____ 2. I cannot recall certain things about my past without experiencing strong, painful emotions (such as guilt, shame, or anger.)

_____ 3. I seem to make the same mistakes over and over again.

_____ 4. I want to change certain aspects of my character, but I don't believe I ever can successfully do so.

_____ 5. I feel inferior.

_____ 6. I cannot accept certain aspects of my appearance.

_____ 7. I am generally disgusted with myself.

_____ 8. I feel that certain experiences basically have ruined my life.

_____ 9. I perceive of myself as an immoral person.

_____ 10. I feel I have lost the opportunity to experience a complete and wonderful life.

_____ Total (Add the numbers you have placed in the blanks.)

My score means—

Interpreting Your Score
If your score is. . .

34-40
God apparently has given you a very strong appreciation for His love and unconditional acceptance. You seem to be free of the shame that plagues most people. (Some exceptions exist: Some people who score this high either are greatly deceived or have turned off their emotions as a way to suppress pain. Examine your heart and talk to your group members to see if these exceptions apply to you.)

28-33
Shame controls your responses rarely or only in certain situations. Again, the only major exceptions are those who are not honest with themselves.

22-27
Emotional problems you experience may relate to a sense of shame. When you think about some of your previous decisions, you probably will relate many of them to your feelings of worthlessness. Feelings of low self-esteem may affect many of your future decisions unless you take direct action to overcome those feelings.

16-21
Shame forms a generally negative backdrop to your life. Probably, few days go by when shame does not affect you in some way. Unfortunately, this robs you of the joy and peace your salvation was meant to bring.

10-15
Experiences of shame dominate your memory and probably have caused you to experience a great deal of depression. These problems will remain unless you take definite action. In other words, this condition will not simply disappear one day; time alone cannot heal your pain. You need to experience deep healing in your self-concept, in your relationship with God, and in your relationships with others.

Effects of Shame

Shame comes from our own negative estimate of 1) our past performance; and/or 2) our physical appearance. Shame leads to the false belief: *I am what I am. I cannot change. I am hopeless.*

Shame often results from instances of neglect or abuse and then is reinforced by failures in our performance or "flaws" in our appearance. Even when others don't know of our failure, we assume their opinion of us is poor, and we adopt what we think their opinion might be.

✎ **Study the paragraph above and check all of the following statements that are part of the paragraph:**

❑ 1. My perception that I am physically imperfect adds to my sense of shame.
❑ 2. Feeling shamed becomes a habit so that I feel others disapprove of me even when they really approve.
❑ 3. My shame will decrease if I can improve my performance enough.
❑ 4. Shame may begin from being ignored or mistreated.
❑ 5. Christians are wrong to feel shame.
❑ 6. The feeling that I have failed feeds my sense of shame.
❑ 7. The only way to be rid of shame is experiencing love and acceptance.

The paragraph makes clear four critical issues concerning shame. Shame comes from not being loved and accepted—usually very early in life. The feeling that our performance and appearance is flawed feeds our sense of shame. Once shame has become our habit, we shame ourselves. Answers 3, 5, and 7 were not in the paragraph. Answer 3 is a lie because working harder will not remove my feeling of shame. Answer 5 is a more damaging lie; you

> **When I experienced shame:**
> _____
> _____
> _____
> _____

cannot get rid of your shame by dumping still more shame on yourself. Answer 7 is the truth. The only way to change the habit of shaming myself is to replace it with the love and acceptance of the Lord and from healthy believers. The answer simply wasn't in the paragraph. In the margin box describe a time when you've experienced shame. We so easily fall for the performance lie that "If only I could make myself feel ashamed enough, I would be motivated to succeed." The truth is that the shame fuels our compulsions and assures our failures.

Shame and Performance

If we base our self-worth on our performance long enough, our past behavior eventually becomes the sole basis of our worth. We see ourselves with certain character qualities and flaws because that's the way we always have been. We then have included Satan's lie in our belief system: "I always must be what I have been and live with whatever self-worth I have, because that's just me."

We then risk going to one of two extremes. Some act out our low self-worth through false humility and become self-abusers. Others go to the opposite extreme and become arrogant. We may think that humility is belittling ourselves, but true humility is an accurate appraisal of our worth in Christ.

Shame and Appearance

Another aspect of poor self-concept relates to personal appearance. Most of us have some aspect of our appearance that we wish we could change but can't. We may not only base our self-worth on our appearance, but we may tend to base our acceptance of others on how they look—even on the color of their skin. We can be very cruel when we accept or reject others based on their appearance.

> **A time I've compared my appearance with that of others:**
> _____
> _____
> _____
> _____

Are you angry with God for the way He made you? Do you compare and rank your appearance with that of others? In the margin box describe a time when you've done this. If you do, at some point in your life you will suffer because someone prettier, stronger, or more handsome always will be around. Even if you are beautiful or handsome, you still will suffer because you will be afraid of losing your good looks—the basis of your self-worth. If we insist on valuing our worth by our appearance and performance, sooner or later God will graciously allow us to see the futility of that struggle. God created our need for a sense of significance. However, He knows we will never come to Him until we find the importance of people's opinions to be empty and hopeless. At that point, we can turn to Him and find comfort and encouragement in the truths of His Word.

Jesus answered and said to him, "Truly, truly I say to you, unless one is born again, he cannot see the kingdom of God."
     –John 3:3

Therefore, if any man is in Christ, he is a new creature; the old things passed away; behold, new things have come.
     –2 Corinthians 5:17

put on the new self, which in the likeness of God has been created in righteousness and holiness of the truth.
     –Ephesians 4:24

God's Answer: Regeneration

Regeneration is the renewing work of the Holy Spirit by which a person literally becomes a new creation. Our regeneration occurred at the instant of our conversion to Christ. In John 3:3 which appears at left, Jesus called this regeneration a new birth. The Holy Spirit has been joined to our human spirit. This has formed a new spiritual entity. A new birth has produced a new being. Read more about this in the second and third verses at left.

Satan victimizes us with lies. We not only can recognize and reject them but replace them with the truth of God's Word. We can replace the self-defeating message of shame with the life-giving truth of regeneration.

> **Key Concept for Lesson 5**
> I am complete in Christ.

 Please pray and ask God how this concept can apply in your life. Now please review this lesson. What has God shown you that you can use?

LESSON 6

Key Concept:
I can cooperate with God as He renews my mind.

Making new paths

Taking the Step

We humbly ask God to renew our minds so that our codependent patterns can be transformed into patterns of righteousness.

Finally, brethren, whatever is true, whatever is honorable, whatever is right, whatever is pure, whatever is lovely, whatever is of good repute, if there is any excellence and if anything worthy of praise, let your mind dwell on these things.

–Philippians 4:8

In this Step you examined in detail the effects of the key false beliefs. You have considered the truths needed for recovery. Now you can do the work necessary to apply these truths. That work includes: making a truth card, exposing ungodly thoughts, and identifying and stopping the bargaining process.

Speaker and author Earnie Larsen compared codependent habits to a ravine washed out by desert rains. For years we have thought, felt, and acted in certain ways. When the rains fall, the water naturally runs in the same channel. The false beliefs are the channels for our guilt, shame, and dysfunctional behaviors. Now we want to change our behavior, thinking, and feeling.

When the pressure builds up, we naturally will fall back into the old channels. We can decide what is more healthy behavior and begin to scratch out a new channel. When the rains come, much of the water still will run in the old ditches, but with time and persistence, we will make new paths.¹

 We begin to create that new channel by feeding our minds with the truth. Here is an exercise in how to do just that: Make a Truth Card.

A simple three-by-five-inch card can be a key factor in helping you base your self-worth on the liberating truths of the Scriptures. To make the Truth Card, use a three-by-five-inch card. On the front, write the following truths and their corresponding verses from Scripture.

Step 7 157

- I am deeply loved by God (1 John 4:9-10).
- I am completely forgiven and fully pleasing to God (Romans 5:1).
- I am totally accepted by God (Colossians 1:21-22).
- I am a new creation, absolutely complete in Christ (2 Corinthians 5:17).

On the back of the card, write out the four false beliefs.

Carry this card with you at all times. For one month, each time you do a routine activity, like drinking your morning cup of coffee or tea, look at the front side and slowly meditate on each phrase. The Scripture at left tells us how we are to meditate on God's Word. Thank the Lord for making you into a person with these qualities. By doing this exercise for the next month, you can develop a habit of remembering that you are deeply loved, completely forgiven, fully pleasing, totally accepted, and complete in Christ. If you have not already done so, memorize the supporting verses listed on the card. Look in your Bible for other verses that support these truths and commit them to memory. Doing this will establish God's Word as the basis for these truths. Also memorize the false beliefs. The more familiar you are with these lies, the more you will be able to recognize them in your thoughts. Then, as you recognize them, you can more readily replace them with the truths of God's Word.

Let the word of Christ richly dwell within you, with all wisdom teaching and admonishing one another with psalms and hymns and spiritual songs, singing with thankfulness in your hearts to God.
–Colossians 3:16

Exposing Ungodly Thoughts

Habitual lies

One reason the lies we believe are so destructive is because they are habitual rather than conscious. We have a running conversation with ourselves, often without even realizing it. When we make a mistake we begin to call ourselves names. Our thoughts reveal what we really believe, yet it is difficult for most of us to be objective in our thinking simply because we haven't trained ourselves to be. We usually let any and every thought run its course in our minds without analyzing its worth.

We need to develop the skill of identifying thoughts that reflect Satan's deceptions. Then we can reject those lies and replace them with scriptural truth.

✎ **As a first step in developing this skill, write down your thoughts in response to the four truths we've examined. For example, you might respond to the truth that you are fully pleasing to God by thinking, "No, I'm not! I mess up all the time, and to be fully pleasing, I'd have to be perfect!" When we see it written out, we more easily recognize that response as a lie.**

I am deeply loved by God: _____

_____

_____

I am completely forgiven and fully pleasing to God: _____

_____

_____

I am totally accepted by God: _____

_____

_____

I am complete in Christ: _____

_____

_____

Thoughts that contradict these truths are lies. Reject them and replace them with passages of Scripture to reinforce the truth in your mind. Below are some passages on which to reflect:

> **Propitiation:** Matthew 18:21-35; Luke 7:36-50; Romans 3:25; 8:1-8; Colossians 3:12-14; Hebrews 2:17
>
> **Justification:** Romans 3:19-24; 4:4-5; 5:1-11; Titus 2:11-14; 3:4-7
>
> **Reconciliation:** John 15:14-16; Romans 5:8-10; Ephesians 2:11-18
>
> **Regeneration:** 2 Corinthians 5:17; Galatians 5:16-24; Ephesians 2:4-5; 4:22-24; Colossians 3:5-17

Identifying and Changing Bargaining Behavior

Christy's dilemma

When people see how codependency affects their lives, they often respond by trying to bargain with themselves, their family, and God. After learning about dysfunctional families, Christy quickly saw those painful effects in her own life. She asked a friend, "How can I get my father to love me?" Her friend explained, "Christy, it's not up to you to get your father to love you. It's up to you to be secure in the Lord, whether or not your father ever loves you."

Bargaining takes many shapes and forms, but its goal is to get other people to change by offering some change in ourselves. We say, "I'll be a better husband to her," or "I won't nag him anymore, then he'll love me the way I want to be loved." We can come up with all kinds of "deals" to get people to love us, but bargaining still is not totally objective. The responsibility still remains on us alone, and we are still believing the best about the other person. Believing the best of others usually is good and right. But when a person by months and years of irresponsible, manipulative behavior proves he or she is emotionally unhealthy, then believing the best is naive and foolish.

An act of worship

Bargaining expresses hope—hope that the other person will change and give us the love and worth that we need. But it is a false hope. Observing objectively leads us to a painful but honest conclusion: We need to give up the vain hope that the other person will change and give us what we need. Giving up doesn't sound very godly, but it is. Giving up reflects reality. It is an act of abandoning the idol of pleasing others and being accepted and loved by them as the way to win self-worth. Actually, it is an act of worship to the Lord.

The Awkwardness of Change

Many of us will experience wide swings in feelings and behavior during these early stages of growth. As we take the cap off our emotions for perhaps the first time, we may feel more hurt, anger, and fear than we ever thought possible. We may become afraid of how intense our emotions are, and we may put the cap back on until we have more courage to experiment again with these feelings. We also may feel more joy and freedom and love than ever before. We may cry for the first time in years. These wide swings in mood and behavior are understandable. Don't try to clamp them; instead, realize that surges of emotion are perfectly understandable for someone who has repressed them for years. Be patient.

Expect wide mood swings

Key Concept for Lesson 6
I can cooperate with God as He renews my mind.

✎ Please pray and ask God how this concept can apply in your life. Now please review this lesson. What has God shown you that you can use?

_____

_____

✎ Please review this Step. Pray and ask God to identify the Scriptures or principles that are particularly important for your life. Underline them. Then respond to the following:

Restate Step 7 in your own words:

_____

_____

What do you have to gain by practicing this Step in your life?

_____

_____

Reword your summary into a prayer of response to God. Thank Him for this Step, and affirm your commitment to Him.

_____

_____

Memorize this Step's memory verse:
And do not be conformed to this world, but be transformed by the renewing of your mind, that you may prove what the will of God is, that which is good and acceptable and perfect.

–Romans 12:2

Notes
[1] Earnie Larsen, *Stage II Recovery*, E. Larsen Enterprises, Inc., 1990.

STEP 8

Choosing to Forgive

We make a list of all persons who have hurt us and choose to forgive them. We also make a list of all persons we have harmed, and we become willing to make amends to them all.

Step 8 Into Codependency

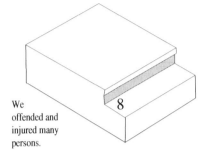

We offended and injured many persons.

Step 8 Out of Codependency

We make a list of all persons we had harmed, including ourselves.

LETTING GOD FILL THE GAPS

Karen felt it was her responsibility to rescue Jack, a co-worker who always was depressed. She put in a good word for him with his boss and spent a lot of unnecessary overtime helping him with his projects so he would look good to the company. Daily she prayed for Jack and his well-being. But the more Karen did for Jack, the more he seemed to abuse her. He made critical remarks about Karen to her co-workers, snubbed her in meetings, and repeatedly canceled social engagements with her.

As she studied about how to untangle from this destructive relationship, Karen learned to detach from Jack to give herself space to learn to relate to him in a more healthy way. To a friend who was helping her in recovery, Karen confided, "I can't even pray for Jack anymore. I know what I'm doing is right, but shouldn't I be able to pray for him?" The friend helped her understand the situation more clearly. "That's OK, Karen. God can take care of Jack without your prayers. For now, He wants you to concentrate on detaching and getting your security from Him. Later, you can start praying for Jack again." Read on the following pages about what happens when we detach.

Owe nothing to anyone except to love one another; for he who loves his neighbor has fulfilled the law.

–Romans 13:8

Overview for Step 8

Lesson 1: Forgiveness, Pathway to Freedom
Goal: You will explain the parts of genuine forgiveness necessary to deal with an abuser.
Lesson 2: Dealing with Our "Other(s)"
Goal: You will describe key principles for dealing with others as you continue in your recovery.
Lesson 3: Faulty Concepts of Forgiveness
Goal: You will describe some defective concepts of forgiveness.
Lesson 4: Reasons for Not Forgiving
Goal: You will evaluate some of the common reasons for withholding forgiveness.
Lesson 5: Results of Not Forgiving
Goal: You will motivate yourself to make amends as you describe the harm unmade amends cause in your life.
Lesson 6: Preparing to Make Our Amends
Goal: You will write an amends list.

LESSON 1

Forgiveness, Pathway to Freedom

We make a list of all persons who have hurt us and choose to forgive them. We also make a list of all persons we have harmed, and we become willing to make amends to them all.

And just as you want people to treat you, treat them in the same way.
—Luke 6:31

Key Concept:
True forgiveness is based upon honesty—about the offense and about myself.

The Two Key Components of Forgiveness

 Study the following paragraph carefully. Then in the exercise below select the statement that most clearly conveys the paragraph's idea.

We can apply the truth of God's love, forgiveness, and acceptance only as deeply as we have experienced the reality of the pain involved. If we only have allowed ourselves to experience superficial feelings of hurt, then we will experience only superficial love, comfort, and forgiveness, though we may think that this level is all that exists.

Check the appropriate summary statement:
❑ 1. We cannot be forgiven until we have admitted fully the seriousness of our offenses.
❑ 2. We cannot fully experience the benefits of forgiveness until we have recognized fully our pain.
❑ 3. We cannot fully extend forgiveness to others until we have acknowledged fully the seriousness of their offenses.

Beyond the surface

Cindy told me, "I'm confused about forgiveness. I've forgiven my father for all he did to me. I've worked through all of that, but I still hate him. I know I've forgiven him. What's wrong with me?" As she talked, I learned that Cindy's father had neglected and verbally abused her. I told Cindy that we often forgive in stages. "Your forgiveness of your father will be only as deep as is your experience of the pain he has caused you," I told her. "You've probably repressed a lot of pain over the years, and that's why you're confused about forgiveness."

I told Cindy that two things are necessary for a person to forgive others genuinely. The person first needs to experience the pain the offense caused. Others' wrongs toward us hurt! If we repress those hurt feelings, it confuses our efforts to forgive. We will think we have forgiven, but we still will have resentment toward the source of our pain. If instead we are open and honest about our pain, we will know exactly why we are extending forgiveness. The correct answer to the exercise above is number 2. In the margin box describe the first thing a person must do to experience the relief of genuinely forgiving.

> **The first thing we must do to experience the relief of forgiving:**
> _____
> _____
> _____

In the psalms David modeled this honesty about his hurt and anger. Christ didn't deny His own feelings either. He experienced anger with those who rejected Him, fear at crucifixion, and hurt that His followers abandoned Him. We first must be honest about our feelings. We cannot forgive while we minimize the seriousness of the hurt and offense. We can remember that our forgiving others depends on our progress in seeing their offenses objectively.

> **God shows me these areas of unforgiveness—**
>
> _____
> _____
> _____

➮ Stop now and pray. Ask God to reveal any areas of incomplete forgiveness in your life that occur because you repressed the pain of the offense. Pray for the courage to face the pain so that you can get to true forgiveness with its relief and joy. Then in the margin box write the areas of unforgiveness God shows you.

A second aspect of forgiveness is to appreciate deeply the forgiveness we have through Jesus Christ. The more we realize that God has forgiven us completely for our bitterness, pride, malice, and neglect of others, the more able and motivated we'll be to forgive those who have hurt us. Read about this in the Scripture appearing below in the margin.

✎ **Explain how appreciating what Christ has done for you will help you to forgive.**

_____
_____
_____

> And be kind to one another, tender-hearted, forgiving each other, just as God in Christ also has forgiven you.
> –Ephesians 4:32

We benefit when we forgive those who have hurt us. We cannot grow unless we forgive. We can forgive when are are honest about how much we hurt and when we experience deeply the forgiveness of Christ. The Lord is gracious. He does not force us to experience all our hurt at once because He knows we would be overwhelmed. Instead He shows us a little at a time. We forgive as much as we can as soon as we can.

✎ **Check all the things you need to do to gain freedom in the area of forgiveness.**

❑ 1. Honestly admit my bitterness and lack of forgiveness.
❑ 2. Pray to identify those people I have forgiven incompletely.
❑ 3. Become objective about just how much I have hurt or am hurting.
❑ 4. Spend some time meditating on God's great forgiveness of me.
❑ 5. Talk with a friend, counselor, or mentor about my need and desire to forgive completely.

How Do I Deal with My Abuser?

The most difficult part

One of the most pressing issues for the person emerging from the darkness of codependency is: "How do I deal with the one who has hurt, neglected, used, and condemned me?" Although you already have studied some of the issues we will examine in this Step, we will look at them again here as we answer this major question about how to treat our abusers. The primary issue in dealing with these individuals is idolatry or independence: Will we continue to let a person determine our behavior and thus, be our lord? Or, will we be independent and make our own decisions, including the decision to have healthy boundaries and yet show love to this person?

Many of us have defined love as rescuing, worrying, feeling guilty, complying with manipulation, and pitying the other person. The desire to be accepted and the desire for intimacy have been so strong that we would do *anything* to make that person happy. We've called it love. It's not. It's idolatry. We have

We have allowed a person to be our lord and to determine our thoughts, feelings, words, and actions.

allowed a person to be our lord and to determine our thoughts, feelings, words, and actions. Comments from people who finally are being objective about this matter reveal the depth of this lordship:

Annette lamented: "I've lived to please my father all of my life. He said, 'Jump!' and I said, 'How high?' I got some praise for what I did—enough to keep me jumping, but not enough to give me a sense of security."

Terry remembered: "My mother always could get me to do anything she wanted me to do. She rarely yelled at me, but just with the expressions on her face she could get a powerful message across."

Brad said of his daughter: "I did everything I could do to get her to stop eating. I begged, I threatened, I hid food, I sent her to classes, I screamed at her, I avoided her. I can't tell you how many nights I lay awake trying to think of ways to get her to stop. I thought she was the one who was 'hooked,' but I was an addict, too—an addict to her performance and happiness." Brad looked puzzled at the thought of letting his daughter live with the consequences of her actions. "She needs me. What would happen to her if I didn't help her?" he asked.

✎ **Were the actions of Annette, Terry, and Brad examples of love or of idolatry? Why?**

_____

_____

Therefore also we have as our ambition, whether at home or absent, to be pleasing to Him.
–2 Corinthians 5:9

For am I now seeking the favor of men, or of God? Or am I striving to please men? If I were still trying to please men, I would not be a bond-servant of Christ.
–Galatians 1:10

Only Jesus Christ is worthy of our ultimate affection and obedience. If we put others in His place, and if we try to please others as a means of gaining love and value, then we are committing idolatry. Pleasing Christ is the one worthy ambition, as the verses appearing in the margin indicate. Remember the difference between pleasing people and pleasing Christ. Once we have trusted Christ and accepted His payment for our sins, our identity is secure in Him. Don't try to bargain. Don't try to get that person to give you the love and acceptance you need. Many of us have tried to obtain real love from a parent, child, or mate who simply did not have it to give. We have sought something that did not exist. You can turn from that idolatry by getting your significance and worth from Christ alone. Then, and only then, can you respond to that person with objectivity, healthy independence, and forgiveness.

Key Concept for Lesson 1
True forgiveness is based upon honesty—about the offense and about myself.

✎ **Please pray and ask God how this concept can apply in your life. Now please review this lesson. What has God shown you that you can use?**

_____

_____

_____

LESSON 2

Dealing with Our "Other(s)"

We make a list of all persons who have hurt us and choose to forgive them. We also make a list of all persons we have harmed, and we become willing to make amends to them all.

Live such good lives among he pagans that, though they accuse you of doing wrong, they may see your good deeds and glorify God.
—1 Peter 2:12, NIV

Key Concept:
I am responsible for my behaviors, not for others' responses.

Responding in a Healthy, Realistic Way

 Think of the person or situation that most brings out your self-destructive behavior. In the paragraph that follows underline every word which applies to that relationship.

Your relationship with the person you care for probably has been characterized by some combination of rescuing, outbursts of anger, displaced anger, compliance, withdrawal, guilt, hurt, loneliness, pity for him or her, and pity for yourself. A sense of loyalty probably has contributed to your inability to see the relationship objectively. You may have thought that any negative thoughts or emotions were signs of something wrong—not with them but with you!

What do you say?

You may have noted any combination of acts and emotions that mark your past relationships. Now you are growing in your objectivity. You are learning that you've repressed emotions that you didn't even know existed.

This is difficult, but you are getting in touch with your feelings. Your source of security is changing. You are learning to make your own decisions. All of these are good, but how do you deal with "that" person: your spouse, your sibling, your parent, your child, your classmate who has hurt you deeply?

To move away from the six characteristics of codependency, you can learn to identify, detach, and decide. The decision will include where to set limits or boundaries. Here's a brief explanation of these three steps:

Get in touch

Identify—Recognize how you feel and how you act when you see or think about that person.

Get some space

Detach—Then detach so you have the time and space necessary to think and feel. You may be able to detach calmly, but you may not. Even if you detach in anger, remember that not detaching is prolonging idolatry.

Get some limits

Decide—Ask yourself questions so you will see what really is happening. Then, make your own choices about what to say and do. Set limits or boundaries. Decide what you can live with for now. Decide on the extent of your communication and contact with that person.

Determine which issues you will discuss and which ones you won't. If you decide ahead of time on these areas, you will be much less likely to give in to the pressure of the moment and give in to manipulation or condemnation.

Step 8

✏️ **To help you develop these skills, write the three-step process just described:**

1. Honestly recognize your feelings and actions: _____
2. Emotionally uncouple from the situation: _____
3. Choose the healthy course of action—setting boundaries and agreeing on what you will or will not do, say or accept. _____

When you go through this process you will 1) *identify* your feelings, 2) *detach* from the situation, 3) *decide* on the proper course of action and set limits or boundaries. This isn't selfish. To insist on making your own decisions based on reality is perfectly good and right. Too often we have believed lies, lived by deception, and made our decisions to rescue and feel guilty based on a world of unreality. This can end now. Base your life on what genuinely is real, not on what that other person believes and says is real.

To insist on making your own decisions based on reality is right.

Express Yourself Appropriately

We often are so excited about the freedom, peace, and joy recovery brings that we have tried to explain it to our family members or friends. In our enthusiasm, most of us have told them things they weren't ready or willing to hear. It took years for God to break down my denial so I could see myself; yet, I want my family members and friends to find the same healing instantly.

How much do you say? Do you tell that person all about codependency and how messed up you've been because of your relationship with him or her? Do you describe your dark thoughts, your bitterness, hatred, and fear? The principle here is: Express yourself fully to God, and express yourself appropriately to the other person.

✏️ **Look at how the Scriptures appearing in the margin state both sides of this principle. In your own words sum up these two verses.**

Psalm 62:8: _____

Proverbs 18:2: _____

Trust in Him at all times. . . .
Pour out your heart before Him.
—Psalm 62:8

A fool does not delight in understanding, but only in revealing his own mind.
—Proverbs 18:2

Jesus warned us not to "give what is holy to dogs, and do not throw your pearls before swine" (Matthew 7:6). We can beware of giving people information they can't appreciate. I paraphrased Psalm 62:8 to say that I need to be open totally and pour out my heart to God, for He is the only one who is totally trustworthy. The proverb warns that we are not to pour out all our hearts to people. Only a fool delights in telling all he knows.

The question is not: "How much can I blast him?" but, "What will help that person? How much does he need to know at this time and place?" As you consider what to do and say, seek the advice of a godly, knowledgeable person to give you perspective and encouragement. Don't expect to do all of this perfectly. Because this is such a contrast to how you have related in the past, you may have all kinds of conflicting thoughts and emotions.

Beware of the Backlash

Don't expect the other person to say, "Well, now I completely understand. Thank you so much for saying all of this. I'll change today and never treat you the same way again." The person may say he'll change, but that's what he's said many times before. The person may weep and try to get you to pity him or her. The person may withdraw from you. The person may say, "Let's talk about this," when the goal really isn't to understand your point of view but to convince you that you are wrong (poor, misguided person that you are) so that you'll return to being the docile, compliant puppet you've always been.

These persons are so steeped in denial that they can't even see how they condemn others.

Or this person may say it's all your fault. These persons are so steeped in denial that they can't even see how they manipulate and condemn others. They may say, "I'm sorry," but what they mean is, "I'm sorry you feel that way. I've never done anything wrong, but you have!"

✎ **Describe your relationship with the person(s) who has hurt you deeply. How has he or she treated you? How have you typically responded? (You likely will need to use extra paper for this exercise.)**

_____

_____

What limits do you need to set in your relationship with that person?

_____

_____

How much should you say to him or her? How and when will you say it? How can you be well-prepared?

_____

_____

You can be independent, healthy, and realistic.

Realistic expectations are vital to your relationship with this person. He or she may change, but don't expect resolution and reconciliation quickly, if ever. Let your identity in Christ and His lordship, not dreams of intimacy with "that person," fill your thoughts. He or she never may change, but you can. Be unhooked. You can be independent, healthy, and realistic.

> **Key Concept for Lesson 2**
> I am responsible for my behaviors, not for others' responses.

✎ **Please pray and ask God how this concept can apply in your life. Now please review this lesson. What has God shown you that you can use?**

_____

_____

LESSON 3

Faulty Concepts of Forgiveness

We make a list of all persons who have hurt us and choose to forgive them. We also make a list of all persons we have harmed, and we become willing to make amends to them all.

> *And whenever you stand praying, forgive, if you have anything against anyone; so that your Father also who is in heaven may forgive you your transgressions.*
>
> –Mark 11:25

Key Concept:
To forgive genuinely we declare the debt paid so that we may be free.

We have great difficulty forgiving. Much of that difficulty comes from our wrong ideas about the nature of forgiveness. Forgiving is not excusing or rationalizing the offense, nor is it saying it's OK to hurt us again. Genuine forgiveness is declaring the debt paid so that we may be free.

Beth's husband Timothy was a compulsive workaholic who spent 80 hours a week at the office and was consumed with work-related problems when he was at home. When the couple visited his parents at Christmas, Beth noticed that Timothy's father was preoccupied most of the time with projects around the house and that he paid little attention to Timothy's mother. Beth thought, "He is a workaholic, too. No wonder Timothy works so hard. That's all he ever has seen in his father." That flash of insight helped Beth put a lot of pieces together. She felt better. She understood.

Like father, like son

At first Beth tried to excuse Timothy's neglect and preoccupation with his work. Soon, however, she realized that excusing him wasn't the same as forgiving him. Instead of continuing to excuse him, Beth forgave Timothy and committed herself to loving him unconditionally. That meant loving him enough to confront him with his workaholism's effects on both of them. At first Timothy was angry and defensive, but he agreed to read a book and to talk to their pastor about their relationship. Gradually Timothy began to recognize he was addicted to performance. Together, he and Beth began to experience healing and intimacy in their relationship.

What Forgiving Is Not

Not understanding
Understanding is not the same as forgiving. Understanding the painful background of those who have hurt us often helps, but most codependents respond in pity. They excuse harmful behavior and feel guilty for being angry. In that case, we have understood, but we haven't forgiven.

✎ Did Beth's understanding the source of Timothy's workaholism improve their relationship? ❏ Yes ❏ No

Why or why not? _____

_____

Do not confuse insight with recovery. Many people join a group, gain insight about their problems, and declare themselves cured, only to go out and crash.

Knowledge makes arrogant, but love edifies.
—1 Corinthians 8:1

parable–n. a narrative drawn from nature or human circumstances in order to teach a spiritual lesson (Vine's)

His fellow servant fell to his knees and begged him, "Be patient with me, and I will pay you back." But he refused. Instead, he went off and had the man thrown into prison until he could pay the debt. When the other servants saw what had happened, they were greatly distressed and went and told their master everything that had happened. Then the master called the servant in. "You wicked servant," he said. "I canceled all that debt of yours because you begged me to. Shouldn't you have had mercy on your fellow servant just as I had on you?" In anger his master turned him over to the jailers to be tortured, until he should pay back all he owed. This is how my heavenly Father will treat each of you unless you forgive your brother from your heart.
—Matthew 18:29-35, NIV

What does the parable mean to you?

_____
_____
_____

Beth thought insight solved the problem, but it only led her to feel superior to and to pity her husband. Read the Scripture at left.

Not excusing

We have been quick to excuse people for how they have hurt us. Excusing, however, is not forgiving. Forgiveness acknowledges that the offense is real and that the wrong has consequences. It then chooses not to hold that offense against the person. When Christ died on the cross, His blood paid for our sins so we could be forgiven and not just excused for our sins. Our forgiveness of others can mirror the depth of that forgiveness.

Not opening ourselves for more hurt

Forgiveness does not mean that you have to trust automatically the one you have forgiven. Some of us believe, "If I can't trust him, then I really haven't forgiven him." That belief is not true, and it causes undue pressure and guilt. If over the course of months or years a person has proven that he is not trustworthy, then he can be forgiven, but he should not be trusted. Trusting a proven liar is foolishness, not godliness.

In Matthew 18:21-35 Jesus told a story about a king whose servant who owed him a large sum of money. The servant was unable to pay, so the king forgave him the debt. Then the servant found one of his fellow-servants who owed him a very small amount of money. The servant who had just been forgiven grabbed his fellow-servant and began to choke him. "Pay back what you owe me!" he demanded. Read the rest of the **parable** which appears in the margin.

 Was it possible for the first servant to pay back the large sum of money that he owed? ❏ Yes ❏ No

Likewise, before you trusted Christ, how great was your debt to God for your sin? Was it possible for you ever to repay it?

_____

The debt of the king's servant was so huge he never could have hoped to pay it. Yet the man whom the king graciously forgave so much refused to forgive even a small debt. In the margin write your own statement about what the parable means.

You may have written that since God has forgiven you of so much, you are responsible to forgive others.

Forgiveness Is Liberating

Sometimes we feel that almost everybody is letting us down. We hurt when the offense happens and when we relive it. Although we can't avoid being offended, we can avoid most of our pain if we learn to deal with offenses rather than reliving them countless times.

 According to the paragraph you just read, who is responsible for the majority of my pain?

❏ 1. Others, for offending me.
❏ 2. Me, for reliving the event.

Step 8 169

When people fail to forgive, what happens to them?

_____
_____
_____
_____

When people fail to forgive, what happens to them in terms of their attitudes toward others, opinions of themselves, quality of relationships? Answer this question in the margin box. You could have answered by citing many things—all of them painful—that happen when we refuse to forgive.

> **Key Concept for Lesson 3**
> To forgive genuinely we declare the debt paid so that we may be free.

 Please pray and ask God how this concept can apply in your life. Now please review this lesson. What has God shown you that you can use?

_____
_____

LESSON 4

Key Concept:
Making excuses not to forgive prolongs my pain and keeps me stuck.

I'm tempted not to forgive—

_____
_____
_____
_____

Reasons for Not Forgiving

We make a list of all persons who have hurt us and choose to forgive them. We also make a list of all persons we have harmed, and we become willing to make amends to all of them.

> *See to it that no one comes short of the grace of God; that no root of bitterness springing up causes trouble, and by it many be defiled.*
> –Hebrews 12:15

We often fail to forgive others, and ourselves, because we don't think we can. We forget how God graciously has forgiven all of our sins through Christ's death and rationalize why we can't forgive. We now will study 12 common excuses we make for our unwillingness to forgive others and ourselves.[1]

1. The offense was too great.
Grant's wife had committed adultery, and he was bitter toward her. Her infidelity was too great a sin for him to forgive. Two years after the incident, God began to impress Grant with the idea that he should forgive his wife "just as God in Christ also had forgiven him." When Grant finally did forgive, he pledged to rebuild his relationship with her so that she would not be compelled to repeat the incident with someone else. In the margin box write about an offense you are tempted not to forgive because it is too great.

2. The person won't accept responsibility.
Danny told fellow church members some very harmful things about Jerry. Later Danny came to apologize . . . almost. He said he was sorry people misunderstood and thought he said hurtful things, but that really he hadn't done anything wrong. Having others agree that they've offended us isn't necessary for us to respond properly to their offense.

3. The person isn't truly sorry.
John pulled a practical joke on you which caused you to be late for class, and your professor refused to accept your paper because you didn't have it in on

Common excuses

does not act unbecomingly; it does not seek its own, is not provoked, does not take into account a wrong suffered.
—1 Corinthians 13:5

time. John doesn't see anything wrong with a little joke. Oh, he made some rather insincere statements about being sorry, but he still thinks the incident was hilarious. Even if John doesn't recognize the pain he's caused you, you still can forgive him and can refuse to hold the offense against him.

4. The person never asked for forgiveness.
For whatever reason, the offender never got around to asking you for forgiveness. Are you going to withhold forgiveness until someone requests it? Who is suffering, you or the offender? What would God want you to do? (Read 1 Corinthians 13:5, which appears in the margin, and Ephesians 4:32, which appeared earlier in this lesson.)

5. The person did it too many times.
Candy's husband had been out late playing cards every Friday night for three years. Some nights he didn't come home at all. "Me? Forgive that jerk?" Candy asked. "Look how many times he's wronged me." Jesus said the number of times we need to forgive is seventy times seven—in other words, regardless of the number of offenses. Forgiveness doesn't mean accepting unacceptable behavior. Some situations calling for forgiveness also require us to confront and/or allow the offender to experience the consequences of his or her wrongful behavior. For Candy, failing both to forgive and to confront her husband will cause her to be the bitter loser.

✏️ **Does forgiving mean lying down to be a doormat?** ❏ Yes ❏ No

Explain: _____

_____

The paragraph above explains that sometimes when we forgive, we also need to confront wrong behavior.

But God demonstrate His own love toward us, in that while we were yet sinners, Christ died for us.
—Romans 5:8

✏️ **Read Romans 5:8 in the margin. Did God wait for us to act before He paid for our sin?** ❏ Yes ❏ No

✏️ **Explain what you think this statement means: "The-12 Step program is a selfish program, and forgiving is the most selfish thing I can do."**

_____

_____

God forgives entirely

The last two excuses make forgiveness depend upon the actions of the offender. Those reasons trap us in a situation in which we have to live with bitterness until someone else changes. The difference between God's attitude and ours is that He forgives us entirely because of Himself, not because of our actions. You may have answered the last question by saying that the best thing for us is to forgive. If we refuse to forgive, we hurt ourselves.

6. I simply don't like the person.
Generally, we don't have a great deal of appreciation or tolerance for the person who has wronged us. In fact, every emotion within us may call for getting back at the creep! Only when we realize that forgiveness is an act of the will, and not of the emotions, will we choose to forgive those who have hurt us.

> **Forgiving a deliberate wrong is difficult because—**
>
> _____
> _____
> _____

7. The person did it deliberately.
George's best friend, Hal, swindled George out of $10,000. Hal had used him. George felt he never could forgive Hal. Whether or not the offense was deliberate, God still wants George to forgive Hal. In the margin box explain why you have a difficult time forgiving a wrong like Hal's action. You may have written about the fact that your damaged pride and bruised ego keep you from forgiving.

8. If I forgive, I'll have to treat the offender well.
Ben excused his slander of Steve by pointing out how Steve had offended him. He felt justified in lying to destroy Steve's reputation.

9. Someone has to punish the person.
How often do we want God to be merciful to us and yet want Him to skin other people alive? When we don't see others suffer, we take it upon ourselves to be God's hand of vengeance. For two weeks Shirley had been cold to Greg, who had offended her. She would forgive him all right—as soon as she was through punishing him.

 Explain how punishing those we haven't forgiven fulfills the Proverbs 14:1 passage appearing in the margin.

_____
_____

> The wise woman builds her house, But the foolish tears it down with her own hands.
> —Proverbs 14:1

Each excuse in this group underestimates the importance and difficulty of forgiving. Like the woman in the proverb, they all destroy us as we try to punish others.

 In this last group of excuses—10, 11, and 12—underline the statements that show the true nature of forgiveness.

10. Something keeps me from forgiving.
Satan actively promotes unforgiveness. When you attempt to deal with this problem honestly, you may be in for a tremendous spiritual battle. Don't be surprised if you find yourself resisting the devil at every turn in order to accomplish the task of forgiving the offender. Again, forgiveness is not a warm feeling; it's primarily an act of the will.

11. I'll be a hypocrite if I forgive.
We often think we won't be true to ourselves if we forgive. We are hypocritical only if we do something for selfish gain. For instance, a politician is hypocritical if he or she attends church only to get its members' votes in the next election. This politician actually despises the church and its people. To forgive as an act of the will in obedience to the Lord's command is true spirituality, not hypocrisy.

I underlined the statements that indicated that forgiveness is an act of my will, an act of obedience, and a choice rather than a feeling.

12. I've found an excuse for the offense, so I'll forgive.
Hank was irresponsible early in his marriage. His wife, Sally, always was able to forgive him by blaming his mother, who babied Hank even after he was grown. Sally thought she forgave Hank when she really had just excused him.

When you offend someone, or when someone offends you, do you immediately look for a "reason"? ❏ Yes ❏ No

If you do, you may be rationalizing. If you come up with an excuse for the question, "Why did I forgive the person?" then you have not truly forgiven the offense. You have excused it.

Key Concept for Lesson 4
Making excuses not to forgive prolongs my pain and keeps me stuck.

 Please pray and ask God how this concept can apply in your life. Now please review this lesson. What has God shown you that you can use?

_____

_____

LESSON 5

Results of Not Forgiving

We make a list of all persons who have hurt us and choose to forgive them. We also make a list of all persons we have harmed, and we become willing to make amends to all of them.

> *The heart knows its own bitterness, And a stranger does not share its joy.*
> –Proverbs 14:10

Key Concept:
I have far more to lose by not making my amends than by making them.

When we fail to forgive others, our lives and our relationships suffer. Let's take a look at some problems in our lives that stem directly from a lack of forgiveness.[2]

- **Stress:** Living with the high level of tension brought by an unforgiving attitude exhausts your mental resources, leads to emotional difficulties, brings physical exhaustion, and causes illness.

- **Self-inflicted Reinjury:** In *Search for Significance* LIFE Support Edition, Robert S. McGee recalled this incident: "As I drove home, I saw flashing through my mind the face of a guy I played basketball with in college. He was one of the few people I ever met whom I truly wanted to punch out. I began to remember the unkind things he did to me. Soon anger started creeping up inside of me. I had not thought about this fellow for years, and I'm sure that he doesn't remember me at all. Yet my reliving this event caused me a lot of pain. I had not properly dealt with it in the beginning."[3] How many times are you reinjuring yourself because past offenses haunt you?

We withdraw from those we love when we have not dealt adequately with an offense.

- **No More Love:** "I don't know if I can ever love someone again" is a frequent complaint from those offended by someone about whom they care deeply. One way we deal with the pain of being offended is simply to withdraw and refuse to love anymore. We often make this unconscious decision when we have not dealt adequately with an offense. We desperately may want to love

> **What results of lack of forgiveness do you spot?**
>
> _____
> _____
> _____

again but feel we are incapable of it. Both refusing to experience love and feeling unable to love are devastating conditions. In the margin box describe which of these three problems stemming from lack of forgiveness you most readily spot in your life.

- **Bitterness:** Emotions trace their lines on our faces. We think others don't notice what's going on inside, but even the casual observer usually can detect our anger.

- **Perpetual Conflict:** A husband and wife, both of whom had been married previously, received counseling. Having been hurt in their first marriage, they anticipated hurt again. At the smallest offense each reacted as if the spouse were about to deliver the final blow. They protected themselves from the attacks they imagined their mate would deliver. They reacted in a way that perpetuated the conflict.

- **Walls That Keep Others Out:** Many of us refuse the love others want to give us. We become anxious and threatened when personal intimacy becomes possible. Jane prayed that her husband Frank would come to know the Lord. She thought that if he were a Christian, he would be more loving toward her and toward their children. One day Frank accepted Christ and experienced change. He paid more attention to Jane and started spending time with her and the children. He was sensitive and loving. Was it a dream come true? Instead of rejoicing, Jane deeply resented Frank for not changing sooner! "If Frank is able to love us like this now, then he's always had the ability," she thought. She also felt confused and guilty about her anger. Jane's anger was a defense mechanism to keep distance between herself and Frank. The closer they might get, the more she would hurt if he reverted to his old ways. She never had forgiven Frank, so the bricks of unforgiveness were stacked to form a wall that kept him from getting too close. Hiding behind a wall of unforgiveness is a lonely experience. In the margin box describe a time when one of the last three results of unforgiveness has affected you.

> **How unforgiveness has affected me—**
>
> _____
> _____
> _____
> _____

Forgiveness Is Not Erasure

The modern idea of forgiveness is to approach an offense with a large eraser and wipe it off the books. God has never forgiven like this. For each offense He demanded full payment. This is the reason for the cross. Christ has paid for our sins in full. Christians have a special ability to forgive because they can forgive as God does. God has forgiven us fully and completely. Think of it this way: No one can do anything to me (such as insult me, lie about me, annoy me) that can compare with what Christ has forgiven me for doing. Read the verse appearing in the margin about what Paul said in Ephesians about this kind of forgiveness.

> And be kind to one another, tender-hearted, forgiving each other, just as God in Christ has forgiven you.
> –Ephesians 4:32

✎ **List six things for which you are glad God in Christ has forgiven you. This can prompt you to be willing to forgive everyone who has done wrong to you.**

1. _____   4. _____

2. _____   5. _____

3. _____   6. _____

The popular idea of forgiveness is that one simply erases the debt. The biblical idea is that the debt has been paid by Christ Jesus. Your list has not been removed, it has been paid for "with precious blood, as of a lamb unblemished and spotless, the blood of Christ" (1 Peter 1:19).

✎ **Use the following exercise to recognize any lack of forgiveness in your life and to forgive freely as God in Christ has forgiven you. You may write in the margin or use extra paper as you describe these events.**

Offense: Describe in some detail an event which caused you pain.

_____

_____

Persons to Be Forgiven: List everyone who participated in the offense.

_____

_____

Reasons for Not Forgiving: Review the list of 12 reasons for unforgiveness listed on pages 170-172. List the ones that apply in this case.

_____

_____

✎ **In the statement below insert the person's name and the offense about which you just wrote. Use this prayer as a means for correcting any lack of forgiveness in your life.**

Enabling me to forgive

Dear Lord, I forgive _____ for _____ (offense) because God freely has forgiven me and has commanded me to forgive others. I have the capacity to do this because of Christ's forgiveness in my life. I do not excuse this person's offense in any way, nor do I use any excuse for not forgiving. Thank You, Lord Jesus, for enabling me to forgive. I also confess that I have sinned by using these excuses for not forgiving _____ and _____. Thank You, Lord Jesus, for forgiving me for this sin.

Key Concept for Lesson 5
I have far more to lose by not making my amends than by making them.

✎ **Please pray and ask God how this concept can apply in your life. Now please review this lesson. What has God shown you that you can use?**

_____

_____

Step 8

LESSON 6

Preparing to Make Our Amends

We make a list of all persons who have hurt us and choose to forgive them. We also make a list of all persons we have harmed, and we become willing to make amends to them all.

> *then he shall confess his sins which he has committed, and he shall make restitution in full for his wrong.*
>
> –Numbers 5:7

Key Concept:
Making amends to those I have harmed is a gift I give myself and others.

Having examined the importance of forgiving others, we now can ask, "What have I done to others that merits my seeking their forgiveness?" Step 4 has prepared us for this step by enabling us to see "what" we've done wrong. Now we need to know "whom" we have wronged. We are not yet ready to make amends with these people. Our task here is simply to list their names. In preparing this list, use these guidelines and refer back to Step 4. You may want to add more pages. Some people have come up with 20 pages of names in compiling a list such as this. Take your time in doing this important work. Invite the Lord to remind you of people and situations. Months from now you still may be remembering names and adding to your list.

- Whom did I rescue instead of letting this person be responsible for himself or herself?
- Whom did I control and manipulate through condemnation, praise, or silence?
- Whose separateness did I fail to respect? On whom did I impose my own feelings, thoughts and decisions?
- Whom have I blamed because I was unwilling to be responsible for my own behavior?
- From whom did I cheat or steal?
- What promises and/or confidences did I break (sexual infidelity, lying, sharing something told to me as a secret)? Whom did I hurt or betray?
- For whom did I cause pain by missing family obligations (birthdays, anniversaries) or other special days or commitments?
- What social responsibilities did I break or avoid? Who did this harm?
- What financial obligations did I avoid or wrongly create? Who did my behavior harm or inconvenience?
- What have I done to harm those with whom I've worked?
- What physical damage—either to property or people—resulted from my compulsive behavior? Whom did I harm?
- To whom have I neglected to show gratitude?

Whom did I hurt?

Persons I Have Harmed	**How I Harmed Them**
1. _____	_____
2. _____	_____
3. _____	_____
4. _____	_____
5. _____	_____

Motivations for Making Amends

✎ **As you read the paragraphs that follow, circle the benefits you can gain from making amends.**

Making amends will release us from the control people currently have on us. Think about those persons you have been avoiding, those you've been dodging in hopes they won't see you, or those you've been excluding from your circle of friends altogether. Have you ever considered that your guilt and fear are controls which keep you from the full enjoyment of life and love that God desires for all who know Him?

To make amends is to be released from the past. It releases us from the fear of someone's finding out something about us that we don't want them to know, a fear that will haunt and control us for the rest of our lives if unconfessed. Making amends will enable us to enjoy fellowship with others, a key factor in our continued recovery. Finally, as we act to forgive others and experience their forgiveness, we can forgive ourselves more completely. We will better understand that while our behavior may have been shameful, we as persons are not worthless. Learning how to love and forgive ourselves is a prerequisite for genuinely loving and forgiving others.

✎ **Of the benefits you circled, write the three you most would like to have in your life.**

1. _____
2. _____
3. _____

As I answered the above exercise, I selected these benefits I have seen in my own life from having worked this Step: I am free from the negative control many others had in my life, I am able to enjoy life more than I ever could have imagined, and I am able increasingly to forgive myself.

Congratulations on your courage in making your amends list. You will find great joy, release, and victory in being free from the endless burden of unmade amends.

> **Key Concept for Lesson 6**
> Making amends to those I have harmed is a gift I give myself and others.

✎ **Please pray and ask God how this concept can apply in your life. Now please review this lesson. What has God shown you that you can use?**

_____
_____
_____

Step Review

✎ **Please review this Step. Pray and ask God to identify the Scriptures or principles that are particularly important for your life. Underline them. Then respond to the following:**

Restate the Step in your own words. _____

_____

What do you have to gain by practicing this Step in your life?

_____

_____

Reword your summary into a prayer of response to God. Thank Him for this Step, and affirm your commitment to Him.

_____

_____

Memorize this Step's memory verse:
Owe nothing to anyone except to love one another; for he who loves his neighbor has fulfilled the law.
—Romans 13:8

Notes
[1] Robert S. McGee, *Search for Significance* LIFE Support Edition (Nashville: LifeWay Press, 1992), 130-131.
[2] Ibid., 131-132.
[3] Ibid., 132.

STEP 9

Making Amends

We make direct amends to people where possible, except when doing so will injure them or others.

Step 9 Into Codependency

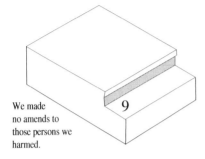

We made no amends to those persons we harmed.

Step 9 Out of Codependency

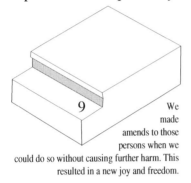

We made amends to those persons when we could do so without causing further harm. This resulted in a new joy and freedom.

MARKING A NEW START

Mike and Steve hadn't had a decent conversation with each other since they were fellow students about to get their degrees from graduate school. When they finished school, Mike and Steve accepted jobs with competing companies. Steve's company eventually put Mike's firm out of business. Mike was angry at Steve. For years he made rude comments about Steve to other people and constantly cut him down. Mutual friends urged Mike to talk with Steve and try to resolve their differences, but Mike refused.

Then one day when Steve was absorbed in a project at his desk, Mike walked into his office. Because he had participated in a 12-Step group, Mike now realized that his hostility to Steve was harming him and was affecting his relationships with others. He confessed to Steve that he had been angry at him for years and asked for Steve's forgiveness. He asked Steve if he could take him to lunch and asked if he could visit with Steve's family and catch up on the details of his one-time colleague's life. Mike also tracked down friends to whom he had spoken rudely of Steve and told them he was wrong for attempting to ruin Steve's reputation.

Although Steve quite honestly had not thought about Mike in years, he was moved by Mike's sincerity and his desire to make amends. This conversation marked the new start of a rewarding friendship between the two men. On the following pages you'll learn more about the importance of making amends.

Therefore, however you want people to treat you, so treat them, for this is the Law and the Prophets.

–Matthew 7:12

Overview for Step 9

Lesson 1: What Amends Are Not
    Goal: You will distinguish the healthy process of making amends from its counterfeits.

Lesson 2: The Mechanics of Amends
    Goal: You will describe the specific actions necessary to make amends.

Lesson 3: Taking the Step
    Goal: You will record the results as you make your amends.

LESSON 1

What Amends Are Not

We make direct amends to people where possible, except when doing so will injure them or others.

For each one shall bear his own load. —Galatians 6:5

Key Concept:
To make amends is to correct a wrong.

Amends: Not Just Apology

Dan said he thought before he entered recovery that Step 9 was the "I'm sorry" Step. He said, "I was like someone with 'I'm sorry' stenciled across my forehead. I was so accustomed to taking the blame that I apologized for anything that I had or hadn't done."

 Many people confuse making amends with confession and apology. These two concepts are not the same. Read carefully Lamentations 3:40 appearing in the margin. Check which of the following statements most nearly reflects the meaning of the verse:

Let us examine and probe our ways; And let us return to the Lord.
—Lamentations 3:40

❏ 1. We are to examine our behaviors and ask forgiveness.
❏ 2. We are to ignore our past actions.
❏ 3. We are to examine our behaviors and take corrective action.

amend–v. to make better by some change; improve; to improve one's conduct (Webster's).

As you see from the definition appearing in the margin, **amend** means to change behavior. Asking forgiveness sometimes is the appropriate change, but the change in behavior is the key. The answer is number 3.

 Read the following true story and answer the question that follows.

An old friend from high school phoned Sue late one evening. He asked her to forgive him for holding resentments and anger toward her for years. In a state of shock she mumbled, "Oh, that's OK," hung up the phone, and stumbled off to a rather sleepless night.

Did Sue's friend's action really amount to an amend? ❏ Yes ❏ No

Why or why not? _____

_____

Paying a debt

We can begin to understand about amends when we think about a debt to be paid. When you owe a debt, the solution is not confession and apology. The debt needs to be paid. Sue's friend was not making an amend for a harm done. He merely was seeking some relief for his real or imagined guilt. It was an apology rather than an amend. His comments to Sue left her feeling bewildered and not necessarily better.

A friend in Alcoholics Anonymous rejoiced that he had completed the final amend on his list. He had paid off the last of the debts he ran up during his drinking days. When someone asked how long he had been paying on the debt, he replied "only 14 years."

> **This story exemplified an amend because—**
> _____
> _____
> _____
> _____

In the margin box describe why you think this story about the friend in Alcoholics Anonymous was a better example of an amend than was the story of Sue's friend.

You may have answered that this was a great example of an amend because he genuinely owed the debt, he accepted full responsibility, and he worked until he could pay off the debt. To the best of his ability he genuinely corrected the offense. The story of Mike and Steve on the unit page also is an example of healthy amends. Mike's apology to Steve was not empty words; he took steps to try to become reacquainted with him, to extend the hand of friendship to Steve's family, and to tell others that he was wrong to speak ill of Steve.

Amends: Not Relapse

Making amends with others does not mean that we go back to old patterns of rescuing and manipulating in our relationships with them, although that is exactly what some people expect and want from us. Making amends involves a break with the past rather than a return to it. We begin here a new life where we act in a way which will earn our own respect and that of others.

A break with the past

Family members rarely applaud when a rescuer stops rescuing. They usually want the rescuers to keep fixing their problems. If the person stops, they grouse, "Who will take care of me?" For that reason family members often attempt to pressure us into going back to the old patterns of behavior. Such pressure may take the form of subtle passive-aggressive manipulation or outright condemnation and ridicule, such as, "How could you be so selfish?"

 We can distinguish clearly between making healthy amends and returning to destructive behaviors. In the following list write "amend" by statements representing healthy actions and "relapse" by those that would return us to our codependency.

_____ 1. Accepting full responsibility for my own past actions.
_____ 2. Allowing others to again manipulate and control me.
_____ 3. Explaining points at which others were at fault.
_____ 4. Paying off the debts I incurred in the past.
_____ 5. Accepting the blame for everything in the family.

"How do people treat each other when they love each other?"

This kind of manipulation worked wonders in the past and will work again unless we prepare for it in advance. We can do so by reflecting on what genuine love is and by asking ourselves questions like: "How do people treat each other when they love each other? How would my family members treat me if they genuinely loved me?" Discussing with a trusted friend or group these kinds of questions will add to our sense of objectivity. We may conclude that our families or others never will love us the way we want to be loved. You may have marked 1 and 4 as examples of healthy amends and answers 2, 3, and 5 as relapses into our old behaviors.

We can base our relationships and our decisions to make amends for our wrongs in those relationships on the firm foundation of security and healthy separateness, not on manipulation and guilt. Then we can make amends because we know that doing so is right, not because we feel someone is forcing us. We make healthy amends with the understanding that we are not responsible for making others happy. We can find a balance between assuming responsibility for our wrongs and avoiding responsibility for someone else's response.

Making amends is a difficult step—with great rewards. As you prepare to take it, follow these suggestions:
1. Pray for strength and courage as you determine to make your amends.
2. You won't make all your amends at once. You may benefit from making the easiest first.
3. Make your amends one by one as the Lord leads.
4. For strength and motivation, keep in mind two pictures: 1. how good you will feel when you have made your amends and 2. how pleased Jesus is as you make the difficult choices to make amends.

> **Key Concept for Lesson 1**
> To make amends is to correct a wrong.

 Please pray and ask God how this concept can apply in your life. Now please review this lesson. What has God shown you that you can use?

_____

_____

LESSON 2

Key Concept:
Amends are actions.

The Mechanics of Amends

We make direct amends to people where possible, except when doing so will injure them or others.

> *If therefore you are presenting your offering at the altar, and there remember that your brother has something against you, leave your offering there before the altar, and go your way; first be reconciled to your brother, and then come and present your offering.*
>
> –Matthew 5:23-24

Direct Amends

In this lesson we'll study reasons to make direct amends to others. Many reasons exist for doing so.

 In the following paragraph circle each reason to make direct amends.

> Be direct in making amends. Avoid making anonymous phone calls, letters, or payments to those we wronged. Unless we're extremely far away, we can go in person. Once we have looked someone squarely in the eye to confess our wrongdoing, we always can look that person and others in the eye. Having gained their respect, we will regain our self-respect. If a personal interview is impossible, a phone call is our second choice. One of our objectives is to open a door for dialogue.

You may have circled: *to confess our wrongdoing*, so we can *look that person and others in the eye*, *to regain our self-respect*, and *to open a door for dialogue*.

182 Step 9

Be direct

Being direct also means assuming complete responsibility for our wrongs. We don't do this by pointing the finger at someone else and saying, "I'm very sorry, but if you hadn't done what you did...." Nor do we want to lessen our responsibility by blaming a third party and saying something like, "Well, I'll admit to using poor judgment, but if Joe hadn't told me...." Your point in making amends is not to admit how you were misled, though this may have been the case. Your point is to confess that you had a choice in the matter and that you made the wrong one.

restitution–n. the act of restoring to the rightful owner that which was lost or has been taken away (Webster's)

Read the definition at left of **restitution**. Then in the margin box write your own definition.

Making amends is more than just making apologies. Restitution means setting things back in order—righting our wrongs. We demonstrate not only that we know we are wrong but also that we have a change of heart that results in a change of action. When our actions demonstrate a positive change of direction, we have repented.

To me restitution means—

_____
_____
_____

✏️ What does the passage in the margin say to you about making restitution with creditors, the government, local law enforcement agencies, or in instances of theft?

_____
_____

What do you owe someone you have controlled and rescued? _____

_____

If a wicked man restores a pledge, pays back what he has taken by robbery, walks by the statutes which ensure life without committing iniquity, he will surely live; he shall not die.
–Ezekiel 33:15

What action—large or small—can accompany your words to show that you really mean what you say?

_____

Indirect Amends

Step 9 states that *we will make direct amends to others where possible*. Again something we cannot change—the past—confronts us. The children we may have wronged now may be grown. We cannot go back and erase the poor example we might have been for them or the abuse we might have given them. Nor can we make restitution with persons who have died or who now have moved to unknown places.

In these instances we can take some positive, constructive steps by way of direct amends: We can learn from our mistakes and apply that knowledge to present and future situations. If people we wronged have moved or died, we can pay what debts we may owe to one of their survivors or make a charitable donation in their name; we can treat their survivors with a special act of kindness.

Pray for people still living but whom we cannot locate.

We can do for other people's children or parents what we wish we'd done for our own. We can do this not as an act of guilt but in love. We can pray for those whom we know are still living but whom we cannot locate.

✎ Below list any other suggestions you can think of about how to make indirect amends.

_____

_____

Avoiding Injury to Others

Some situations call for making partial restitution. This may mean partially disclosing your wrongdoing. Sexual infidelity may be one situation calling for this kind of action. Telling your spouse about your sexual escapades possibly could cause him or her severe mental and emotional anguish and could damage your marriage beyond repair. In the same way, disclosing the person(s) with whom you committed infidelity possibly could damage them. Causing others such pain is both needless and harmful. Our goal in making amends is not to do further damage to others but to right our wrongs.

Our goal in making amends is not to do further damage but to right our wrongs.

How can we make restitution in such instances? First, we can repent. If we haven't already, we can break off the adulterous relationship(s). We can resolve that with God's help, we will remain faithful to our spouse for the rest of our lives (one day at a time). We also can show renewed interest toward our spouse by giving him or her time and attention.

Other situations calling for partial restitution may be those which would threaten our family's well-being. We can avoid taking steps that would result in loss of employment or in a legal implication which would harm family members, co-workers, or friends. Again, our goal is not to avoid reaping the consequences of our sins but to show careful consideration for other people in what we do and don't expose about others and ourselves.

We can avoid taking steps that would threaten our family's well-being.

God knows your own situation. Pray about the matter. Consult an objective minister, a Christian counselor, or your sponsor. Find someone with whom you can talk candidly and from whom you can expect a godly response.

✎ Think about the people or circumstances in your life which may call for making partial amends. Because of the sensitive nature of the information that comes to mind, you may desire to use a separate sheet of paper for this exercise. Using the format below, write down each instance. Then by the side of each instance, identify the possible damage that could result from making full disclosure.

Person or Situation: Specific Action:

_____ _____

As you reread your list, think about ways you can demonstrate partial restitution by a change of action. List those on your separate paper, using the format below.

Person or Situation: Specific Action:

_____ _____

Timing is important

Still other situations may call for delayed restitution. You may have hurt someone so recently that any discussion now might end in a broken relationship. In these cases, you can wait to act. Careful, prayerful consideration, combined with wise counsel and timing, are very important in successfully completing Step 9.

✎ List below the people or circumstances in your life which may call for delayed amends. (These may include situations where you still have not resolved your own negative emotions.) Beside each instance, list the possible harm that you could cause by making amends now:

Person or Situation: Specific Action:

_____   _____

_____   _____

Name some things you can do about these situations while you are waiting for the right time to make amends.

_____

_____

Take all of these issues to your sponsor, pastor, or counselor; ask him or her to pray through each with you, and wait with an open mind for God's direction.

At Peace with All

Making restitution often brings favorable results. Many people are completely disarmed when we are willing to be open and honest and when we admit wrongdoing. These people usually respond with gracious appreciation. But this isn't always the case. Some persons will respond in anger, shock, indifference, or disapproval. The fear of such a response should not deter us from completing our errand. We can remember that we cannot control others' responses. Scripture tells us that "their" response is not the issue. Romans 12:18 says, "... so far as it depends on you, be at peace with all men."

We cannot control others' responses.

```
┌─────────────────────────────────────┐
│        Key Concept for Lesson 2     │
│           Amends are actions.       │
└─────────────────────────────────────┘
```

✎ Please pray and ask God how this concept can apply in your life. Now please review this lesson. What has God shown you that you can use?

_____

_____

_____

_____

LESSON 3

Taking the Step

We make direct amends to people where possible, except when doing so will injure them or others.

> *Let us examine and probe our ways, And let us return to the Lord.*
> –Lamentations 3:40

Key Concept:
We can record our own progress and growth in discipleship.

Creating Your Action Sheet

Turn back to page 176 in Step 8 where you listed all the persons you have harmed. In the spaces provided on the following page, rewrite those names. Beside each, list the action you plan to take, the date the action is to be completed, and the result of your interview with him or her. Use extra pages of paper if necessary for additional names and actions. This exercise may take weeks or even months to complete as you prayerfully determine your best course of action. The point is to have a reminder of both those you need to make amends to and of what you are going to do to demonstrate repentance toward them. Success in smaller amends also will encourage you when you need courage to face more difficult amends.

Name: _____

Action Planned: _____
_____
_____

Date Planned: _____ Completed: _____

Name: _____

Action Planned: _____
_____
_____

Date Planned: _____ Completed: _____

Name: _____

Action Planned: _____
_____
_____

Date Planned: _____ Completed: _____

Respecting ourselves

Remember that we make amends so that we can respect ourselves, not so we can obtain any particular response from others. However, we do often see positive results from making amends. As you make amends, note here any resulting changes. Watch for changes in the response of those to whom you make amends, in your relationships with others, in your prayer life, marriage, or any other result. Below write any observed results. Add extra pages if necessary.

_____
_____
_____
_____
_____
_____

Step Review

✎ **Please review this Step. Pray and ask God to identify the Scriptures or principles that are particularly important for your life. Underline them. Then respond to the following:**

Restate the Step in your own words: _____
_____
_____

What do you have to gain by practicing this Step in your life?
_____
_____
_____

Reword your summary into a prayer of response to God. Thank Him for this Step, and affirm your commitment to Him.
_____
_____
_____

Memorize this Step's memory verse:
Therefore, however you want people to treat you, so treat them, for this is the Law and the Prophets.
–Matthew 7:12

STEP 10

People of the Extremes

We continue to take personal inventory, and when we are wrong, promptly admit it.

Step 10 Into Codependency

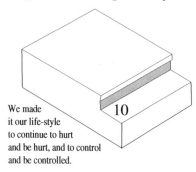

We made it our life-style to continue to hurt and be hurt, and to control and be controlled.

Step 10 Out of Codependency

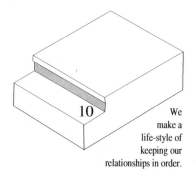

We make a life-style of keeping our relationships in order.

TWO SIDES OF THE COIN

Kathy once shoplifted in the small town where she lived. The store owner who caught her knew that Kathy had been going through an extremely stressful time in her life and decided not to press charges, but Kathy felt totally disgraced by the incident. She refused to go out in public because she thought everyone knew the story. She thought, *What will everyone think of me? I can't face anyone now.* Guilt ate away at Kathy. She felt that God never could forgive her for this act.

Phillip inherited some money when his father died. He went on a spending spree and squandered the money his father hoped he would use to pay college tuition. Phillip realized that his actions were harming him and were dishonoring his father's good intentions for him. He felt sorrow about the destructive things that he had done, and he asked God to forgive him. He accepted God's forgiveness for his actions. He then set out to pay off his credit card bills and began trying to save some money to set his priorities straight.

In the lessons that follow read more about the difference between the destructive guilt that Kathy experienced and the godly sorrow Phillip felt.

Trust in the LORD with all your heart, And do not lean on your own understanding. In all your ways acknowledge Him, And He will make your paths straight.
—Proverbs 3:5-6

Overview for Step 10

Lesson 1: Guilt: A Devastating Burden
　Goal: You will distinguish between guilt and godly sorrow.
Lesson 2: More About the Process
　Goal: You will identify ways that conviction and guilt occur in our lives and how they affect us.
Lesson 3: Identifying False Beliefs
　Goal: You will develop the skill of identifying false beliefs.
Lesson 4: Catching the Signals
　Goal: You will practice identifying the warning signals of harmful behavior.

LESSON 1

Guilt: A Devastating Burden

We continue to take personal inventory, and when we are wrong, promptly admit it.

> *He is on the path of life who heeds instruction, But he who forsakes reproof goes astray.*
> —Proverbs 10:17

Key Concept:
Guilt is destructive to believers, but godly sorrow for our sins is important for us to grow.

Our denial often prevents us from seeing real instances of wrongdoing in our lives. We go to one of two extremes. Some of us have dulled consciences and fail to recognize when we hurt someone or when we sin in some other way. Most of us, however, have overly active consciences. We spend much time reliving and condemning ourselves for many things we've said and done. Our self-worth plummets, and as it does, our sense of guilt rises. We begin to perform for God in a desperate effort to win His approval and boost our esteem. We may feel pretty good for a while, until we sin again or perceive that we've sinned again. Then we repeat the same cycle.

In order to walk by the Spirit in the light of honesty, we can learn to take a daily inventory. Before we do this, however, we can examine the effect of guilt on our lives. The following material in lessons 1 and 2 is adapted from *Search for Significance* LIFE Support Edition. We hope you will find it helpful in coming to understand how you can be free from this always-present burden.

condemnation–n. the sentence pronounced, a verdict, the decision resulting from an investigation (Vine's)

There is therefore now no condemnation for those who are in Christ Jesus.
—Romans 8:1

To begin with, people who accept Christ are free from eternal **condemnation** (see definition appearing in the margin) for their sins. See what Paul wrote about this in the verse at left. Christ removed our condemnation. He took all our guilt upon Himself when He accepted the penalty for our sins and suffered the full punishment. Sometimes we believe that despite our salvation, we still are doomed for our sins. We can be free from that wrong idea. Because of His substitution we are free from the sentence of spiritual death.

Guilt's Destructiveness

If we say that we have no sin, we are deceiving ourselves, and the truth is not in us. If we confess our sins, He is faithful and righteous to forgive us our sins and to cleanse us from all unrighteousness. If we say that we have not sinned, we make Him a liar, and His word is not in us.
—1 John 1:8-10

Even after we've trusted Christ and are freed from eternal condemnation, we still sin. First John 1:8-10 appearing at left tells us about this. We miss the mark; we make mistakes; we turn from God's ways. What happens at that point? Should we then feel guilty about what we've done?

The Bible indicates that God intends for us to feel *something* when we sin, and we don't stop feeling that *something* just because we accept Christ. God doesn't intend that just because we accept Christ, we can go on sinning and sinning without our sins ever bothering us.

confess–v. to declare by way of admitting oneself guilty of what one is accused of, the result of inward conviction (Vine's)

Here's what happens: When we sin, the Holy Spirit urges us to **confess** those sins. (We also studied the term confess in unit 5.) The definition at left says that we confess sin by admitting ourselves guilty of what we are accused. This comes about through **conviction** (see definition on the next page)—the Holy Spirit works in our lives to get us to agree with God about the wrong we've conviction–n. the act of convincing a person of error (Webster's)

I now rejoice, not that you were made sorrowful, but that you were made sorrowful to the point of repentance; for you were made sorrowful according to the will of God, in order that you might not suffer loss in anything through us. For the sorrow that is according to the will of God produces a repentance without regret, leading to salvation; but the sorrow of the world produces death.
—2 Corinthians 7:9-10

done. Our sense that something is wrong occurs because the Holy Spirit is **convicting** us of sin.

God wants us to feel a godly sorrow, or grief, for our sins. He does not want us to experience guilt that eats away at us and destroys our self-esteem. Second Corinthians 7:9-10 at left describes this kind of sorrow. This verse says godly sorrow brings us to the point of repentance.

Once we confess our sin, repent, and accept Christ's forgiveness, we may continue to have regret and remorse, but we can be assured that Christ has forgiven us completely. Forgiveness enables us to lose the fear of condemnation.

What Guilt Does to Us

When people allow guilt to burden them even after God forgives them, they can find themselves harmed emotionally. This kind of lingering guilt causes a loss of self-respect. It causes the human spirit to wither, and it eats away at our personal significance and self-esteem. It causes us to condemn ourselves.

Guilt plays on our fears of failure and rejection; therefore, it never can ultimately build, encourage, or inspire us in our desire to live for Christ.

✎ Go back to Step 4 and select two incidents from your personal inventory that have caused you to feel guilty. List for each the destructive effect this guilt had on your life.

Incident #1: _____

The destructive effect on my life was: _____

_____

Incident #2: _____

The destructive effect on my life was: _____

_____

Describe a time when someone tried to use guilt to motivate you.

_____
_____
_____
_____

Unfortunately, some people tell us that even after God has forgiven us of a particular sin, we still are guilty. And sadly, we hear this statement in churches—places that loudly and clearly should proclaim God's forgiveness. Sometimes people may try to make us feel guilty in order to motivate us to respond in certain ways.

Guilt, however, is not a healthy motivator for us. In the margin box briefly describe a time when you felt that someone tried to make you feel guilty to motivate you to do something.

Perhaps some people think that if they don't use guilt motivation, people won't respond. Because guilt motivation is so deeply ingrained in us, we will require time to develop more healthy motivations. These motivations are produced by the grace of God, who is in us. Be patient with yourself as you learn to develop healthy motivations.

Recognize the Lies

Learn to identify the results of guilt in your thoughts. Then focus instead on the unconditional love and forgiveness of Christ. His love is powerful, and He is worthy of our intense zeal to obey and honor him.

Christians are subject to grief, or sorrow, over our sins. The Bible often speaks of the Holy Spirit's work to convict believers of sin. He directs and encourages our spiritual progress by revealing our sins in contrast to the holiness and purity of Christ. The purpose of conviction is to lead us back to God's way for our lives. The Holy Spirit's conviction is not intended to produce pangs of guilt long after we've been forgiven of our sins. Conviction is the Holy Spirit's way of showing the error of our performance in light of God's standard and truth. His motivation is love, correction, and protection. Reread the story on page 188 about Kathy and Phillip. Phillip experienced a sense of relief at being forgiven. Godly sorrow that comes about through conviction enables us to realize the beauty of God's forgiveness and to experience His love and power. After we repent and God has forgiven us for that sin, no reasons exist from God's perspective for feelings of guilt to be a part of our lives.

In the margin box describe a time when conviction caused you to experience godly sorrow for a sin.

> **A time when I felt godly sorrow for sin:**
> _____
> _____
> _____
> _____

> **Key Concept for Lesson 1**
> Guilt is destructive to believers, but godly sorrow for our sins is important for us to grow.

✏️ Please pray and ask God how this concept can apply in your life. Now please review this lesson. What has God shown you that you can use?

_____

LESSON 2

More About the Process

We continue to take personal inventory, and when we are wrong, promptly admit it.

Sanctify them in the truth; Thy word is truth. –John 17:17

How Guilt Affects Us

Key Concept:
I can understand that I am forgiven, accepted, loved, and totally secure because of Christ.

Although Christians no longer are subject to condemnation, we probably won't be free from its destructive power until we learn that we no longer have to fear judgment. The Holy Spirit wants us to be convinced that we are forgiven, accepted, loved, totally secure because of Christ. The Holy Spirit is the Paraclete, or "one called alongside," to lift us up and encourage us. He faithfully makes us aware of any behavior that does not reflect the character of

Christ. He helps us understand both our righteousness before God and the failures in our performance.

Knowing this, how can we deal with feelings of guilt? First, we can study here a little more about how guilt affects us.

> # GUILT
>
> **Basic Focus**—Guilt focuses on self-condemnation. We believe, "I am unworthy."
>
> **Primary Concern**—Guilt deals with the sinner's loss of self-esteem and wounded self-pride. We think, "What will others think of me?"
>
> **Primary Fear**—Guilt produces a fear of punishment. We believe, "Now I'm going to get it!"
>
> **Behavioral Results**—Guilt leads to depression and more sin. We think, "I am just a low-down, dirty, rotten sinner." Or, it leads to to rebellion. We believe, "I don't care; I'm going to do whatever I want to do."
>
> **Interpersonal Results**—The interpersonal result of guilt is alienation, a feeling of shame that drives one away from the person wronged. We think, "I never can face him again."
>
> **Personal Results**—Guilt ends in depression, bitterness, and self-pity. We think, "I'm just no good."
>
> **Remedy**—The remedy for guilt is to remember that if you have repented of your sin, Christ has forgiven you and remembers your sin no more.

 Look back in the box at the statements about guilt. Check any that you might have experienced in your life.

> Father, I affirm that I am deeply loved by You, fully pleasing to You, and totally accepted in Your sight. You have made me complete and have given me the righteousness of Christ, even though my performance often falls short. Lord, I confess my sins to You. (List them. Be specific.) I agree with You that these are wrong. Thank You for forgiving me for these sins. Do I need to return anything, repay anyone, or apologize to anyone in order to fully make amends? Give me the courage to take these steps. In Jesus' name. Amen.

To deal with feelings of guilt, we first can affirm that Christ has forgiven us. As believers we are not condemned when we sin, but that sin is harmful and dishonors God. We can confess our sin to God, claim the forgiveness we already have in Christ, and then move on in joy and freedom to honor Him. The following prayer expresses this attitude. You may want to pray the words of this prayer of confession—like those found in the margin—or use similar words of your own.

We can affirm our righteousness in Christ as well as confess our sins. God does not need to be reminded of our right standing in Him, but we do. Make this prayer a daily experience and let it fill every corner of your thoughts.

As you yield to the gentle urging of God-given conviction, confess your sins and affirm your true relationship with Him, you gradually will be shaped and molded to increasingly "honor Him who died and rose again on (our) behalf" (2 Corinthians 5:15).

> **Key Concept for Lesson 2**
> I can understand that I am forgiven, accepted, loved, and totally secure because of Christ.

✎ Please pray and ask God how this concept can apply in your life. Now please review this lesson. What has God shown you that you can use?

_____

_____

_____

LESSON 3

Identifying False Beliefs

We continue to take personal inventory, and when we are wrong, promptly admit it.

For the mouth speaks out of that which fills the heart. —Matthew 12:34

Key Concept:
Changing my belief system is the key to changing my behavior.

You brood of vipers, how can you, being evil, speak what is good? For the mouth speaks out of that which fills the heart.
—Matthew 12:34

You earlier identified how our belief system is the key to our behavior. In this lesson you will further develop this process and begin to practice identifying the beliefs that control your life from behind the scenes. By taking a personal inventory we learn to identify the false beliefs that govern our actions, so that we can replace them with the truth of God's Word. We can recognize the source of our emotions and actions. Read Matthew 12:34 appearing in the margin to learn about what Jesus said about this. Our communication, which reveals our thoughts, emotions, and the intent of our actions, comes from our heart or belief system. What we believe interprets the events in our lives; therefore, our belief system, not the situation, usually is the key to our response! The following diagram helps us understand our thinking process from situation to action.

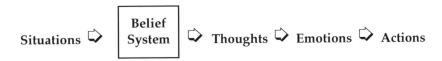

Tracing Emotions to Root Beliefs

Let's suppose Bill picked you up late, so you are late to work (or school, church, committee meeting). You respond in anger. You can trace that anger

Step 10 193

back to its root false belief in order to replace it with corresponding truths from the Scriptures or a characteristic of Christ presented in Step 3.

"Why am I angry?"

How do you determine the false belief responsible for your anger? Ask yourself, "Why am I angry? Am I angry because . . .

- . . . I hate to be late (your "certain standard") and my lateness makes me feel badly about myself? (*I must meet certain standards. . .*)

- . . . my boss will be displeased with me because I'm late, and her opinion of me means so much? (*I must be approved by certain others. . .*)

- . . . Bill failed by being late to pick me up? It was *his* fault, that creep! (*Those who fail are unworthy of love and deserve to be punished.*) No matter what I do, something always goes wrong? (*I am hopeless. I cannot change.*)

Note that the proper response is not "I'm not angry." You *are* angry. Denial only compounds our problems; it is not a solution. We can be honest with the Lord and with ourselves about our feelings.

✎ **If the situation about being picked up late in the previous example had happened to you, what would your emotion(s) likely have been?**

_____

To which false belief(s) could you trace it? _____

_____

_____

Learned Habits We Can Overcome

The process described above works in every person's life, but it may be more difficult for those of us who come from hurtful backgrounds. Our emotions also are habits, products of our family backgrounds, our past experiences, relationships, and patterns of responses. They are learned habits we can overcome.

We use many different methods to block pain in our lives, but we can begin reversing this trend by finding someone who will encourage us to be honest about our feelings. We can then use our feelings as a gauge to determine if our response to a situation is based on the truth or a lie.

Feelings are signals which tell us something about our environment.

Only by getting in touch with our feelings will we overcome these self-destructive defense mechanisms. Feelings are neither right nor wrong. They are signals which tell us something about our environment. Without awareness of those feelings we miss an entire range of information we need to live life effectively. When we are honest about our emotions, these emotions can tell us what we need to know about our perceptions. When our emotions are painful or distressing, we can ask, "Why am I responding this way? Am I believing a lie? If so, which one?" Learning to take a daily inventory—to take Step 10—is our path to a growing life-style of victory and obedience.

> **Key Concept for Lesson 3**
> Changing my belief system is the key to changing my behavior.

 Please pray and ask God how this concept can apply in your life. Now please review this lesson. What has God shown you that you can use?

_____

_____

LESSON 4

Catching the Signals

We continue to take personal inventory, and when we are wrong, promptly admit it.

Do not reprove a scoffer, lest he hate you, Reprove a wise man, and he will love you.
—Proverbs 9:8

Key Concept:
In recovery we recognize and deal with the codependent behaviors in our lives.

The Book of Proverbs gives a test for a wise person. Proverbs states this test repeatedly. Can you figure it out from reading the passage above?

 Look at the verse above. What is the one difference between a wise and a foolish person?

_____

_____

A wise person can take correction and apply it to his or her life.

Step 10 is about looking at myself honestly and regularly. A wise person is one who can take correction and apply it in his or her life.

Warning Signs

Throughout these pages, we have looked at many examples of harmful behavior—these represent warning signs for us. As we read them we may identify by saying, "That's me; that's what I do!" or "My wife does that to me!" or "I respond that way to my husband."

We can learn to see the truth about ourselves. Some of us see a few particular events but don't see any deep-rooted patterns in our behavior.

Do we feel people can't do without us? Or do we feel like we're always at fault?

A friend named Ralph told me about his relationship with his condemning, manipulative father. "I've been angry with my father several times, so I guess I'm pretty objective," he surmised. He didn't see the obvious—that his life was

Step 10 195

filled with insecurity and all sorts of defense mechanisms that he had developed. We need to see both the patterns of our behavior and the specific events that make up those patterns.

We have divided the following chart into the two extremes of savior and Judas thinking. Sometimes we act as if we are the Savior—faultless and indispensable. Other times we act as if we are a Judas—always at fault. Review these common feelings and behaviors and determine which of these, or variations of these, you can identify in your life. Do you find a pattern?

✎ **Circle the feelings you identify in your own life.**

> *Sometimes I think I'm God and at other times I think I'm pond scum!*

Savior	Judas
Feelings: grandiose, important, superior, certain, euphoric, confident, appreciated, angry, self-righteous, jealous, possessive, easily hurt	**Feelings:** depressed, lonely, angry, helpless, confused, afraid, hurt, inferior, hopeless, guilty, numb, trapped, martyred, persecuted, lethargic, worthless, ashamed, tired
Thoughts and Words: *It's all your fault.* *You made me fail.* *I can help.* *He (she) needs me.* *Why aren't people as perceptive as I am?* *I deserve their respect and love.* *I can make life good.*	**Thoughts and Words:** *It's all my fault.* *I'm a failure.* *I can't do anything right.* *Everything I do is wrong.* *Yes, but I mean no.* *No, but I mean yes.* *I don't deserve their respect and love.* *Life never will be good for me.*
Black-and-White: *People really need me.* *I am indispensable to the kingdom of God.* *People won't be helped and the Great Commission can't be fulfilled without me.*	**Black-and-White:** *People really need me, but I'll only let them down.* *Good Christians wouldn't think or act this way.* *God must be mad at me. He'll punish me.*
Actions: positive exaggeration, self-promotion, overcommitment, workaholism, susceptibility to manipulation, control of others through praise and condemnation, rescue of people without being asked, denial of reality, compulsion to avoid failure, giving, helping, trying to please people, defensiveness, overly responsible, prone to outbursts of anger.	**Actions:** negative exaggeration, self-denigration, withdrawal, avoidance of people and risks, susceptibility to manipulation, control of others through self-pity, denial of reality, passive-aggressive behavior, fear of failure leading to passive behavior, defensive, irresponsible, prone to outbursts of anger, rationalizing.

Growing in objectivity

Did you identify with several of the feelings, thoughts, and actions in both columns? Identifying this behavior indicates your growing honesty and objectivity.

 Pray and ask God to give you insight and objectivity. This exercise is not about putting yourself down but about honestly identifying the patterns in your life. Using the Savior/Judas chart, describe your feelings, thoughts, statements, and actions. Be specific. Use an extra sheet of paper, or write in the margin, if necessary.

When I feel like a savior, I:

Feelings: _____

Thoughts and words: _____

Actions: _____

When I feel like a Judas, I:

Feelings: _____

Thoughts and words: _____

Actions: _____

Identifying our behaviors usually brings out a flood of emotions as we realize how deeply we have been affected. The Lord can give us wisdom and strength, and a friend can give us the encouragement we need to fight our battles. However, what you see probably is only the first layer of the onion. As you deal with these hurts, fears, anger and habits, you will expose yet another layer. The Lord will give you the grace to endure and progress. Be encouraged by what Paul said to the believers in Corinth. Read the verse at left.

> No temptation has overtaken you but such as is common to man; and God is faithful, who will not allow you to be tempted beyond what you are able, but with the temptation will provide the way of escape also, that you may be able to endure it.
> –1 Corinthians 10:13

The way of escape so that we may endure begins when we *identify* our destructive behavior; *detach* and reflect on reality; and finally, *decide* on the best course of action. For the next 15 days, develop a habit in your scheduled activities which can change your life permanently. Select a specific time and place to complete the daily inventory that follows. Everything else of value in your life—a time to eat your meals, a time to rest, a time to begin the work day—usually happens as a result of scheduling.

Schedule a time to take a daily inventory in which you—

- seek to *identify* situations that bring out a codependent response.

- *detach* to reflect on the situation. Were you acting like a savior or a Judas? What were you thinking? What did you say? How did you feel? Which false belief(s) were you believing? What is God's truth?

- *decide*. For what are you responsible in this situation? What will be your plan of action? How will you implement it? Finally, pray. Thank God for the insights He has given you. Claim the truth of His Word, and ask Him to provide what you need to gain victory over a similar situation in the future.

✎ Use the chart that follows to help you identify, detach, and decide. Use extra paper if you need to. Copy the chart for the remaining 14 days in which you take your daily inventory.

Identify

Situation: _____

_____

Destructive response: _____

_____

Detach

Were you acting like a savior or a Judas? _____

Feelings: _____

_____

Thoughts and Words: _____

_____

Actions: _____

Which of Satan's lies apply to this situation? How? ____

_____

Which of God's truths apply to this situation? How? ____

_____

Decide

What are you responsible for in this situation? _____

_____

What are you not responsible for? _____

_____

What would have been a healthy response to this situation? ____

_____

What is your plan of action? _____

_____

> **Key Concept for Lesson 4**
> In recovery we recognize and deal with the codependent behaviors in our lives.

✎ Please pray and ask God how this concept can apply in your life. Now please review this lesson. What has God shown you that you can use?

_____

_____

Step Review

✎ Please review this Step. Pray and ask God to identify the Scriptures or principles that are particularly important for your life. Underline them. Then respond to the following:

Restate the Step in your own words.

_____

_____

What do you have to gain by practicing this Step in your life?

_____

_____

Reword your summary into a prayer of response to God. Thank Him for this Step and affirming your commitment to Him.

_____

_____

Memorize this Step's memory verse:
Trust in the LORD with all your heart, And do not lean on your own understanding. In all your ways acknowledge Him, And He will make your paths straight.
—Proverbs 3:5-6

STEP 11

A Growing Relationship

We seek to grow in our relationship with Jesus Christ through prayer, meditation, and obedience. We pray for wisdom and power to carry out His will.

Step 11 Into Codependency

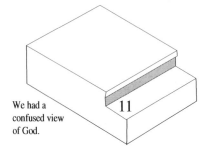

We had a confused view of God.

Step 11 Out of Codependency

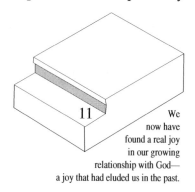

We now have found a real joy in our growing relationship with God—a joy that had eluded us in the past.

WHY THE WAIT?

When Andrea first began working the Steps, she said the placement of Step 11 was a mystery. *We've all heard about how important prayer is, so why is it placed so far down the list in the Steps?*, she wondered. She discovered two very wise reasons—the garbage reason and the grabby reason. The garbage reason is because of all the trash we've begun to remove by working the first 10 Steps. The baggage and garbage from the past interferes with our concept of God. Before recovery Andrea tried to have a meaningful prayer life, but she failed again and again. She felt more guilty after each attempt. When she began to work the Steps, her prayer life improved amazingly.

The grabby reason has to do with control. We are compulsive controllers. We even think that God needs someone to control Him. By now we are ready to understand that God is looking for worshippers, not advisors. The AA statement of this Step emphasizes "praying only for a knowledge of His will for us and the power to carry that out." We can learn to pray asking: "Father, please show me what you want me to do, and give me the power to do it."

A friend in the program said, "I once thought I might have made a couple of mistakes, but I never had done anything wrong." Until she found recovery, she thought she was equipped perfectly to run everyone's life—even God's. As you work this Step, you may find the answer to why your prayer life has been such a source of pain and frustration instead of being the joyous relationship God has in store for you.

But seek first His kingdom and His righteousness; and all these things shall be added to you.

–Matthew 6:33

Overview for Step 11

Lesson 1: **What Is Prayer?**
 Goal: You will identify the primary purpose of prayer.
Lesson 2: **God's Requirements for Prayer**
 Goal: You will describe the requirements God places on those who pray.
Lesson 3: **How to Begin**
 Goal: You will describe a practical plan for developing your relationship to God through prayer.
Lesson 4: **God's Word and Obedience**
 Goal: You will examine some methods to help you work Step 11.

What Is Prayer?

Key Concept:
The essence of prayer is a loving relationship with God.

We seek to grow in our relationship with Jesus Christ through prayer, meditation, and obedience. We pray for wisdom and power to carry out His will.

But if any of you lacks wisdom, let him ask of God, who gives to all men generously and without reproach, and it will be given to him. But let him ask in faith without any doubting, for the one who doubts is like the surf of the sea driven and tossed by the wind.

–James 1:5-6

 Read the Step above very carefully. Except for the name of Jesus, what do you think is the most important word in the Step?

_____

Oscar Thompson was a wonderful Christian pastor, author, and seminary professor. Oscar said the most important word in the language is the word *relationship*. Love only exists within relationships.

Jesus Christ's primary purpose in allowing Himself to be made human and to be crucified on our behalf was to reconcile us to God. He desires to have a relationship with us.

 Think of a time when you desired to have a relationship with someone—possibly a person you admired or a person you wanted to date. What did it feel like to desire to have that relationship? Did you feel—

❏ shy and afraid to speak?
❏ fearful of rejection?
❏ hopeful that you would be accepted?
❏ excited?
❏ happy?
❏ other? _____

Can you carry that feeling over to your relationship to God? He desires to have an intimate love relationship with you. He cares for you so deeply that He was willing to give His Son to die in your place. In the above exercise one thing you probably did not write was that you felt critical of the person you love. In the margin box write why you think we so quickly assume God desires to reject us.

> **We assume God desires to reject us because—**
>
> _____
> _____
> _____

 In the verse at left the sheep described follow—

❏ 1. because they fear the shepherd, or
❏ 2. because they love and trust the shepherd.

To him the doorkeeper opens, and the sheep hear his voice, and he calls his own sheep by name, and leads them out . . . he goes before them, and the sheep follow him because they know his voice. I am the good shepherd; and I know My own, and My own know Me.
–John 10:3-4,14

Mark prayed regularly each night before he went to bed. One night after he stayed up late reading, Mark fell asleep without having his prayer time. The next morning when he realized what he had done, Mark was terrified. He was

Step 11

> We love because He first loved us.
> —1 John 4:19

afraid something horrible would happen to him because he slept through his prayer time the previous evening. He felt that God never would forgive him for getting off his schedule. Many of us try to build a prayer life out of fear. We think God will be disappointed in us or punish us if we don't pray. We can learn from the sheep to follow and pray because we love our Shepherd and respond to His love. See what the verse at left says about this.

Scripture describes Jesus as the Good Shepherd who is faithful to lead and to provide for His sheep. Just as sheep know the shepherd's voice, we can know Jesus' voice. We can't distinguish His voice from any other voice unless we develop an intimate relationship with Him. Such a relationship takes time, but God clearly wants this relationship. He took the initiative to have a relationship with us.

We're Not Alone

> And in the same way the Spirit also helps our weakness; for we do not know how to pray as we should, but the Spirit Himself intercedes for us with groanings too deep for words.
> —Romans 8:26

> for through Him we both have our access in one Spirit to the Father.
> —Ephesians 2:18

When we begin to pray, we may feel lost and alone. Remember that God is on our side. His Holy Spirit lives in believers and helps us pray. Read what the Scriptures appearing in the margin say about this.

The Holy Spirit intercedes for us in prayer. He can speak to God on our behalf. To pray in the Spirit is to pray with His guidance and wisdom; with an open mind which allows Him to place on our hearts those people and things about which we need to speak to God.

God's Response to Prayer

Some of us are uncomfortable with prayer. We find it difficult to concentrate on conversation with a God we can't hear or see. Perhaps, too, we are disappointed with our prayer lives. Perhaps we feel frustrated because we can't seem to get any answers.

 In the following Scriptures underline God's response to prayer.

> *'For I know the plans that I have for you,' declares the LORD, 'plans for welfare and not for calamity to give you a future and a hope. Then you will call upon Me and come and pray to Me, and I will listen to you. And you will seek Me and find Me, when you search for Me with all your heart. And I will be found by you,' declares the LORD.*
> —Jeremiah 29:11-14

> *Thus says the LORD who made the earth, the LORD who formed it to establish it, the LORD is His name, 'Call to Me, and I will answer you, and I will tell you great and mighty things, which you do not know.'*
> —Jeremiah 33:2-3

You may have underlined the fact that God will be found and will answer prayer. Those are sources of encouragement as you work this Step.

Reasons for Prayer

> It will also come to pass that before they call, I will answer, and while they are still speaking, I will hear.
> —Isaiah 65:24

Before we call on Him, God is in the process of answering our prayers (see the verse appearing in the margin). If He hears us even before we speak, why should we pray? Does it really make a difference? Let's examine what the Scriptures say.

✎ **Read the following passages. In the margin write the benefit(s) of praying you find in each.**

(If) My people who are called by My name humble themselves and pray, and seek My face and turn from their wicked ways, then I will hear from heaven, will forgive their sin, and will heal their land.
–2 Chronicles 7:14

And call upon Me in the day of trouble; I shall rescue you, and you will honor Me.
–Psalm 50:15

For the eyes of the LORD are upon the righteous, And His ears attend to their prayer, But the face of the LORD is against those who do evil.
–1 Peter 3:12

Among the things we can gain through prayer are: strength; forgiveness and healing from sin; rescue in times of trouble; and the certainty of our Lord's attention and favor. Like any healthy father, God desires to build strong character in you through prayer.

Key Concept for Lesson 1
The essence of prayer is a loving relationship with God.

✎ **Please pray and ask God how this concept can apply in your life. Now please review this lesson. What has God shown you that you can use?**

LESSON 2

God's Requirements for Prayer

We seek to grow in our relationship with Jesus Christ through prayer, meditation, and obedience. We pray for wisdom and power to carry out His will.

Who may ascend into the hill of the LORD? And who may stand in His holy place? He who has clean hands and a pure heart, Who has not lifted up his soul to falsehood, And has not sworn deceitfully. He shall receive a blessing from the LORD And righteousness from the God of his salvation.
–Psalm 24:3-5

In the last lesson we looked at God's great desire to have an intimate relationship with us. In this lesson we will look at the other side of the issue.

Key Concept:
God gives us clear instructions and encouragement for prayer.

> If I had cherished sin in my heart, the Lord would not have listened.
> —Psalm 66:18, NIV

Those of us who feel we are doing God a great service when we pray may be surprised to learn that He has requirements for prayer. Although He wants to hear from us, God also is holy. He is God, and He maintains very healthy boundaries. He has given instructions for how to approach Him most effectively. These instructions include telling us what He does and doesn't like to see when we pray. Read the verse at left.

✎ **In Psalm 66:18 that you just read, what boundary does God enforce if we choose to love sin more than we love Him?**

_____

The New American Standard translation of the first part of this verse uses the phrase "regard wickedness in my heart." I cannot expect God to respond if I am praying with a divided heart. He demands my first love.

> If therefore you are presenting your offering at the altar, and there remember that your brother has something against you, leave your offering there before the altar, and go your way; first be reconciled to your brother, and then come and present your offering.
> —Matthew 5:23-24

✎ **According to Jesus' statement appearing at left, do broken relationships with others hinder prayer?** ❑ Yes ❑ No

Explain _____

_____

> Again I say to you, that if two of you agree on earth about anything that they may ask, it shall be done for them by My Father who is in heaven.
> —Matthew 18:19

God has given us His people—other Christians—as supporters in prayer. He truly honors a network of prayer. See what the verse at left says about this. This does not mean, of course, that we should rely solely on the prayers of others for our needs. God desires for each one of us to be in direct contact with Him (see Colossians 4:2; 1 Thessalonians 5:17).

✎ **Do you have a prayer network of believers with whom you can pray?** ❑ Yes ❑ No

Whom can you enlist for prayer support? _____

_____

Ted's father was critically ill. Ted felt very helpless because he lived many hours away from the city where his father was hospitalized. He went to several Christian friends who had been through the same experience with elderly parents and asked them if they would pray for him and his father regularly during his father's illness. He specifically sought them out and asked for their prayer support. Knowing that his friends regularly lifted him and His family up to the Lord in prayer brought great comfort and strength to Ted during those trying days.

Priority of Prayer

We need a personal relationship with God, but we are so busy, even in Christian service, that we just don't seem to have time to pray. We also may think our prayers need to be long to be effective. Later in this Step we will discuss the time element. Let's look first at the priority Jesus placed on prayer.

And in the early morning, while it was still dark, He arose and went out and departed to a lonely place, and was praying there.
—Mark 1:35

And immediately He made His disciples get into the boat and go ahead of Him to the other side to Bethsaida, while He himself was sending the multitude away. And after bidding them farewell, He departed to the mountain to pray.
—Mark 6:45-46

But He Himself would often slip away to the wilderness and pray.
—Luke 5:16

✎ **Read the Scriptures at left and answer the questions that follow.**

What did Jesus do to make sure that He could be alone with His Father?

_____

Why do you think it was important for God the Son to spend time alone with God the Father?

_____

Jesus made prayer a priority. He slipped away to be with the Father. Jesus prayed in the normal course of life and at critical points in His ministry.

✎ **From the verses below about Martha and Mary, do you gain any new insights about service—even Christian service—and its priority with God as it relates to prayer? If so, what are they?**

_____

_____

_____

Now as they were traveling along, He entered a certain village; and a woman named Martha welcomed Him into her home. And she had a sister called Mary, who moreover was listening to the Lord's word, seated at His feet. But Martha was distracted with all her preparations; and she came up to Him, and said, "Lord, do You not care that my sister has left me to do all the serving alone? Then tell her to help me." But the Lord answered and said to her, "Martha, Martha, you are worried and bothered about so many things; but only a few things are necessary, really only one, for Mary has chosen the good part, which shall not be taken away from her."
—Luke 10:38-42

God values your time with Him even more than He does your dutiful service for Him.

Key Concept for Lesson 2
God gives us clear instructions and encouragement for prayer.

✎ **Please pray and ask God how the concept you just read can apply in your life. Now please review this lesson. What has God shown you that you can use?**

_____

_____

_____

Step 11

LESSON 3

How to Begin

We seek to grow in our relationship with Jesus Christ through prayer, meditation, and obedience. We pray for wisdom and power to carry out His will.

> And it came about that while He was praying in a certain place, after He had finished, one of His disciples said to Him, "Lord, teach us to pray just as John also taught his disciples."
>
> –Luke 11:1

Key Concept:
Prayer is a learned skill which requires a plan and practice.

Great is the Lord, and greatly to be praised.
—Psalm 48:1

Enter His gates with thanksgiving, And his courts with praise. Give thanks to Him; bless His name.
—Psalm 100:4

Essentials of Prayer

Many methods and varieties of prayer exist. God certainly does not restrict us to any one formula! We should feel free to communicate with Him in the ways His Spirit leads us. However, for those who may be getting started, we offer a simple suggestion which we easily can remember by using the acronym, A.C.T.S. See this acronym explained in the margin.

Adoration

✎ **Read the verses appearing in the margin below about adoration. Do you look forward more to talking with—**
  ❑ 1. a person who always begins a conversation with "I want" or
  ❑ 2. a person who begins with "I appreciate, honor, or praise."

Adoration involves praising God for His virtues, characteristics, and abilities. It is that act by which we state that He is the living God who deserves our single-minded worship and devotion.

For those of us who have known mostly criticism, praising is a skill we can use greatly. As we learn to praise God, we can become better able to praise others and to accept praise. When Tad was a child, his parents pointed out his faults but seldom mentioned his strengths. When he married, his wife wondered why he never complimented her. Because Tad had not grown up with praise, he never learned this skill. In his recovery Tad learned how to praise God. This skill helped improve his marriage because it helped him learn to affirm his wife—and learn how to receive a compliment as well.

✎ **As practice in praising God please write at least three praises. I have written one to get you started.**

1. *Lord, I praise Your grace I have seen through my Christian brothers and sisters in recovery.*

2. _____

3. _____

Confession

> Behold, the Lord's hand is not so short that it cannot save; neither is His ear so dull that it cannot hear. But your iniquities have made a separation between you and your God, and your sins have hidden His face from you, so that He does not hear.
> —Isaiah 59:1-2

> If we confess our sins, He is faithful and righteous to forgive us our sins and to cleanse us from all unrighteousness.
> —1 John 1:9

Remember that confession does not provide forgiveness. Christ's work on the cross accomplished that. Read the verses at left. To confess is to agree with God and to acknowledge under the Holy Spirit's leading that we have missed the mark. In so doing we become aware of how much we desperately need God to intervene in our sinful patterns of behavior; we recognize patterns of behavior that He can transform; we see situations that in the future we can avoid; we become aware of those with whom we can make amends; and we realign our purposes with the purposes of God.

✎ **Do you have any sinful thoughts or behaviors you may need to confess to God right now? If so, what are they?**

_____

_____

Can you identify one or more false beliefs which prompted your sinful behavior? If so, list the belief(s):

_____

_____

Which of God's truths can you substitute for the false belief(s)?

_____

_____

Thanksgiving

> In everything give thanks, for this is God's will for you in Christ Jesus.
> —1 Thessalonians 5:18

We can be thankful for *something* in any situation, as the verse at left describes. We often miss this truth because the enemy, Satan, makes every effort to call our attention to what we lack in life, rather than what we have.

I was puzzled when I first heard someone in a meeting say: "Hi, I'm _____, and I'm a grateful recovering alcoholic (overeater, codependent, etc.)." Looking at all the addiction had cost them, how could they be grateful for the worst source of pain in their lives? Eventually I came to understand and identify. My addiction is what caused enough pain to get me to turn to Christ. Even the most painful experiences can be sources of praise when we allow them to point us to Jesus.

Even painful experiences can be sources of praise.

✎ **For which of the following can you give thanks? Check all that apply.**

- ❏ Spiritual blessings (such as answers to prayer, salvation, forgiveness, acceptance)
- ❏ Physical blessings (such as eyes, ears, health)
- ❏ Relational blessings (such as family, friends, co-workers)
- ❏ Material blessings (such as home, job, money, car)
- ❏ Intangible blessings (such as freedom of speech, freedom of worship)

From the list on the previous page, for what are you most thankful?

_____

Make a habit of thanking God daily for at least one of the blessings listed in each category above.

Supplication

> If you abide in Me, and My words abide in you, ask whatever you wish, and it shall be done for you.
> –John 15:7

Read the first verse at left, which will help you understand supplication. Supplication means "to kneel down and ask for, to beg." Two forms of supplication are intercession and petition. Intercession is praying on behalf of others; petition is asking God to meet our own needs. We will consider intercession first.

Intercession

> we are members of His body.
> –Ephesians 5:30

Praying for others is an outgrowth of remembering that we are the body of Christ, as the second verse states. The parts of the physical body need each other for survival. The body of Christ is the same. We need each other. God doesn't intend for us to do His work alone!

 In the following Scripture underline those for whom we are to pray.

> *I urge that entreaties and prayers, petitions and thanksgivings, be made on behalf of all men, for kings and all who are in authority, in order that we may lead a tranquil and quiet life in all godliness and dignity. This is good and acceptable in the sight of God our Savior, who desires all men to be saved and to come to the knowledge of the truth.*
>
> –1 Timothy 2:1-4

In the verse you just read, the apostle Paul certainly encourages us to pray: for one another, for those in authority, and for those who need to know Jesus.

We can pray that God will grant others the same blessings for which we are thankful: spiritual blessings; physical blessings; relational blessings (support, friendships, family); material blessings (job, home, money); and intangible blessings (traveling safety, for example).

 Ask the Holy Spirit to guide you as you answer the following. Beside each name you list, write what you think God might be asking you to pray in each situation.

What political authorities need your prayers?

Persons: Requests:

_____   _____

_____   _____

_____   _____

Step 11

What family members need your prayers?

Persons: Requests:

_____   _____

_____   _____

_____   _____

For what other "saints" (such as friends, ministers, Sunday School teachers, missionaries, Christians who have fallen into sin) might God want you to pray?

Persons: Requests:

_____   _____

_____   _____

_____   _____

What unbelievers (friends, family members, supervisor, co-workers, neighbors) may need your prayers?

Persons: Requests:

_____   _____

_____   _____

_____   _____

You have just completed a very practical exercise in praying for other people. By writing down your requests, you already have made them known to God! You also have a list to refer back to and pray from. Making a list can help us in two ways: it enables us to remember what we need to pray for, and it enables us to see God's answers! Pray each day for one person in each of the above categories. As you see answers to your prayers, you may decide to begin your own prayer journal so that you can record the persons needing prayer, your requests, and God's answers. This can be a very exciting way to pray!

Petition
Many of us have a tendency to approach God as if He were Santa Claus. We may read a passage such as John 15:7, the verse appearing at left, and wonder why we do not get everything we wish. When Jesus said the words in John 15:7, He knew that if we would abide in Him, in His Word, and in His Spirit, we would pray according to His will, with a view not only to our best but also to what might be best in God's eyes. Because we often don't know what to pray for, we can pray for a knowledge of God's will and the power to carry out that will. Certainly we can bring our physical, spiritual, emotional, relational, and material needs before God, remembering that sometimes His answer is no, and sometimes the answer is wait.

If you abide in Me, and My words abide in you, ask whatever you wish, and it shall be done for you.
–John 15:7

Has God said no or wait to your request(s)? If so, name some of those occasions.

_____

What might God have wanted to teach you through those situations?

_____
_____

> to keep me from exalting myself, there was given me a thorn in the flesh, a messenger of Satan to buffet me—to keep me from exalting myself! Concerning this I entreated the Lord three times that it might depart from me. And He has said to me, "My grace is sufficient for you, for power is perfected in weakness." Most gladly, therefore, I will rather boast about my weakness, that the power of Christ may dwell in me. Therefore I am well content with weakness, with insults, with distresses, with persecutions, with difficulties, for Christ's sake; for when I am weak, then I am strong.
> –2 Corinthians 12:7-10

Read the aspostle Paul's words at left about how God answered one of his requests. Whether God's answer is no or wait, we can remember the words He spoke to the prophet Isaiah. The words appear in the bottom verse at left. God's plan and timing are perfect. As we continue to seek Him and walk with Him, we will continue to realize that He can be trusted. Make it your habit to pray for two of these needs each day. Then use a separate piece of paper (or a journal including intercessory prayers) to record God's answers to you.

Key Concept for Lesson 3
Prayer is a learned skill which requires a plan and practice.

> " 'For My thoughts are not your thoughts, neither are your ways My ways,' " declares the LORD. " 'For as the heavens are higher than the earth, so are My ways higher than your ways, and My thoughts than your thoughts.' "
> –Isaiah 55:8-9

 Please pray and ask God how this concept can apply in your life. Now please review this lesson. What has God shown you that you can use?

_____
_____

LESSON 4

God's Word and Obedience

We seek to grow in our relationship with Jesus Christ through prayer, meditation, and obedience. We will pray for wisdom and power to carry out His will.

I will meditate on Thy precepts, And regard Thy ways. I shall delight in Thy statutes; I shall not forget Thy word.
—Psalm 119:15-16

Meditation

For the non-Christian meditation is a human attempt to get in contact with an unknown. For the believer meditation is a discipline of getting to know and obey the God we know and who knows us. Christian meditation centers on

Key Concept:
Building relationships takes time, effort, and commitment.

God's Word. In the last lesson you studied prayer, our communication with God. We are ready to examine God's communication with us through His Word.

> The grass withers, the flower fades, But the word of our God stands forever.
> —Isaiah 40:8

> All Scripture is inspired by God and profitable for teaching, for reproof, for correction, for training in righteousness; that the men of God may be adequate, equipped for every good work.
> —2 Timothy 3:16-17

✏️ **As you look at the verses appearing at left and find reasons to study God's Word, respond to the questions in the margin.**

From reading in Isaiah 40:8, what can you count on to endure in your life? _____

From reading Isaiah 40:8, what can you count on to never fail? _____

From reading 2 Timothy 3:16-17, name several things God's Word can do in your life:

_____
_____
_____

I trust you recognized the responses were: God's Word or the Bible for questions 1 and 2; the things the Word does include: teaches, trains, corrects, equips, and makes us adequate. The passage below describes a wonderful attitude we can have about studying God's Word.

O how I love Thy law! It is my meditation all the day. Thy commandments make me wiser than my enemies, For they are ever mine. I have more insight than all my teachers, For Thy testimonies are my meditation. I understand more than the aged, Because I have observed Thy precepts. I have restrained my feet from every evil way, That I may keep Thy word. I have not turned aside from Thine ordinances, For Thou Thyself hast taught me. How sweet are Thy words to my taste! Yes, sweeter than honey to my mouth! From Thy precepts I get understanding; Therefore I hate every false way. Thy word is a lamp to my feet, And a light to my path.
—Psalm 119:97-105

✏️ **Does Psalm 119 describe the attitude you have toward God's Word?**
❏ Yes ❏ No

Explain _____

Would you like to love God's Law in the way the psalmist describes?
❏ Yes ❏ No

Explain _____

Remember that victorious living is largely a learned, practiced habit.

✏️ **Turn back to the list of personal prayer requests you made on pages 208-209. For which requests are you seeking guidance from the Scriptures?**

_____

Step 11

➪ **Stop and pray, asking the Spirit of God to build faith in you through His Word.**

Obedience

As we mentioned earlier, we can't hope to obey God without knowing His commands. Our goal in Christian living is not perfection. We progress in our relationship with God as we practice obeying Him in our daily lives.

✎ **From the passage appearing in the margin it is better to—**

❑ 1. do great things for God or
❑ 2. obey God's words.

> And Samuel said, "Has the LORD as much delight in burnt offerings and sacrifices as in obeying the voice of the LORD? Behold, to obey is better than sacrifice, and to heed than the fat of rams."
> –1 Samuel 15:22-23

I think we could agree that Samuel would say it is better to obey (answer 2). We by no means imply that we are saved or lost by whether we obey. Jesus Christ has paid for our sins, averted for us the wrath of God, and made us dear, beloved children of God. We want to grow in obedience for another reason. He is worthy of our obedience! He is Lord! He truly is excellent, and He deserves our affections and our efforts. As Christians, we have the unspeakable privilege of representing the King of kings. We can do this effectively for eternal purposes only as we allow the Holy Spirit to teach and guide us through prayer and personal Bible study. Let's look at some ways we can make both a part of our daily routine.

Getting Started

Many of us are eager to know the Scriptures. We may even envy those who can rattle off verses at the mention of any given topic, but we don't often do anything about this desire to know. Instead, we often are intimidated by how many Scriptures exist and by how complex they seem.

Read regularly

Two tips for personal study are 1) get started and 2) ask the Holy Spirit to teach you and help you understand what you read. Read on a regular basis. You may start with the Book of Matthew and read one chapter each day until you get to Mark, and then continue through the four Gospels and the New Testament until you are finished. Then turn to Genesis and read through the Old Testament, or start again with Matthew and reread the New Testament.

Don't hurry

Do not hurry or rush your way through. The point of reading is learning, not finishing. Why? So you can begin to apply God's truths to your life. You may want to join a Bible study so that you will have some accountability for reading and studying. Join a study such as *Step by Step Through the Old Testament* and *Step by Step Through the New Testament*. Some Bibles offer a format for reading through the Scriptures in a year. The Bible often becomes more meaningful for us when we have something to look for. Here are some ideas for ways to study the Bible personally.

- **Attributes of God.** We have given you some of these already. Many others exist. Look for them as you read, and write them in a notebook.
- **God's commands.** Learn God's commands in order to fulfill them. As you read, you may want to ask the Holy Spirit to call your attention to His commands, and then ask God's help to keep them.

New ways to study

- **God's promises.** The Scriptures contain thousands of promises God makes us. He is faithful. He never breaks one of His promises. Read these and underline in your Bible those that mean the most to you. Try to memorize some so that you will know them when you need them.
- **God's warnings.** What warnings from God do you need to read and then heed? Watching for them and absorbing them is another way to study His Word effectively.
- **Word studies.** Take a word in one passage and compare it to other passages using the same word. An example of this is the word *shepherd* in Psalm 23. How is it used in this passage? How is it used in other Scripture passages? Does it always mean the same?
- **Character traits.** Who were the great leaders in the Bible? What were they like? What were their assets? weaknesses? What do you learn from them?
- **Asking questions.** Using a topic like the one given above, you may want to personalize your reading by asking, "In what ways has God demonstrated His love to me?" Or, in the case of a word study, "In what ways has God been a shepherd to me?" Or, "Am I acting as a shepherd to God's people?"

✎ From the list above pick out at least three new ways you would like to study God's Word. Write them here. Add any other ideas God brings to mind.

_____

_____

_____

✎ Now write on a card the methods you have chosen. Place the card in your Bible. The next time you read God's Word, use the card as a reminder to look for these things in God's Word.

These are a few of the many possibilities for personal study. Use any method you like, but above all, get started.

Making Time for God

Earlier, we mentioned that an obstacle to our personal relationship with God is T-I-M-E. Many of us resist approaching God because we feel like we owe Him a large chunk of our time. We do owe everything to God, but truthfully, He is delighted with any effort we make to spend time with Him, especially if it means having to say no to something else to keep the appointment. These are some suggestions for pursuing time alone with God:

- **Start slowly, but be consistent.** Each day at first you may want to spend 10 minutes with God. You can read five verses of Scripture and spend the rest of your time in prayer. The point is: do it every day.
- **Make an appointment and keep it.** Set aside one special time each day reserved specifically for you and God.
- **Find a quiet place.** If necessary take the phone off the hook. Choose a time when you will be free of interruptions.
- **Ask the Holy Spirit for help and guidance.**
- **Remember that every relationship takes time.** God knows this more than anyone else does. As you continue to grow in Him, you will find yourself wanting to spend more time with Him.

> **Key Concept for Lesson 4**
> Building relationships takes time, effort, and commitment.

✎ Please pray and ask God how this concept can apply in your life. Now please review this lesson. What has God shown you that you can use?

_____
_____
_____

Step Review

✎ Please review this Step. Pray and ask God to identify the Scriptures or principles that are particularly important for your life. Underline them. Then respond to the following:

Restate the Step in your own words: _____
_____
_____

What do you have to gain by practicing this Step in your life?
_____
_____

Reword your summary into a prayer of response to God. Thank Him for this Step, and affirm your commitment to Him.
_____
_____
_____

Memorize this Step's memory verse:
But seek first His kingdom and His righteousness; and all these things shall be added to you.

–Matthew 6:33

STEP 12

Practicing and Sharing

Having had a spiritual awakening, we try to carry the message of Christ's grace and power to others who struggle with codependency and to practice these principles in every aspect of our lives.

Step 12 Into Codependency

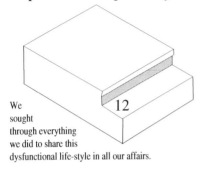

We sought through everything we did to share this dysfunctional life-style in all our affairs.

Step 12 Out of Codependency

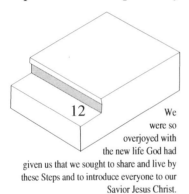

We were so overjoyed with the new life God had given us that we sought to share and live by these Steps and to introduce everyone to our Savior Jesus Christ.

GAIN OUT OF PAIN

At the time Marjorie couldn't imagine how any good could come from the pain she experienced in recovery. She remembered one especially hurtful day at a family reunion when her brother and sister sat across the room and glared at her after she set healthy boundaries with them for the first time. When she asked them to help with the care of their elderly mother instead of her carrying the entire load, they lashed out at her verbally. Her 12-Step group helped support Marjorie during this trying period and assured her that she had taken the right step in asking for help instead of continuing to be the family "doormat."

Marjorie now marvels at how freely she can talk about her recovery from destructive behavior in the situation with her siblings and in other situations like it. At her church, Marjorie has become a facilitator of a 12-Step group. Now she reaches out to others to help them through recovery in the same way others once assisted her.

Because she feels a wholeness in her life and understands herself now as never before, Marjorie feels closer to God and feels motivated to share His Word. Marjorie now works in an outreach program at her church and has helped several individuals come to know the Lord. "I don't think God caused the painful events in my life, but I'm glad that He can help me use my experiences to serve others," Marjorie says. In this Step you'll learn about sharing your recovery story and your Christian story.

---

but sanctify Christ as Lord in your hearts, always being ready to make a defense to everyone who asks you to give an account for the hope that is in you, yet with gentleness and reverence.

–1 Peter 3:15

Overview for Step 12

Lesson 1: Genuine Recovery
  Goal: You will identify the boundary between healthy and codependent caring.
Lesson 2: Carrying the Message
  Goal: You will identify the two greatest obstacles to overcome in sharing your recovery.

LESSON 1

Genuine Recovery

Having had a spiritual awakening, we try to carry the message of Christ's grace and power to others who struggle with codependency and to practice these principles in every aspect of our lives.

Key Concept:
Healthy caring is other-centered; codependent caretaking is self-centered.

For whoever wishes to save his life shall lose it; but whoever loses his life for My sake and the gospel's shall save it.
—Mark 8:35

In the Scripture above, Jesus stated the principle behind Step 12. The paradox is: to keep a victorious life, you have to give it away. One way to keep a vibrant relationship with God is to share Him with others. One way to keep a victorious recovery is to work the twelfth Step by continuing to give it away.

A Tale of Two Drunks

A solution to addiction

Alcoholics Anonymous originated from two men who learned that a set of Scriptural principles were the keys to victory over alcoholism. Bill W. and Dr. Bob both were hopeless drunks who felt they could not possibly ever remain sober. They discovered that a relationship with God was the solution to their addiction. But one element still was missing. That remaining element was the 12th Step. They found that they could remain sober as long as they practiced and *shared* the first 11 Steps.

✏️ **Place a check by the statement which most accurately represents the principle of Step 12.**

❑ 1. You have to work to earn grace.
❑ 2. Grace is God doing for us what we cannot do for ourselves.
❑ 3. God's grace works powerfully when we get outside of ourselves by sharing our salvation and recovery.
❑ 4. Helping others keeps us emotionally healthy by reminding us how far we've come.

All the answers but the first are true. I think answer 3 is the best statement of the principle.

The Boundary Between Sharing and Controlling

Like healing a broken leg

Some people believe recovery is just an excuse for self-indulgence. They think recovery validates selfishness. As we become more aware of the deep hurts that stem from these family disorders, we become more self-absorbed for a while. Like anything else, emotional healing requires time and attention. Consider someone who has a broken leg. Before the leg even can begin the process of healing, the person sees a doctor, has the leg examined and x-rayed, possibly has surgery, and gets a cast for the leg. For a while the patient will be unable to walk because of the pain. After some time the person will regain some ability to walk and will become more productive and less preoccupied with the leg. That doesn't mean the person can forget about the leg, of course.

After the cast comes off, the person rebuilds the leg muscles through therapy. Like the time and attention required for a broken leg to mend, the time and attention to heal a broken heart isn't selfishness; it's reasonable.

✎ **Write a paragraph comparing the time and attention a person needs to rebuild an injured body to the time a person needs to heal from emotional injuries.**

_____

_____

_____

_____

A healthy level of activity

You may have written several comparisons. One important similarity is the activity level. First you stop and see the extent of the damage. Then you slowly work up to a healthy level of activity. You focus your time and attention on the healing process and slowly increase your level of activity.

✎ **The following paragraphs describe what happens in healing. Circle the parts of the recovery process.**

The initial preoccupation we all experience in recovery is only the first stage in a process that will lead to a strong sense of biblical identity, genuine love, and selfless service. This process results in authentic Christianity. This process begins and continues with a growing sense of reality about life. Our denial wears away; we become more aware of our sins and the sins others commit against us. We begin to experience forgiveness for our wrongs and comfort for the hurts we have endured.

Our view of God evolves from that of an aloof or cruel Master to that of a just and merciful Father. Our black-and-white, extreme perspectives often are shaded with gray as we become more comfortable with the many things unclear about life. We develop relationships that are more authentic. These are based on honest communication, respect for one another's separateness, and genuine love.

✎ **In the margin beside the paragraphs above, write key statements from the paragraphs in an outline you could use to describe the healing process.**

Addressing the root issues of our destructive behavior—including the spiritual, emotional, physical, and relational factors—may take time and attention, and it may be somewhat complicated, but it is the key for genuine change and progress.

In the past we may have spent enormous amounts of energy "helping" others. What we really were doing was helping ourselves and seeking to build our own sense of worth. Recovery makes it possible to serve or not to serve based on others' needs. As rescuers, we tend to cite Jesus' command not to judge as an excuse to avoid seeing reality. "I shouldn't even think about my father's alcoholism," one woman told me. "That would be judging him, and that's wrong!" We also tend to view loving others, doing good, and lending as virtues without analyzing the deeper motivation that the Scriptures address. The Scriptures command us to please others but also make it clear that we do this for their good, not so we will receive appreciation. We can love, give, and serve without the twisted motives and deceptions common to destructive behavior.

> For the love of Christ controls us, having concluded this, that one died for all, therefore all died; and He died for all, that they who live should no longer live for themselves, but for Him who died and rose again on their behalf.
> –2 Corinthians 5:14-15

The growth that accompanies recovery frees us from being imprisoned by hurt, bitterness, shame, and manipulation so that we can live more wholeheartedly for Christ. A deep experience of God's love has a powerful, liberating and motivating influence, as the Scripture in the margin states.

Authentic Christianity. Changed lives. Is this phony? No, not at all. Is it attractive? Yes, very attractive! Therein lies the difference between Christian witness and destructive controlling. When we are living out of our grace relationship of recovery, a beauty and a joy that is attractive happens in our lives.

Key Concept for Lesson 1
Healthy caring is other-centered; codependent caretaking is self-centered.

✎ Please pray and ask God how this concept can apply in your life. Now please review this lesson. What has God shown you that you can use?

_____

_____

_____

LESSON 2

Carrying the Message

Having had a spiritual awakening, we try to carry the message of Christ's grace and power to others who struggle with codependency and to practice these principles in every aspect of our lives.

> *Blessed be the God and Father of our Lord Jesus Christ, the Father of all mercies and God of all comfort; who comforts us in all our affliction so that we may be able to comfort those who are in any affliction with the comfort with which we ourselves are comforted by God.*
> –2 Corinthians 1:3-4

Key Concept:
The balance of Step 12 means overcoming the fear of sharing while avoiding controlling others.

Why Share Recovery?

We find many benefits when we share with others the comfort we have received through recovery. It aids our own recovery and serves as a sharp

Propelling us to action

reminder of our former state when we still were compelled to rescue and control. Such reminders make us aware of how much we need humility. We so easily can fall back into the habit of rescuing and controlling again. Working this Step propels us into action. Helping others is, in part, the telling of a story—the story of your progress toward health through the 12-Step program. In the exercises below you will prepare your story. Use more paper if necessary to tell your story.

✎ **How has the 12-Step program deepened your faith in Jesus Christ?**

_____

_____

How is the power of Jesus Christ transforming your life?

Emotionally: _____

_____

Relationally: _____

_____

Spiritually: _____

_____

Mentally: _____

_____

Physically: _____

_____

Describe any changes in your behavior resulting from identifying false beliefs and replacing them with the truths of God's Word.

_____

_____

_____

Have other people noticed changes or improvements in your behavior? If so, describe some of the changes they have mentioned.

_____

_____

By writing down some of the many changes that have occurred in your life since you entered recovery, you are gathering some good material to share with others. Two dangers exist for us in working this Step. The first: Sharing our recovery can become a reason to slip back into our controlling, rescuing behaviors. The opposite danger is fear. We may be afraid that others will focus on our past faults and sins or on behaviors we haven't quite overcome yet. We may fear they will condemn us. Our fear of what others will say can keep us from sharing our faith and our recovery.

> The things you have learned and received and heard and seen in me, practice these things; and the God of peace shall be with you.
> –Philippians 4:9

✎ **Plan ahead for the dangers of slipping back into destructive behavior. List as many practical actions as possible that you can take to ensure that helping others won't cause a downfall in your own life. You will find at least one idea in Philippians 4:9 at left.**

_____

_____

_____

Philippians 4:9 suggests how important it is to practice the things you have learned. My answer to the question included: feeding on the Word of God and reading good books, maintaining a support group of persons who will pray for me and be honest with me, and having a mentor who will help me to be accountable.

The second hurdle to overcome is fear. As we experience the joys of giving comfort to others, and as we mature in our own relationship with God, we likely will begin to feel compelled to share His transforming love and power with others. This is the work of the Holy Spirit, yet some of us shy away from this responsibility because we fear rejection. Christ has assured us that at least some people will reject us when we take a stand for Him, but we no longer have to accept others' opinions as the basis of our significance. Instead, the love and acceptance of the infinite, Almighty God frees us to live unreservedly for Him. We can step out in faith and lovingly tell people about Christ's offer of forgiveness. Billions of people are waiting to hear His message!

Your Christian Testimony

To share your faith, you can use an outline similar to the one you used to describe your recovery. The easy-to-remember outline is: 1) what my life was like before I met Christ, 2) how I came to realize that I needed Christ, 3) how I received Christ, and 4) what my life is like now. Try to avoid using religious or "churchy" language. Write your testimony. Then share it with your sponsor and possibly your pastor. Enlist their aid to help you make it as clear and easy to communicate as possible.

✎ **What my life was like before I met Christ—(Hint: think of what motivated you to trust Christ, such as "I was fearful, lonely, or lacked purpose.")**

_____

_____

_____

How I came to realize that I needed Christ—

_____

_____

_____

How I received Christ—(Hint: people don't automatically understand what receiving Christ means. Explain how you prayed to ask Christ to forgive your sins and to come into your life.)

_____

_____

_____

What my life has been like since I received Christ—(Hint: this is not designed to paint a false picture of life "happily ever after." What change does having Christ in your life make? Does He strengthen you in your troubles, encourage you in your times of depression?)

_____

_____

_____

Your job—to tell

God always provides the resources for the tasks He calls you to do. His Spirit will give you the power to share your testimony effectively and to overcome the fear of talking to others. Your job simply is to tell the story—what you've seen, heard, and experienced through His healing touch. Don't worry if others reject your message; your role is not to change other people but to share what God has done in your life.

For Further Study

Sheryl worked diligently for many months on her Steps. She had used a workbook like this one to guide her study. Finally she shared with her sponsor her written work on Step 12. With mixed feelings she walked out of the office where she and her sponsor had met regularly. She felt accomplishment; but she also felt cut adrift. Using her workbook had helped her to grow. It had built the discipline of working daily. "Now what shall I do?" she thought. Don't be surprised if you feel a bit like Sheryl did.

Where do you go from here? Many people choose to go through the 12 Steps again. They realize they still need to work on some important issues in their lives, and they want the encouragement and accountability of a 12-Step group to help them. Other people need new material. On the next page we have listed for you some resources you may find helpful. Each is written in the interactive format to which you have become accustomed in studying *Conquering Codependency*. You will benefit most by studying these with a group.

To help you understand God's will for your life:
- *Experiencing God: Knowing and Doing the Will of God*, by Henry Blackaby and Claude V. King. This study helps Christians discover God's will and obediently follow it. (Nashville: LifeWay Press), product number 0767390873; Leader's Guide, product number 0805499512.

To help you grow in your prayer life:
- *Disciple's Prayer Life: Walking in Fellowship with God*, by T.W. Hunt and Catherine Walker. This course helps adults strengthen and deepen their prayer lives. (Nashville: LifeWay Press), product number 0767334949.

Learning more

To help you know more about the Bible:
- *Step by Step Through the Old Testament*, by Waylon Bailey and Tom Hudson. This workbook surveys the Old Testament and provides a framework for understanding and interpreting it. (Nashville: LifeWay Press), product number 0767326199; Leader's Guide, product number 0767326202. *Step by Step Through the New Testament*, by Thomas D. Lea and Tom Hudson. This workbook surveys the New Testament and provides a framework for understanding and interpreting it. (Nashville: LifeWay Press), product number 0805499466; Leader's Guide, product number 0767326210.

To help you learn how to disciple others:
- *MasterLife* by Avery T. Willis, Jr. guides both new and experienced believers to develop a lifelong, obedient relationship with Jesus Christ. The resource includes four six-week sequential studies. For more information about this resource PHONE 1-800-458-2772.

Congratulations, you have completed the Steps! But in a larger sense your study is just beginning. The Steps are the basis for the rest of your life. May it be a life of joy and victory.

✎ **Please review this Step. Pray and ask God to identify the Scriptures or principles that are particularly important for your life. Underline them. Then respond to the following:**

Restate the Step in your own words: _____

_____

What do you have to gain by practicing this Step in your life?

_____

Reword your summary into a prayer of response to God. Thank Him for this Step, and affirm your commitment to Him.

_____

_____

Memorize this Step's memory verse:
but sanctify Christ as Lord in your hearts, always being ready to make a defense to everyone who asks you to give an account for the hope that is in you, yet with gentleness and reverence.   —1 Peter 3:15

The Twelve Steps of Alcoholics Anonymous*

1. We admitted we were powerless over alcohol—that our lives had become unmanageable.

2. Came to believe that a Power greater than ourselves could restore us to sanity.

3. Made a decision to turn our will and our lives over to the care of God *as we understood Him.*

4. Made a searching and fearless moral inventory of ourselves.

5. Admitted to God, to ourselves, and to another human being the exact nature of our wrongs.

6. Were entirely ready to have God remove all these defects of character.

7. Humbly asked Him to remove our shortcomings.

8. Made a list of all persons we had harmed, and became willing to make amends to them all.

9. Made direct amends to such people wherever possible, except when to do so would injure them or others.

10. Continued to take personal inventory and when we were wrong promptly admitted it.

11. Sought through prayer and meditation to improve our conscious contact with God *as we understood Him,* praying only for knowledge of His will for us and the power to carry that out.

12. Having had a spiritual awakening as the result of these steps, we tried to carry this message to alcoholics, and to practice these principles in all our affairs.

*From *Alcoholics Anonymous*, 3d ed. (New York: World Services, 1976), 59-60. The Twelve Steps are reprinted here and adapted on the following pages with permission of Alcoholics Anonymous World Services, Inc. Permission to adapt the Twelve Steps does not mean that AA has revised or approved the content of this workbook, nor that AA agrees with the views expressed herein. AA is a program of recovery from alcoholism. Use of the Twelve Steps in connection with programs and activities which are patterned after AA but which address other problems does not imply otherwise.

The Christ-Centered 12 Steps for Codependency

Step 1
We admit that we were powerless over other people; our needs to be needed and our compulsions to rescue others have made our lives unmanageable.

Step 2
We increasingly believe that God can restore us to health and sanity through His Son Jesus Christ.

Step 3
We made a decision to turn our will and our lives over to God through Jesus Christ.

Step 4
We make a searching and fearless moral inventory of ourselves.

Step 5
We admit to God, to ourselves, and to another person the exact nature of our wrongs.

Step 6
We commit ourselves to obey God and desire that He remove patterns of sin from our lives.

Step 7
We humbly ask God to renew our minds so that our codependent patterns can be transformed into patterns of righteousness.

Step 8
We make a list of all persons who have hurt us and choose to forgive them. We also make a list of all persons we have harmed, and we become willing to make amends to them all.

Step 9
We make direct amends to people where possible, except when doing so will injure them or others.

Step 10
We continue to take personal inventory, and when we are wrong, promptly admit it.

Step 11
We seek to grow in our relationship with Jesus Christ through prayer, meditation, and obedience. We pray for wisdom and power to carry out His will.

Step 12
Having had a spiritual awakening, we try to carry the message of Christ's grace and power to others who struggle with codependency and to practice these principles in every aspect of our lives.

Made in the USA
Lexington, KY
29 June 2018